GW-BASIC® and PC BASIC® programming
for beginners

F. Kampow   N. Szczepanowski

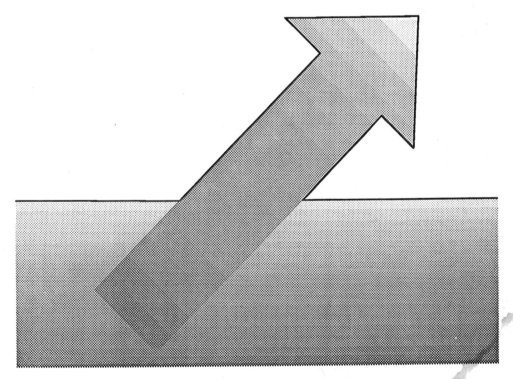

Abacus
A Data Becker Book

First Printing, March 1989
Printed in U.S.A.

Copyright © 1988,1989   DATA BECKER GmbH
Merowingerstr. 30
4000 Düsseldorf, West Germany

Copyright © 1988,1989   Abacus, Inc.
5370 52nd Street, S.E.
Grand Rapids, MI 49512

IBM, PC-AT, PC-XT, PC-BASIC and PC-DOS are trademarks or registered trademarks of International Business Machines Corporation.

Microsoft, MS-DOS and GW-BASIC are trademarks or registered trademarks of Microsoft Corporation.

ISBN   1-55755-062-X

Table of Contents

	Foreword	vi
1	Fundamentals of programming	1
1.1	Starting GW-BASIC	1
1.1.1	Loading GW-BASIC	1
1.1.4	Entering your first BASIC program	7
1.2	Algorithms and programs	7
1.3	The BASIC language	8
1.4	Data flowcharts, program flowcharts, and documentation	10
1.4.1	Data flowcharts	11
1.4.2	Program flowcharts	12
1.4.3	Documentation	15
1.5	ASCII codes	18
2	Introduction to programming in BASIC	19
2.1	The first BASIC program	19
2.1.1	Entering values with INPUT	21
2.1.2	Value assignment with LET	23
2.1.3	Output with PRINT	24
2.1.3.1	PRINT USING	27
2.1.4	Comments with REM	32
2.2	Variables and their use	33
2.2.1	Calculations with variables	34
2.3	Numerical functions	36
2.3.1	Functions with DEF FN	40
2.3.2	Random numbers	41
2.3.3	More commands for variables	42
2.3.4	ASC(X$) and CHR$(X)	43
2.4	TAB and SPC	45
2.5	Strings	46
2.5.1	LEFT$	47
2.5.2	RIGHT$	48
2.5.3	MID$	48
2.5.4	LEN(X$)	49
2.5.5	VAL(X$)	50
2.5.6	STR(X$)	51
2.5.7	INSTR	51
2.5.8	STRING$	52
2.5.9	SPACE$	52
2.6	Editing programs	54

2.6.1	Editing keys	57
2.6.2	Shortcuts with the Alt key	59
2.7	Screen Control	60
3	Extended program structures	61
3.1	Unconditional program jumps	61
3.2	Conditional program jumps	64
3.2.1	`IF...THEN...ELSE`	64
	Exercises	68
3.2.2	`FOR...TO...NEXT`	69
3.2.3	Loops with `WHILE...WEND`	74
3.3	Calculated jump commands	81
3.3.1	Example program `MATH TUTOR`	83
3.3.2	Program jumps with `ON... ERROR`	91
	Exercises	93
3.4	Reading the keyboard	94
3.6	`FRE`, `POS`, `CALL`, and `WAIT`	95
3.7	`READ`, `DATA`, and `RESTORE`	97
4	Advanced BASIC applications	103
4.1	Arrays	103
4.1.1	One-dimensional arrays	103
4.1.2	Examples of one-dimensional arrays	110
	Exercises	116
4.1.3	Multi-dimensional arrays	117
4.2	Subroutines	125
4.3	Menu techniques	144
4.3.1	Cursor positioning with `LOCATE`	148
4.3.2	Using input routines in the menu	148
4.4	Sorting methods	153
5	Working with the disk drive	157
5.1	Program management	157
5.1.1	Saving programs	157
5.1.2	Loading programs	158
5.1.3	Displaying the disk contents	158
5.1.4	Erasing files	159
5.1.5	Renaming files	159
5.2	Sequential file management	160

6	Music and graphics	165
6.1	Sound	165
6.1.1	The SOUND statement	165
6.1.2	The Play statement	167
6.2	Graphics	171
6.2.1	Text mode graphics	172
6.2.2	CGA Graphics	174
	Appendix A: GW-BASIC Commands	181
	Appendix B: Reserved BASIC Words	271
	Appendix C: Exercise Solutions	273
	Appendix D: ASCII Characters	283
	Appendix E: BASIC Error List	285
	Appendix F Number Systems	291
	Index	330

Foreword

The IBM PC and compatibles are quite capable computers. The purpose of this book is to make you a capable BASIC programmer. We intend to present the fundamentals of BASIC—from simple screen output with PRINT to complex program algorithms such as sorting.

Chapter 1 gives you the fundamentals of programming, such as good programming style and program documentation. In addition, you will learn the theoretical and practical foundations of data processing.

In Chapter 2 and 3 you begin your actual programming. First you will learn how various BASIC commands are used and applied by means of numerous examples.

At the conclusion of the individual sections you will find exercise problems for you to solve. This lets you check your comprehension of the preceding material. The exercise solutions are found in Appendix C. We suggest you work through the solution to all the problems before proceeding, because the problem solution will help with the transition to the following section.

Chapter 4 consists of more complex problems and hence more complex programs. Again, the chapter contains many examples and problems—you won't be just reading, but will get actual hands-on experience working with BASIC on your computer.

Chapter 5 introduces you to the principles of file management and operation of the disk drive.

Chapter 6 explains some of the sound and graphics commands of the GW BASIC, and includes many examples.

Appendix A is a convenient alphabetical list of all GW BASIC commands and instructions, with explanations and examples of their use. Appendix C contains the solutions to all of the sample problems in the book.

We'd like to wish you lots of fun and success while working with this book and with GW BASIC.

Throughout this book you will notice icons, small descriptive pictures, in the margin. These icons tell you what to do, whether it is to simply read, note important information or actually enter something at your computers keyboard.

Reading icon.

Note important information icon

Exercise icon.

Keyboard entry icon

Disk icon

Program listing icon

Sincerely,

Frank Kampow
Norbert Szczepanowski

1.   Fundamentals of programming

1.1   Starting GW-BASIC

PC BASIC is the name of the BASIC programming language for the IBM PC, PC-XT and PC-AT. GW-BASIC™ is the version of BASIC for PC compatibles. For all intents and purposes, the two are identical. We'll take the liberty of referring to the programs by the generic name GW-BASIC.

GW-BASIC has more than 230 commands, statements and functions. This makes it a very comprehensive programming tool. This book is designed not only to teach you how to use these commands, but also as a permanent reference, containing many charts and tables of the commands and functions used in conjunction with GW-BASIC.

Although we call it a generic version of the BASIC programming language for the IBM PC, XT, AT and compatibles, GW-BASIC has subtle differences depending on the particular computer for which it is configured. We have noted many of these differences in this book, but refer to your original BASIC handbook or system manual if you encounter a major difference.

1.1.1   Loading GW-BASIC

Before you can begin using BASIC, you must load it into memory. Prior to loading BASIC, you'll need to turn on your computer and load the operating system. This is usually accomplished by placing your system disk into your startup disk drive (drive A:) and turning on your computer system power. If you have a hard disk system with the operating system installed on the hard disk, you may just turn on your power. Often you will need to enter the current date and time when starting your system. See your system manual if you run into problems starting your system. When your system is loaded and ready for use, it will display a prompt on the screen, usually A: for single and dual floppy systems or C: for hard disk systems, to indicate the current disk drive in use. If the prompt shown is not for drive A, then type the following:

    A:

Then press <ENTER> or <RETURN>

Now place your BASIC disk into drive A and type the following (substitute the name of your version of BASIC where we have used GWBASIC if you don't have GW-BASIC):

    A:GWBASIC   <RETURN>

If your computer responds with a message similar to 'BAD COMMAND OR FILE NAME', check to be sure you have the disk containing BASIC in drive A. You can also try entering BASIC or BASICA. If you continue to have problems, check your BASIC manual for information on loading BASIC.

If GWBASIC loaded correctly your screen should appear similar to the following, don't worry if your screen is slightly different:

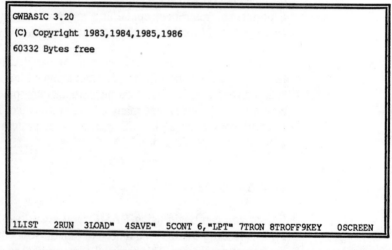

```
GWBASIC 3.20
(C) Copyright 1983,1984,1985,1986
60332 Bytes free




















1LIST    2RUN   3LOAD"   4SAVE"   5CONT 6,"LPT" 7TRON 8TROFF9KEY    0SCREEN
```

A number of operating parameters and options may be specified along with the filename when loading most versions of BASIC. The examples in this book will not require any of these parameters, but you should be aware of them. The following is a breakdown of the syntax used in loading BASIC, and descriptions of the additional parameters which may be specified.

```
BASIC|BASICA|GWBASIC[prog][<stdin][>stdout][/C:buffer]
[/D][/F:files][/M:[address][,blocks]][/S:buffer][I]
```

prog   Specifies the name of a BASIC program that is executed after the BASIC interpreter is loaded. If omitted, BASIC displays the READY prompt and is in the command mode.

<stdin   Specifies the name of the file or device from which GW-BASIC reads input.

>stdout   Specifies the name of the file or device to which GW-BASIC directs output.

/C:buffer

Specifies the size of the data transfer buffer when the asynchronous communication adapter is used. The default size is 256 bytes. The maximum is 32767.

/D   Specifies that the mathematical functions ATN, COS, EXP, LOG, SIN, SQR, TAN are performed using double-precision arithmetic.

/F:files   Specifies the maximum number of files that can be accessed. The default is 3. The maximum is 15.

/M:address,blocks

GW-BASIC normally has 64K of memory available for data and stack space. If your application requires some of this memory (e.g. machine language routines), you can protect a portion of this space. Specify *address* to set the highest memory location available to GW-BASIC.

To reserve memory above GW-BASIC, blocks must be byte multiples of 16 (paragraphs). For example, /M:&H1010 reserves 64K (&H1000 (=4096*16) for BASIC, plus 256 bytes (&H10 (=16*16) for machine language routines.

/S:*buffer*

Specifies the maximum record length for a random access file. The default is 128. The maximum value is 32767.

/I   Dynamically allocates the memory space that is required to support file operations.

1.1.2   Entering your first BASIC program

To demonstrate how to enter and edit a program line, type the following example. First type the following:

```
20 print "hi, i'm your friendly personal computer"
```

To store the line into the computer's memory, press the <RETURN> or <ENTER> key, whichever your computer is equipped with. Any further references to the <RETURN> key should be interpreted as the <ENTER> key if your computer is so equipped. Now, to see if our program works, type:

```
run
```

and press the <RETURN> key. After you type a command or a program line you must press the <RETURN> key to tell the computer to interpret it. The following should be displayed on your monitor screen:

```
hello, how are you?
```

The RUN command tells BASIC to execute whatever program is in memory. Let's explain the program that you just typed in.

```
20 print "hi, i'm your friendly personal computer"
```

To enter a program into memory, the program must have a number in front of it (20 in our example). This number is appropriately called a *line number*. The purpose of line numbers is to put the program lines into a desired order. BASIC stores the program in memory in ascending sequence according to the line number. As you enter a program line, BASIC places that line in sequence with the other lines in memory as determined by the line numbers. Therefore, you can enter program lines in any particular order and BASIC will put them into the proper order in memory. Type the following:

```
10 print "this is the first line"
30 print "this is the third line"
```

To see the entire program in memory type:

```
list
```

Notice how the line numbers are displayed in sequence. LIST displays your current program. If you enter a program line with a duplicate line number, the new program line replaces the one in memory. To demonstrate, type the following:

```
20 print "hi, i'm replacing the second line"
```

Enter the LIST command and notice that what you just typed replaced the second line. If you enter just a line number followed by <RETURN>, the program line with that line number is removed or deleted from memory. Type the following to see this occur:

```
20
```

Notice that only lines 10 and 30 remain. To change a line without having to type the whole thing over again, you are able to edit it. Enter the following command:

```
edit 30
```

Remember to press the <RETURN> key after entering a command. Line 30 should appear with the cursor positioned on the first character. Now we can edit our program. To do so we will need to use the cursor keys. The cursor keys are located in different places on different keyboards. Often they are either separate keys, or located on the numeric keypad, and are identified by arrows pointing up, down, left, and right or are labeled CRSR UP, CRSR DOWN, CRSR LEFT, and CRSR RIGHT. If you have trouble locating these keys, or any keys discussed throughout this book, check the manuals supplied with your computer.

The cursor is moved in the direction indicated by the arrow on the key. Press the right-cursor key (the key with the arrow pointing to the right) 15 times. The cursor should now be on the i in the word is. Locate the <INSERT> key. On some keyboards this is a shifted function and is activated by being pressed while the <SHIFT> key is being held down. If this is the case on your computer, the word INSERT or INS will be written on the key above some other function name. To insert a blank space, activate the insert mode by pressing <INSERT> or <SHIFT>+<INSERT>. Now press the space bar. Notice how the rest of the line shifted to the right to allow a space to be inserted. Return to overstrike mode by pressing <INSERT> again. Insert mode is toggled on and off using the same key sequence. The line should now have two spaces between the words **this** and **is** like this:

```
30 print "this  is the third line"
```

Now locate the <BACKSPACE> key. Sometimes this key is identified as <DEL> or <DELETE> with an arrow pointing to the left. This key performs a different function than the regular <DELETE> key or the <DELETE> key with an arrow pointing to the right. The <BACKSPACE> key moves the cursor one position to the left. In doing so, it also moves the character the cursor is on and the remainder of the line one position to the left, erasing the character previously located to the left of the cursor. Press <BACKSPACE> once. The line should now look as it did before you inserted the extra space.

Locate the regular <DELETE> key or <DELETE> key with an arrow pointing right. Press this key once. The character the cursor was resting on is removed by this function. The line should now read:

```
30 print "this s the third line"
```

Activate the insert mode again using the <INSERT> key. Now type:

```
wa
```

Be sure to turn off insert mode using the <INSERT> key. Press the <RETURN> key to enter the line. The line should look as follows:

```
30 print "this was the third line"
```

Type RUN to execute the edited program.

Congratulations, you have entered and edited your first BASIC program.

1.2 Algorithms and programs

This chapter is about the fundamentals of programming. In particular, we're going to learn about the GW-BASIC language.

But before we begin our BASIC programming, we must first clarify some terminology. We'll be giving you a little theory of programming—it may sound a little dry at first, but will be necessary for solving more complex problems later.

Just what is programming?

A computer is a "dumb" machine, unable to do anything unless it's carefully instructed. While some computers have a programming language built into them, your computer requires you to first load BASIC from diskette. But even then, you can't just type in your request at the keyboard:

```
"Calculate the surface of a sphere."
```

To solve this problem, you must first define a plan outlining how to solve the problem in a clear and logical ordered set of instructions. This plan is called an *algorithm*. Next you must convert this plan into the commands of the computer language. This set of commands is called a *program*.

1.3   The BASIC language

The most widely used programming language is called BASIC. BASIC was developed in 1961 at Dartmouth College in New Hampshire. BASIC is an acronym for:

Beginner's **A**ll-purpose **S**ymbolic **I**nstruction **C**ode

BASIC has its roots in the FORTRAN programming language. Since its inception, many different dialects of BASIC have been developed for different computers. For the IBM line of personal computers and compatibles, we refer to the specific version developed for that computer, GW-BASIC.

GW-BASIC is an interpreted language and, while it retains most of the language elements of BASIC from other computers, some programs from other computers must be modified to run under GW-BASIC.

As with all interpreted languages, the computer cannot immediately understand a BASIC command. A command must first be converted to a form which the computer can understand—machine language. The conversion is performed by the BASIC interpreter. When you type in a BASIC command at the keyboard and press the <RETURN> key, the interpreter converts the command into machine code. Only after the computer has done this preliminary work can it understand and execute the command.

To recap, an algorithm is an ordered set of instructions to solve a problem. A program is a translation of the algorithm into a programming language, in our case GW-BASIC.

Let's take a specific problem to further illustrate these two concepts. Suppose you want to determine the volume of a sphere knowing only its radius. Let's carry it a bit further, and say you want to do this for twenty different radii. Remember, an algorithm is an ordered set of instructions to solve a problem. In this case you might proceed like this:

For each of 20 values do the following:
- input the radius
- calculate the volume of the sphere
- display that volume

A program is the translation of the algorithm into a programming language. Here's a program to solve our problem:

```
10 PI=3.14159265
20 FOR I=1 TO 20
30 INPUT"RADIUS (IN CM)";R
40 V=4*PI*R^3/3
50 PRINT"THE VOLUME IS ";V;" ccm"
60 NEXT I
```

The program works perfectly and you have your answers. You decided upon an algorithm and then translated it into BASIC. This all appears very straightforward and easy. Because of the simplicity of your problem, you were able to formulate a solution quickly.

But this does not hold true as you tackle more complex problems. Even the smallest logic or translation error may lead to incorrect results.

A more general approach to computer problems is to divide the problem into small subprograms. You can then think of these smaller pieces as smaller problems having easier solutions.

One difficulty of this method is that you have to make sure that all of the pieces fit together again afterwards. The next section describes two tools that help us do this—data flowcharts and program flowcharts.

1.4   Data flowcharts, program flowcharts and documentation

Data flow and *program flow* are terms that describe a programming solution to a complex problem. We'll describe both in detail.

A *flowchart* is a pictorial representation of the programmed solution to a problem. Flowcharts are made up of different geometrical symbols. Each symbol represents a specific type of program element. A calculation is one program element; printing the result to the screen is another program element.

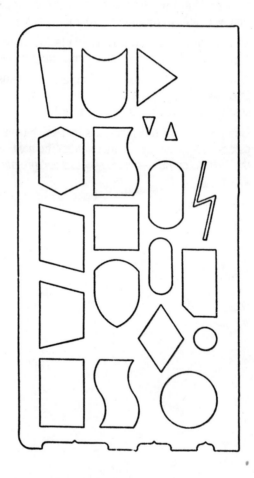

Figure 1: Programming Template

1.4.1   Data flowcharts

A data flowchart is a pictorial representation of the data elements involved in the program. Again, various different symbols represent the flow of the data within a program.

A data flowchart describes the flow of data within a program. But more precisely, it shows which data item is being used (value of the radius), how it is entered into the computer (by keyboard input), what calculations are performed with the data (finding the value of the sphere) and how the results are output (to the screen).

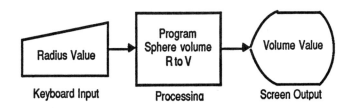

Figure 2

As you can see, we've created a data flowchart for a problem as small as this one. You may think it unnecessary or trivial, but it helps you see the overall program. Without such a tool, it might be impossible to write more complex programs. For longer programs these charts may be several pages long. In these cases, they make it easier to understand the flow of the data to be processed. If you become accustomed to creating data flowcharts, it will make your programming task much easier.

Figure 3 illustrates the different symbols used in data flowcharts.

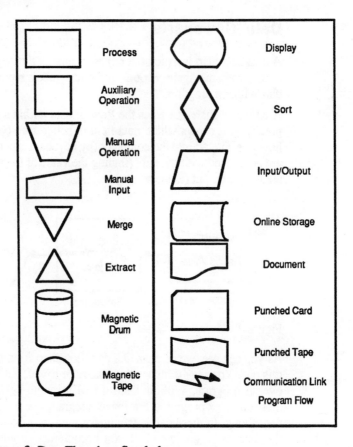

Figure 3: Data Flowchart Symbols

For practice, create a data flowchart for a program to convert miles to kilometers and display the result on the screen. Compare your data flowchart with the suggested solution in Figure 6 on page 17.

In this section we have learned:

- data flowcharts clearly show how data is used in a program
- how data items are used by the program
- how the data is entered into the computer (source)
- how the data is used by the program (processed)
- how the data is output (destination)

In the next section we'll talk about the program flowchart. The data flowchart does not give information about how, for example, the radius values are converted into the volume values. We need a second form of symbolic representation that tells us the individual steps the computer uses to solve a problem. This is the purpose of the program flowchart.

1.4.2   Program flowcharts

In the data flowchart for the calculation of the volume of a sphere, the only item listed for "processing" was Program sphere volume R to V. There is no information about what happens to the data. The problem has not been divided into individual steps. You can do this with the help of the program flowchart. It shows in clear, individual steps what to do in order to solve a specific problem. The symbols on the programming template are also used for the program flowchart. These are explained in Figure 4.

We will use our previous example to create our first program flowchart. You should practice making program flowcharts for small examples so that you don't run into difficulties when making flowcharts for larger programs. The adage "practice makes perfect" applies here.

Program flowcharts are always drawn from top to bottom. When you reach the bottom of the page, you can use a connector symbol to indicate the continuing page. The connector is placed at the lower end of the chart and designated with a number or letter. The second connector is designated with the same letter and placed at the start of the second section. Take a look at the following example of a program flowchart in figure 5.

☐	Internal Process	◇	Program Decision Branch
▱	Input or Output	▯	Subroutine
⬭	Start or End	}	Comments
○	Connector	│	Flow Line

Figure 4: Program Flowchart Symbols

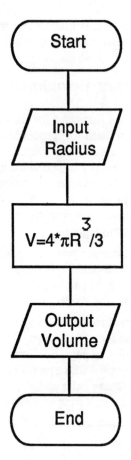

Figure 5: Program Flowchart

The start/end symbol does not have to be translated into BASIC. The input symbol "Input radius" can be translated into the BASIC command `INPUT`. This can also be provided with a prompt like:

```
ENTER RADIUS IN CM?
```

The formula for calculating the volume of the sphere can be placed directly in the symbol for the internal processing. For the output symbol "Output volume" we use the `PRINT` command, which is provided with the appropriate text. In contrast to our short example program, a `FOR...NEXT` loop is not used here. When a program flowchart has reached a given level of refinement, the individual symbols need only be translated into the corresponding language statements.

Once you have reached this point in programming, you can think about the first test run of your program. This is done first on paper, that is you follow the data by means of the data flowchart and check the program flow with the program flowchart. If everything is to your satisfaction, you can start the program by typing RUN.

Try to draw your own flowchart for the following problem:

Write a program to convert temperatures from Celsius into Fahrenheit. The formula for this is:

F=1.8*C+32

Compare your result with the suggested solution in figure 7.

The advantages of program flowcharts will become clear with larger programs. They are easy to read because of their graphic representation, something that can't necessarily be said of a program listing. Another advantage that's often overlooked is that flowcharts are independent of specific computers. The end result of this is that your flowchart is usable on any computer. Furthermore, it represents a useful tool for documenting your programs.

Documentation is a narrative description of the program. The writer describes the program's approach in plain English.

Too many programs lack documentation. But if a program has to be modified some time after it's written, even the original programmer may not be able to understand it. This is because you simply cannot remember all the details that were put into the program, perhaps a year ago. For this reason, you should get into the habit of documenting your programs. This should be done so that the program can be understood several months later.

1.4.3 Documentation

Documentation is another tool to help with problem solving by computer. To be precise, program and data flowcharts are a type of documentation for a program—but documentation also includes a narrative of the program.

The narrative is an English language description of the program. It describes:

- the problem being solved
- the approach being used
- any special or unique attributes of the problem
- results to be expected

Here's an example narrative:

"This is a generalized program to determine the volume of a sphere. It calculates the spherical volume from the radius entered at the keyboard, for up to twenty different radii. The result is displayed on the screen. It is written in GW-BASIC. The formula for spherical volume is from Geometric Encyclopedia, R. Chemedes, 1942."

The five fundamental programming rules for good programming are:

- Definition of the problem (acquire the problem statement, problem analysis)
- Development of the algorithm for solution (data and program\flowcharts)
- Translation of the algorithm into a programming language (creating the program)
- Test run of the program
- Documentation

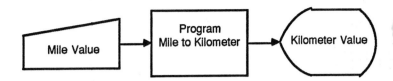

Figure 6: Example data flowchart for mile to kilometer

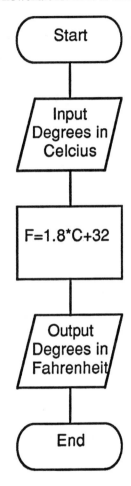

Figure 7: Program flowchart for Celcius to Fahrenheit program

1.5   ASCII codes

Your computer cannot directly process the characters which you enter on the keyboard. These are translated into numerical codes. The most widely used numerical code is called ASCII. ASCII stands for American Standard Code for Information Interchange. It was developed to standardize the exchange of data between different information carriers. For example, the character "A" always has the ASCII value 65. If this number is sent to a computer or printer that also works with ASCII, this value is always interpreted as the letter "A". The circumstances of the transfer make no difference. No matter whether you enter characters into the computer with the keyboard or send your data across the country with a telephone modem, as soon as the receiver gets the value 65 it will be translated into an "A". The standard ASCII code uses the values from 0 to 127.

Most computer manufacturers have decided to use an extended ASCII code so that other characters can be represented as well. This code is also called ASCII, although not all of the values agree with the standard ASCII.

In the standard ASCII, the values 65-90 are used for uppercase letters and the values 97-122 for lowercase letters and other characters. The ASCII code of your computer is identical to the standard ASCII code for codes 0-127, which consists of the upper and lowercase letters. Codes 128 through 255 make up an extended ASCII characters set. There are some differences in the way BASIC handles certain codes in the range of codes 8-32. Some of these codes can be useful in BASIC for positioning the cursor.

When working with BASIC you will encounter the term ASCII codes quite often. Appendix E contains an ASCII table of the IBM character set.

2.

Introduction to programming in BASIC

In this chapter you will learn how to use simple BASIC commands. Later you'll learn more complex commands by writing several BASIC programs. You'll write the first program by following the five fundamental programming rules presented in Chapter 1.

2.1   The first BASIC program

Let's assume that you want to calculate the surface of a sphere for 10 different radii. Since you already solved a similar problem in the previous chapter, you should have a good feeling for the approach to a solution.

First you'll have to define the problem.

1) Definition of the problem

Determine the surface area S of a sphere from the given radius, specified in centimeters. The formula for the spherical surface is:

$$S = 4 * \pi * r^2$$

2) Develop the algorithm

    a)   Start
    b)   Input r
    c)   Calculate $S = 4 * \pi * r^2$
    d)   Output S on the screen
    e)   End

On the following page are the data flowchart (figure 8) and the program flowchart for a solution to the problem. This program flowchart (figure 9) is a linear flowchart—that is, there are no branches in the form of subroutines or loops. If the terms subroutine and loop are unfamiliar to you, it doesn't matter at the moment. They will be explained in the Chapter 3.

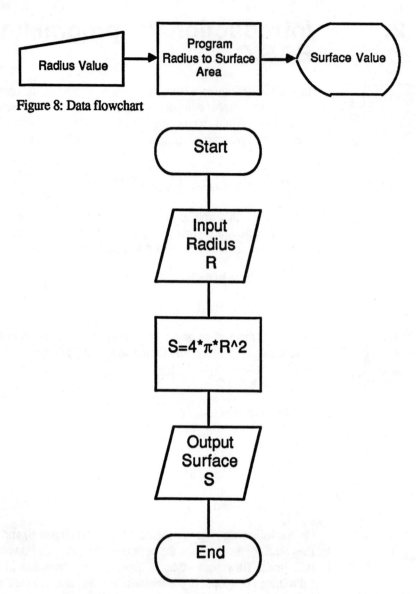

Figure 8: Data flowchart

Figure 9: Program flowchart

3) Creating the program

Enter the following program from the keyboard:

```
10 INPUT"ENTER RADIUS IN CM";R
20 LET S=4*3.14159*R^2
30 PRINT S
40 END
```

4) Test run of the program

Next you must check the data flowchart and program flowchart to verify if all details of the program were planned in a sound, logical manner. Then you can start the program with RUN. Since our program can be checked at a glance, we can enter RUN directly.

5) Documentation

The documentation of a program should be written so that other programmers will be able to understand the program and be able to make changes. For our short program, the data and program flowcharts and the short description in step 1, (definition of the problem) suffice for documentation.

As you have seen, each statement is written on a separate line in our program. This greatly increases the readability of programs. Avoid putting multiple statements on a line. With larger programs you won't be able to understand your commands later on. If you become accustomed to using line numbers in increments of ten, it will ease the insertion of new lines when required.

You can first enter line 20 into the computer and then line 10 if you like. The computer will sort out the line automatically according to the size of the line numbers. The computer also executes them in this order, provided other BASIC commands do not change this order through program jumps.

Now to the discussion of the commands used in our program: INPUT, LET, PRINT and END.

2.1.1   Entering values with INPUT

The INPUT statement is used in a program to read values from the keyboard during a program run. By entering values the user can affect the results of the program.

If a string of text within quotation marks follows the INPUT keyword, then this is displayed on the screen as a prompt. This prompt assists the user, by asking him to enter a particular value, or set of values. The program waits until the user enters this information and presses the <RETURN> key.

Here are a few examples. Enter the following in direct mode.

```
INPUT S
```

Only a question mark (?) is displayed. A question mark is automatically displayed when the computer is waiting for data input. The user may type a number followed by <RETURN>. The number is then assigned to the variable (S). Since (S) is the type of variable which may only contain a numeric value, if the user inputs the wrong type of information (such as a letter or symbol), the message "?REDO FROM START" will be displayed. The program will then return to another question mark prompt, and wait once again for proper input.

```
INPUT"ENTER RADIUS";S
```

The following text appears on the screen as a prompt:

```
ENTER RADIUS?
```

If you type 3 and <RETURN>, the value 3 is assigned to the variable S.

```
INPUT A,B,C
```

In this case, the user of the program may enter three values, each separated by a comma. The variables A, B, C are assigned the values one after the other. The comma serves to separate the values entered as well as the variables. It is important to note that without a prompt it is difficult for the user to determine what value (or how many values) needs to be entered.

```
LINE INPUT ; A$
```

This is another form of the INPUT statement, LINE INPUT. It is distinguished from the INPUT statement by the fact that if a comma is entered, it is passed to the variable. This means that only one variable can be assigned a value with LINE INPUT, whereas a list of variables can follow INPUT. Another difference with the LINE INPUT statement is that no question mark (?) prompt is displayed. Furthermore, LINE INPUT can be used only with string variables.

2.1.2   Value assignment with LET

The LET statement assigns a value to a specific variable. The expression to the right of the equal sign (=) is evaluated, and the variable to the left of the equal sign receives the value of that expression. The LET statement is also called "value assignment". The keyword LET is often omitted from assignment statements and is therefore considered optional. Some BASIC dialects do require its use but in GW-BASIC it is optional. The following examples should clarify this:

```
LET A=10          or      A=10
```

Assigns the value 10 to the variable.

```
LET A=A+5         or      A=A+5
```

Adds 5 to the variable A. The new value is again stored in A.

```
LET A=A*B-8       or      A=A*B-8
```

The value of A is multiplied by the value of B. Eight is then subtracted from the result. This new result is again assigned to the variable A.

In assignment statements, any arbitrary mathematical expression may stand to the right of the equal sign. Only one variable may be on the left of the equal sign.

Let's take another look at the second example above. Mathematically the expression is incorrect. If the value A is 4, then A=A+5 is false. How can we explain this? In BASIC, the expression is not considered an equality. Rather, it is an assignment. You might think of variables as a dresser full of drawers. Each drawer has a label on it. Therefore, the assignment A=A+5 means:

Take the contents of drawer A, add five to the contents and put the result back into drawer A.

2.1.3   Output with PRINT

The PRINT statement is one of the first commands which the beginner uses in programming. But at the same time it's one of the most versatile commands of GW-BASIC. You can use this statement to output text or the values of variables. You can combine the two and output the values of variables and text.

Here's a few examples of the use of the PRINT statement. The variables to be used have the following values:

```
A=10 : B=20 : C=30
```

Enter the line shown above and press <RETURN>.

Examples:

	Command	Output
a)	PRINT A	10
b)	PRINT "A"	A
c)	PRINT A*B	200
d)	PRINT A,B	10 20
e)	PRINT B;C	20 30
f)	PRINT "B";B	B 20
g)	PRINT "A EQUALS";A	A EQUALS 20

You will learn more about the uses of the PRINT statement in later programs. Before we discuss the examples above, we want to say something about the notation in the examples.

In the first mode, the direct mode, you enter the statements from the keyboard. They are immediately executed after you press the <RETURN> key. If you enter:

```
PRINT A <RETURN>
```

then the value of A is immediately displayed.

In the second mode, the program mode, the statements are prefixed with a line number. These statements are not executed at this time. Instead they are entered into the computer's memory as part of a program. The statement is stored in memory in ascending order according to the statement line number.

If you enter:

```
10 PRINT A
```

BASIC will store this statement in memory. The statement is not executed until the program is later RUN.

Now we come to example a) above. This notation of PRINT is used to output the value of a variable. The number 10 appears since we previously set A=10.

When printing numbers, note that a position is always reserved for the sign (+/-) of the number. If the number is positive, a space is placed before the number. If the number is negative, a minus sign is placed before the number. The numbers 10 and -10 always occupy the same number of positions.

Since no characters follow the variable A in example a), a carriage return and linefeed are performed automatically. This has the result that the next output will appear at the beginning of the following line.

To explain the terms carriage return and linefeed, we'll use the typewriter as an example.

Imagine that you have typed the number 10 on the paper. You then move the lever on the platen to the right. The roller moves the paper one line forward through the machine (linefeed), and the typewriter carriage is returned to the start of the line (carriage return). You can then start typing at the start of this new line.

The computer does the same sort of thing when it performs a carriage return and linefeed, except that you don't have to move a lever and there is no carriage to move to the right. The linefeed forces the cursor down one line. The carriage return forces any further output to begin at the first position in the line.

In example b) the character A appears between quotation marks. This causes the character A to be printed and not the value of the variable A. All characters enclosed in the quotation marks are printed verbatim except for certain special characters such as the <ESC> or <TAB> key. It is not possible to enter these keys directly.

Example c) shows you that calculations can also be performed within a PRINT statement. First the product of the variables A*B (10*20) is evaluated and then it is printed. Here too, a carriage return and linefeed are generated.

Example d) illustrates the ability of the PRINT statement to print several variable values from one statement. The comma supresses the carriage return/linefeed after printing the value of the first variable (A). It also affects the position at which the values are displayed.

Your computer divides each output line into 14 character long TAB positions. If a comma is placed between two variables, the second variable is printed at the start of the next tab, at the 15th column on the screen line. If several variables are separated by commas, they are printed at the successive TAB positions.

Enter the following into the computer:

```
PRINT "1","2","3","4","5","6","7","8"
```

When you press the <RETURN> key the positions of the individual tabs are displayed. If we had not put the numbers in quotation marks, they would have been moved one position to the right because of the space reserved for the sign.

Example e) illustrates the effect of the semicolon. The semicolon supresses both the carriage return and linefeed. It also supresses the tab function. The characters are printed in succession in the order in which they appear in the PRINT statement. This makes it possible to include descriptive text following the value of a variable.

Example f) is similar and shows you how to display descriptive text before the value of a variable. In this case, the descriptive text is the name of the variable whose value follows. Again, the semicolon separates the descriptive text from the variable.

Example g) is similar to f) and merely shows you that the descriptive text can be of any arbitrary length. The text can be as detailed as you wish.

The END statement in the last program line of our example program (in section 2.1) designates the logical end of the program. This statement is usually found at the end of the program. It can also be placed elsewhere within the program. If you have written a program and do not place the END statement in the last line of the program, no harm is done. This is because the computer automatically indicates the end of the program in memory (and not in the program listing itself). Despite this, you should become accustomed to using the END statement for the sake of good, complete programming style.

Our next topic is the PRINT USING statement, since it is very closely related to the PRINT statement.

2.1.3.1   PRINT USING

The PRINT USING statement represents a modified form of the PRINT statement. You will want to learn how to use this statement to output formatted numbers and strings, such as dollar amounts. The following control characters are available for PRINT USING:

For numerical output:

#	indicate position of digit
+	print + sign with positive numbers
−	print - sign with negative numbers (+ and - are mutually exclusive)
.	designate position of decimal point
**	fill with * instead of spaces
$$	print $ as the first character
**$	fill with * and print $ as first non-numeric character
,	place a comma (,) 3 places before decimal point
^^^^	print values in scientific notation (e.g. 1.23 E+02)
_	Suppress control function of the next character, such as for #

For text output:

!	print only the first character of string
\ \	print selected number of characters as determined by the number of characters between \\+ 2
&	print the entire string variable

Let's further clarify the use of the PRINT USING with some examples. First enter the following into the computer:

```
A   = 12345.678    <RETURN>
B   = 34.34555     <RETURN>
C   = -520         <RETURN>
D$  = "IBM PC"     <RETURN>
```

Enter the following statements. Press the <RETURN> key after each one.

```
PRINT USING "#####.##";A
```

As output you get the value rounded to two decimal places, displayed on the screen:

Output: 12345.68

Now input:

```
PRINT USING "#####.##";B
```

Output: 34.35

Note that the decimal point is printed in the exact same position for both values. This would not happen with the ordinary PRINT statement.

If the specified format is exceeded by the value of the number, the number is printed with a preceding percent sign. The specified format cannot be followed in this case.

The following PRINT statement:

```
PRINT USING "####.##";A
```

causes this output:

Output: %12345.60

The percent sign tells you that the value does not fit in the format field you choose for the PRINT USING statement.

If you want to emphasize positive vs. negative results, the following combinations will work:

```
PRINT USING "+#####.##";A
```

Output: +12345.68

```
PRINT USING "#####.##+";A
```

Output: 12345.68+

```
PRINT USING "#####.##-;C
```

Output: 520.00-

Here the negative designation is printed following the number. Normally it is placed in front of the number.

The next example shows you how to fill the output of numbers in the given format with asterisks.

```
PRINT USING "**#####.##";A
```

Output: **12345.68

```
PRINT USING :**#####.##";B
```

Output: *****34.35

The next form of the output places a dollar sign in front of the number.

```
PRINT USING "$$#####.##";A
```

Output: $12345.68

```
PRINT USING "$$#####.##";B
```

Output: $34.35

Naturally, the dollar sign and asterisk sign can be combined with each other, as the following example shows.

```
PRINT USING "**$#####.##";B
```

Output: *****$34.35

Furthermore, you can have commas automatically placed at every third place before the decimal point. Additional designations like "dollars" are also possible.

```
PRINT USING "**##,###.## dollars";A
```

Output: **12,345.68 dollars

To output the number values in exponential notation, the following form of the PRINT USING statement is used:

```
PRINT USING "##.##^^^^";A
```

Output: 1.23E+04

You can also determine how many places appear before or after the decimal point, as the following example shows.

```
PRINT USING "###.##^^^^";A
```

Output: 12.34E+03

The _ character is used in order to output control character like #.

```
PRINT USING "FILE NUMBER _###";B
```

Output: FILE NUMBER #34

This concludes the explanations of the numerical output forms of PRINT USING. Now let's take a look at the options for text output.

```
PRINT USING "!";D$
```

Output: I

By using the exclamation point, only the first character of the string variable D$ is printed. Remember that we assigned the string IBM PC to D$.

The next form allows us to output an arbitrary number of characters of a string.

```
PRINT USING "\ \";D$:REM backslash one space backslash
```

Output: IBM

A total of three characters are given between the quotation marks (including the two slashes). This causes the first three characters of D$ to be printed. This use of the PRINT USING statement is related to the LEFT$ function, which will be discussed later.

The last option outputs the entire string.

```
PRINT USING "&";D$
```

Output: IBM PC

This could also be done with:

```
PRINT D$
```

You may need the & character within a PRINT USING instruction.

For the sake of thoroughness, we should also mention the WRITE statement: this statement also has a close relationship to the PRINT statement. However, its output is somewhat different. Enter the following statement:

```
WRITE "IBM PC"
```

Then press the <RETURN> key. "IBM PC" is displayed. The quotation marks are not displayed by the PRINT statement. If numbers or variables separated by commas follow the WRITE statement, the comma does not have a tab function, but is also displayed.

```
WRITE 2,3,4
```

Output: 2,3,4

Now we have described all the commands that occurred in our example program, including two close "relatives." You shouldn't have any great difficulty using these commands.

In order to make programs understandable to others—and also for yourself—we will take a look at the REM statement.

2.1.4   Comments with REM

REM allows you to place comments in your program at any desired location. REM is short for REMember. Everything that follows a REM statement in a program line will be ignored by the computer, including other BASIC commands.

We will now expand our example program and also make it more understandable for others. This is part of documenting the program, by the way. Here is the modified program listing with descriptions of the individual program lines:

```
1      REM 2.1.4
10     REM CALCULATE SURFACE OF A SPHERE
20     REM INPUT RADIUS IN CM
30     INPUT "INPUT RADIUS (IN CM)";R
40     REM CALCULATE SURFACE
50     LET S=4.*3.14159527*R^2
60     REM OUTPUT SURFACE IN CM^2
70     PRINT" THE SURFACE IS ";S;"CM^2"
80     END
```

Lines 10-20 serve to tell the reader what the program does and what input is required. In line 30 the input of the data is done with INPUT, and a prompt is also printed for the user. This could also have been done by outputting the text with the PRINT statement in a separate program line and the INPUT statement by itself in a program line. The comment in line 40 refers to the calculation in line 50.

In line 50 the variable S is assigned the value of the surface through the computation of the mathematical expression. Line 60 makes references to the output of the CM^2 in line 70. The text and value of the variable are printed in line 70. Line 80 concludes the program with the END statement.

2.2   Variables and their use

Before we give you some sample problems to solve, we must discuss the various types of variables. Variables are used to store different types of information.

In GW-BASIC there are four types of variables, each designated with a different symbol placed at the end of the variable name.

Integer - This variable type can represent only whole numbers. The designation is made with the percent sign, which is simply appended to the name of the variable (such as A% or C4%). If this variable type is assigned a non-integer value, only the places before the decimal point are taken into account. A further restriction is placed on the values of variables of this type, in that only values between -32768 and 32767 are allowed.

Single-precision real - This variable type is used to represent decimal numbers. The variable designation is an exclamation point placed after the variable name, although this is not absolutely necessary. Examples of the permitted designations are A! or B2! (A or B2). Single precision numbers are accurate to 6 decimal places. The published range is -1E-38 to 1E+38. The actual range may vary in different versions. Our version allowed a range of -2.938736-39 to 1.701411+38.

Double-precision real - This is similar to the single-precision real type of variable, with the exception of being accurate to 15 decimal places. Double-precision variables are designated using the number symbol (#). The range is approximately the same as for single-precision.

String - This variable type is designated by the dollar sign ($). String variables can store arbitrary strings of characters. No more than 255 characters may be placed in a string variable or the following error message will be printed:

```
String too long
```

Certain things must be taken into account when using variable designations. GW-BASIC recognizes variable names of up to 40 characters. Many computers cannot distinguish between such long variable names. This makes programs easier to read and understand, because variables can be assigned intelligent designations like payment, exchange, or name%. BASIC keywords may also be found within variable names. The variable name LAND *is* legal, despite the fact that the keyword AND is contained within it. It is preferable to avoid using most keywords in variable names.

Furthermore, digits may be used in the name with the limitation that the first character must be a letter. Names like Amount1, A9, and other are allowed. It is not permitted to have a number in the first location. For instance, a name like 9Amount is illegal. You must also be careful not try to use BASIC keywords as variable names, like OR, FN, or ABS.

2.2.1   Calculations with variables

If you want to perform calculations with the variables in your programs, you must first become acquainted with the rules of the individual computation operations. The order of execution of the operations is just like it would be in algebra. The following listing gives more information.

Operator	Precedence	Meaning
^	First	Exponentiation
*	Second	Multiplication
/		Division
+	Third	Addition
-		Subtraction

There is also an order to the execution of logical operators, which is described in the Appendix.

You now have enough knowledge to solve the following exercises. They contain questions about specific sections as well as small programming problems for you to solve on your own. First try to solve the exercises on your own without referring to the corresponding sections. It won't hurt if you make mistakes, since we learn best from our own mistakes. And you won't be graded here. If you are unsure, you can work through the appropriate sections again.

Try your best to follow the five steps of programming when solving the exercises. Before each new program you type in, enter the command NEW to clear the BASIC memory and erase the old program. In the following section we'll learn some new commands and how they apply in programs.

Exercises

1. Test the following variable names for validity and give reasons for your decision. See Appendix B for reference.

a)	X1	b)	WORLD$	c)	AUTO
d)	ORR%	e)	IF	f)	DATE$
g)	4NAME%	h)	255	i)	MONDAY

2. Write a program that reads the four values A, B, C, and D and outputs the values A and B on one line followed by the values C and D in the next line.

3. Write a program that calculates the surface of a right-angle triangle in square inches and include appropriate text with the output (Area=1/2 base*height).

4. Write a program that calculates the ideal weight (height in cm minus 100 minus 10 percent) of a person. The height input should be required in cm and the output of the body weight should appear in kilograms. (We're using metric figures to keep the calculations simple here. After you've written the program, try modifying it by converting the measurements to US Customary: one inch = 2.54 cm, one pound = 2.2 kilograms).

5. Write a program that calculates the number of liters in an aquarium after the program has asked for the length, height, and width in cm (Liters = Volume divided by 1000).

6. Change problem 2 so that the program prints each value on a separate line, together with the name of the variable.

2.3   Numerical functions

Up to now we have concerned ourselves with assignments of values to variables. The mathematical functions of GW-BASIC were not used; only the four basic computations were used.

In this section we'll talk about the built-in functions like COS (X) or SIN (X). To do this we'll take a short excursion into mathematics. But don't worry—we won't hit you with any long-winded mathematical proofs, or beat you over the head with formulas. This is a BASIC book and will remain as such.

In many BASIC books and in the manual provided with your version of BASIC, you'll note that the arguments for trigonometric functions like SIN(X), COS(X), or TAN(X) are specified in radians. What exactly are radians?

Most of us know that a circle can be divided into 360 degrees. One degree is 1/360th of a circle. Ninety degrees is a quarter of the circle, 180 degrees is a half circle, and so on.

Radian measurement is based on the circumference of a circle. Recall that the circumference of a circle is as follows:

Circumference = $2\pi r$ (r = radius)

If we use a circle with a unit radius (radius=1), the calculation is simplified to:

U=$2\pi1$ (or) U=2π

A circle has 360 degrees, or 2π (6.2831) radians. Ninety degrees would be $2\pi/4$ or $\pi/2$ radians. The advantage of radians is that you can directly determine the length of the arc cut off by the angle. Calculations with radians takes getting used to, since you can more easily imagine 90 degrees than $\pi/2$ radians.

This short excursion into mathematics is enough for now. Let's write and use a couple of example programs so that these ideas become clearer to you.

Enter the following example program into your computer:

```
10   INPUT "ENTER ANGLE IN DEGREES";DG
20   REM CALCULATE THE SINE
25   PI=3.1415927
30   SI=SIN(DG*PI/180)
40   PRINT USING "THE SINE OF ####.##"+CHR$(248);DG;
45   REM THE CHARACTER CODE FOR DEGREE IS 248
50   PRINT" IS =";SI
60   END
```

Start the program by typing RUN and enter the value 90 for the angle. You should get the value 1 as the result. The programs expects the angle in degrees and calculates the corresponding sine. Since the variable π is not directly available in GW-BASIC, it must first be defined in line 25. If you want to enter the angle in degrees, you must use the conversion in line 30. For calculating the cosine, simply replace SIN with COS. The variable SI can stay the same.

In order to make clear the difference from radians, enter the program in the following version. But first enter NEW and press <RETURN>. The NEW command clears any current program lines from memory, so be sure to use this command before entering any new program.

```
10     INPUT "ENTER IN RADIANS";RD
20     REM CALCULATE THE SINE
30     SI=SIN(RD)
40     PRINT"THE SINE OF";RD;"RAD ";
50     PRINT"IS =";SI
60     END
```

As you see, line 25 is omitted from our previous example and line 30 has been changed a little. Start the program and enter the value 1.57079633 (which corresponds to $\pi/2$). Again, the result should be 1.

The use of the other functions is quite simple. These numerical functions are passed just one variable, which is then used to make a calculation. SQR(X) calculates the square root of X and ATN(X) the arctangent of X. The functions EXP(X) and LOG(X) calculate the Xth power of e=2.71827183 and the natural logarithm of X (base e). The one function is the inverse of the other. Enter the following command in the direct mode and press <RETURN>:

```
PRINT EXP(1)
```

As a result you get the number:

2.71828

Repeat the same process with the following command:

```
PRINT LOG(2.718282)
```

You again get the value 1. If you want to calculate the logarithm of base 10, you need only divide LOG(X) with LOG(10).

The following example program calculates both the logarithm base 10 and the natural logarithm.

```
10   INPUT "INPUT THE VALUE";N
20   REM CALCULATE NATURAL LOG
30   LN=LOG(N)
40   REM CALCULATE LOG BASE 10
50   LO=LOG(N)/LOG(10)
60   PRINT "LN(";N;") =";LN
80   PRINT
90   PRINT"LO(";N;") =";LO
110  END
```

You see that it is relatively simple to make use of these functions in programs. The only difficult part is the conversion of the values.

The function SGN(X) returns the sign of X. The result is 1 if X is positive, 0 if X=0, and -1 if X is negative. Any number can be used in place of X. The function INT(X) is another very useful function for rounding numbers. With an appropriate routine, we can round to any number of places after the decimal. The following program should clarify this.

```
10   INPUT" HOW MANY DECIMAL PLACES";X%
20   INPUT "NUMBER TO ROUND";N
30   REM ROUND OFF
40   N=INT(N * 10^X% + .5) / 10^X%
50   REM OUTPUT ROUNDED OFF NUMBER
60   PRINT N
70   END
```

rounding off numbers

Or use

CINT

The program is quite simple, but we would like to explain the most important lines. Line 10 asks for the number of places to which the decimal number will be rounded. This value is assigned to the variable X%. This is an integer variable, since only integers can be used as input.

Line 20 asks for the number to be rounded off. Enter a decimal number here having more places *after* the decimal than the number to be rounded.

The actual rounding off is performed in line 40. N is first multiplied by 10 to the X% power. This moves all of the places to be rounded out in front of the decimal point. Then .5 is added in order to round off the final place, since INT simply truncates the number at the decimal point. The integer value of this number is then taken. This is divided by 10 to the X% power to move the digits back behind the decimal point—but this time only the digits that were moved out in front by the multiplication.

Start the program with RUN and the <RETURN> key. Enter some values in order to see what results you get. Examine line 40 carefully, the line in which the number is rounded off. You can use such routines in your own programs later.

You can also round off numbers with the function CINT (Convert to INTeger). But here the numbers may only be in the range from -32768 to +32767.

```
PRINT CINT(-35.6)
```

Output: -36

The functions CSNG and CDBL convert double-precision variables to single-precision, and single-precision variables to double-precision. It is important to note that single-precision variables converted to double-precision will only be as accurate as the original single-precision form of the variable.

The FIX function will also return an integer value from a floating point number. The difference in the way FIX operates is that it simply chops off the decimal value, as shown by the following example:

```
PRINT FIX(3.99)
```

Output: 3

With the function MOD you can calculate the remainder of a division. Enter:

```
PRINT 32 MOD 7
```

Output: 4   (32=4*7 rem 4).

The ABS, or absolute function always returns a positive number with the same value as the argument. An argument is the value which is placed in parenthesis after the keyword. In the statement, N = ABS(X), the variable X is the argument. Here is an example of how the ABS function operates:

```
PRINT ABS(-3.99)
```

Output: 3.99

2.3.1   Functions with DEF FN

The DEF FN function is a practical way of saving space. With it you can assign complex mathematical functions to the expression FN. This expression is called when needed. At the same time, a parameter used as an argument to the function is passed to it. The following example should make this clear.

```
10   REM DEFINITION FUNCTION
20   DEF FNF(X) =X^2 + 2*X+4
30   REM INPUT PARAMETER
40   INPUT"ENTER VALUE";X
50   REM OUTPUT
60   PRINT FNF(X)
70   END
```

In line 20 the mathematical function X^2+2X+4 is assigned to the expression FN F(X). The values of X in FN F(X) determines the result of the function. If other variables are used within the function, they are not affected by X—they retain their current values.

This function gives you the ability to create your own functions within a program. You can then call up your function with a parameter just like the built-in functions. This saves typing and memory space, and also makes formulas using the custom function easier to read.

2.3.2   Random numbers

GW-BASIC has a built-in random number generator that can be called with the function RND or RND(X). This function is required in certain types of simulation in which chance plays a role. This function is often used in games in order to introduce random elements. There are 3 possible argument types which may be used with RND(X). X may be positive, negative, or zero. Using RND without an argument is the same as using a positive argument. The random number will always be generated by using the argument in a formula with a random seed value. Using a negative argument introduces the last temporary value left over from the most recent floating point operation into the random formula. Using zero as the argument causes the last random number generated to be repeated. The random seed value is initially set by GW-BASIC. It may be changed at any time by using the RANDOMIZE statement. The RND function will always return a value between 0 and 1. This number may then be multiplied by some other value to achieve a number in the desired range, as shown by the following example:

```
10   REM GENERATE RANDOM NUMBER
15   RANDOMIZE 0
20   A = INT (6 * RND(1)) + 1
30   PRINT A
40   END
```

Start the program with RUN and <RETURN>. Execute the program several times in a row and note the numbers printed. You will notice that the same number is generated each time the program is run. This is because the values used to generate the random number are the same each time. To generate truly random numbers, the random seed value should be based on some value which will be different each time the program is run. We'll look at just such an example later on.

A combination of RND and INT was used in line 20 in order to output numbers between 1 and 6, since we need integer numbers. The 1 is added so that zero does not occur (lower bound) and the maximum value of 6 can be reached.

With this type of random number generation you can create random numbers in any range. The 6 represents the upper bound of the interval and the +1 is the lower bound. If you want to create random numbers in the range from 100 to 150, line 20 must look like this:

```
20 A=INT((50+1)*RND(1))+100
```

or in general notation, in which U represents the upper bound and L the lower bound:

```
A=INT((U+1-L)*RND(1))+L
```

In the simpler examples you don't always recognize this general form. The following line:

```
20 A=INT(6*RND(1))+1
```

should be written as:

```
20 A=INT((6+1-1)*RND(1))+1
```

in general form. But since the lower bound is one, the formula can be simplified.

2.3.3   More commands for variables

GW-BASIC has a set of commands that can be used to affect variables or variable formats. GW-BASIC offers two functions that allow you to convert decimal numbers into hexadecimal or octal. These number systems are commonly used in computer calculations, see the Appendix for more information. The function HEX$(X) converts decimal numbers into hexadecimal numbers. Here X stands for the number to be converted. X may assume values between -32768 and +32767.

Example:

```
PRINT HEX$(60)
```

Output: 3C

The function OCT$(X) converts decimal numbers to numbers in the octal system (base 8). Again, X stands for the number to be converted. A value between -32768 and +32767 must be passed to the function. For example:

```
PRINT OCT$(16)
```

Output: 20

In both examples, variables can be used instead of constants. As already mentioned, there are four different types of variables in GW-BASIC. If you want to assign specific variable names with specific variable types within a program, the following commands are at your disposal:

    DEFDBL, DEFINT, DEFSNG, DEFSTR

For example, if you define:

    DEFSTR A-B

within a program, all variables that start with A or B will be treated as string variables. You need not append a dollar sign to these variables within a program to use them as string variables. The instruction:

    DEFSNG C-D

defines all variables starting with C or D as real (single-precision) variables. The other commands are used similarly.

2.3.4   ASC(X$) and CHR$(X)

GW-BASIC can output numbers, letters, and certain special characters on its screen when these symbols are placed between the quotation marks in a PRINT statement.

But not all characters can be printed with this method. The CHR$ function is used here. With this function you have the ability to output any character of the character set. Enter the following in the direct mode:

    PRINT CHR$(65)

When you press the <RETURN> key, the character A appears on the screen.

The function ASC represents the reverse of the CHR$ function. For example, if you want to know the ASCII value of the letter A, you would enter the following command into the computer in the direct mode:

    PRINT ASC("A")

If you press the <RETURN> key, the value 65 appears on the screen. See the Appendix for a chart of ASCII values.

Exercises

To give you a chance to use your newly-acquired knowledge, we want to give you some exercises to solve. Compare your results with the suggested solutions and explanations in Appendix C. Then you can work through the next chapter.

In these exercises you will have to use commands that were discussed on the preceding pages. Also, remember to take the five rules of programming into account here.

1. Write a program that simulates throwing two dice. The results should be printed, with appropriate spacing, on a single line.

2. Write a program that calculates the surface of a triangle according to the formula:

    F=SQR (S* (S–A) * (S–B) * (S–C))

    where S=1/2(A+B+C) (and A, B, and C are the lengths of the three sides).

    Note that the formula cannot be directly inserted into the program in the form it stands. The program should ask for the values of A, B, and C in inches. The result should be labeled appropriately.

3. Write a program that asks for the input of a character and then prints the ASCII value of this character, together with the input character, on the same line.

4. Write a program that calculates the height from the time an object takes to fall from that height. The measured fall time should be requested. Air resistance will not be taken into account. The formula is $D=.5*g*t^2$. The value of the constant g is 9.81. The result is to be printed in meters/second.

5. Write a program that calculates the gasoline consumption per 100 miles using the following formula:

    usage per 100 = total usage / miles traveled * 100

2.4 TAB and SPC

These two functions are used to output data or characters at specific positions on a screen line. TAB and SPC are very similar in their uses, but quite different in their effects. The TAB function and the parameter in parentheses always position the output relative to the start of the line. Enter the following command sequence in the direct mode:

```
PRINT TAB(15) "TEST"
```

The output you get is the word TEST at position 15 of the screen line. Now enter the line again replacing TAB with the SPC function. After pressing the <RETURN> key you get the same result. When using the functions in this manner, they both have the same effect. In the next example you will see the difference. Enter the following commands:

```
PRINT TAB(5) "TEST 1" TAB(20) "TEST 2"
```

After pressing the <RETURN> key the word TEST 1 will appear at the fifth position and the word TEST 2 at the 20th position. Enter the command sequence again and change the second TAB to SPC. Your line should then look like this:

```
PRINT TAB(5) "TEST 1" SPC(20) "TEST 2"
```

Now when you press the <RETURN> key, you will see the difference in the output on the screen. The second word TEST 2 is not printed at the 20th position from the start of the line, but at the 20th position from the last character of TEST 1. This means that the TAB function always works with the *absolute* position in the screen line, and the SPC function with the *relative* position from the last character printed. The values passed to either function may not be larger than 255.

When using these functions in connection with output on the printer, TAB has no real use. This is because, in conjunction with the PRINT# statement, it is either not interpreted or interpreted as SPC. For this reason, the TAB function should only be used with the normal PRINT statement.

2.5 Strings

A string refers to a string of characters that can contain up to 255 of the characters from the character set. The string variable is designated with the dollar sign. A$ would represent a normal designation of a string. The assignment of a character to a string variable is done in the same manner as with the numeric variables. The sole difference is the characters are enclosed in quotation marks. The following example shows a valid assignment:

```
A$="IBM PC"
```

If you try to assign a numerical value to a string variable (e.g. A$=2), the following error message appears:

```
Type mismatch
```

The same error message is printed if you try to assign a string to a numerical variable:

```
A="TEST"
```

When using strings, the plus sign is the only computation operator allowed. This character chains two strings together. If we define A$="DISK " and B$="DRIVE", the computation with + yields the string "DISK DRIVE". A short example program will make this clear.

```
10 A$="DISK ":B$="DRIVE"
20 DL$=A$+B$
30 PRINT DL$
40 END
```

In line 10 the string variables A$ and B$ are first initialized. Line 20 assigns the concatenation (linked series) of variables A$ and B$ to the variable DL$. Line 30 then outputs the new string.

Not only can you combine strings with each other, but check for equality or compare the number of characters. We will get to this, but not until the compare commands are discussed (see IF...THEN...ELSE). When comparing, only strings may be compared with strings. Comparing a string variable to a numerical variable is not legal.

2.5.1   LEFT$

GW-BASIC has other functions for manipulating strings. The first
function we'll look at is LEFT$. This function returns a portion of the
designated string. Enter the following program to make this clear:

```
10   A$="COMPUTER"
20   B$=LEFT$(A$,1)
30   C$=LEFT$(A$,2)
40   D$=LEFT$(A$,3)
50   E$=LEFT$(A$,4)
60   F$=LEFT$(A$,5)
70   G$=LEFT$(A$,6)
80   H$=LEFT$(A$,7)
90   I$=LEFT$(A$,8)
100  PRINT B$:PRINT C$:PRINT D$:PRINT E$
110  PRINT F$:PRINT G$:PRINT H$:PRINT I$
120  END
```

Start the program with RUN. The result of the program is shown
below. This example clearly shows how LEFT$ works. In line 10 the
character string COMPUTER is assigned to the string variable A$. Line
20 forms a left partial string of A$ with one character and assigns it to
B$. Line 30 then forms a string containing the 2 leftmost characters of
A$. Lines 40 to 90 are interpreted in the same manner. This means that
the statement LEFT$(A$,X) generates the leftmost X characters of
A$. Lines 100 to 110 output the results to the screen.

Here is the result of the program:

```
C
CO
COM
COMP
COMPU
COMPUT
COMPUTE
COMPUTER
```

As you see, we can have some fun with this function. But it's also
intended for serious applications as well, especially in data processing.

2.5.2   RIGHT$

The next function is similar to the LEFT$ function in the way it works. It differs from LEFT$ only in that is takes the characters starting at the right end of the string instead of the left. Let's change all references to LEFT$ in the previous example program to RIGHT$, starting in line 20 with RIGHT$(A$,1). Start the program again with RUN. You should get the following output on the screen:

```
R
ER
TER
UTER
PUTER
MPUTER
OMPUTER
COMPUTER
```

Now change the order of the numbers in the RIGHT$ statement. Starting with eight and then counting backwards to one so that you get the reverse result. You first get the expression COMPUTER, and last just the letter R. These examples should clarify the use of these functions.

2.5.3   MID$

One of the more interesting functions used in string processing is MID$. With this function you can isolate one or more characters of a string. First we want to look at the operation of this function by means of simple examples.

Enter the following program into your computer:

```
10  A$="THIS IS A SAMPLE STRING"
20  B$=MID$(A$,1,4)
30  C$=MID$(A$,6,4)
40  D$=MID$(A$,11,6)
50  E$=MID$(A$,12,6)+MID$(A$,20,4)+MID$(A$,11,1)
60  PRINT A$
70  PRINT B$
80  PRINT C$
90  PRINT D$
100 PRINT E$
```

```
110 END
```

Run the program and take a close look at the result. With the MID$ function you can isolate a specific number of characters from a specific position in a string. These are then placed in a new string. The general syntax is:

```
MID$ (M$,X,Y)
```

M$ is the name of the string, X designates the position at which character it will begin, and Y determines the number of characters. The positions are always counted from left to right. So line 20 assigns the substring to B$. A new string is generated from A$ which is to contain four characters and starts with the first character of A$.

The string C$ is formed in the same manner. Here we start with the sixth character so that the string IS A is generated. Line 40 is self explanatory. Line 50 is interesting. Here again we use a *concatenation*, or linked series, to make a string not directly readable from the original string—namely AMPLE RINGS.

You can see that the LEFT$ and RIGHT$ functions can be replaced by the MID$ function. In our examples, the position and number of characters were designated by constants. It is also possible to specify these through variables and arithmetic expressions. In addition, you can not only read characters within a string with MID$, but also change or reassign them. For example, write:

```
MID$ (A$,3,2)="AT"
```

This changes the third and fourth characters to "A" and "T", creating "THAT IS A SAMPLE STRING".

2.5.4   LEN(X$)

Before we look at the next function, try to figure out how many characters (without quotation marks) are contained in the string in our last example. The answer? It's 23 characters. You've probably guessed that this has something to do with the next function we want to discuss.

You can determine the length of a string with LEN(X$). The result is numerical and can be assigned to a corresponding variable. If you have not yet entered NEW (erasing the program and variables), and CLR (setting the variables to zero) since the last example program, enter this in direct mode:

```
PRINT LEN(A$)
```

and press <RETURN>. The result should be 23. You have determined the number of characters in A$. When using this function it doesn't matter what characters the string is made up of. All characters in the string are counted, including spaces.

2.5.5   VAL(X$)

The VAL(X$) function converts a string X$ into a numerical value. If the string starts with a character that cannot be converted to a number, such as a letter, the result will be zero. If a letter or other characters which cannot be converted to a number are found within the string, only the first part of the string is converted to a number. The following examples should clarify this:

a)
```
10 A$="343.45"
20 A=VAL(A$)
30 PRINT A
```

Output: 343.35

b)
```
10 B$="D38.47F"
20 B=VAL(B$)
30 PRINT B
```

Output: 0

c)
```
10 C$="234FFC54"
20 C=VAL(C$)
30 PRINT C
```

Output: 234

d)
```
10 D$="33,221"
20 D=VAL(D$)
30 PRINT D
```

Output: 33

if D$ = 33.221

output =
33.221

Enter these examples into your computer and try them out. Example a) shows what happens when an entire string can be converted. The string in example b) starts with a character which cannot be converted into a number, and is therefore interpreted as zero. Example c) shows a "mixed" string, in which only the first group of digits is converted. Example d) is intended only to show that the comma is simply seen as a non-convertable character, and only the first group of digits is converted.

2.5.6   STR$(X$)

The STR$(X) function has exactly the opposite effect of VAL$—it converts a numerical expression into a string.

The string which is produced may start with a space. If the number is positive, the first character will be space. Two examples should clarify this:

a)   10 A=1234
      20 A$=STR$(A)
      30 PRINT A$

Output: 1234

b)   10 B=-1234
      20 B$=STR$(B)
      30 PRINT B$

Output: -1234

Both of the strings contain five characters each. The values of the numbers themselves could also be converted to strings instead of assigning them to variables first. STR$(1234) could be used in example a) instead of STR$(A).

2.5.7   INSTR

GW-BASIC offers us another useful function for working with strings:

        INSTR

This allows you to search through a string for a desired substring of characters. The syntax of the function looks like this:

INSTR(X,A$,B$)

Here the X stands for the position at which the string A$ is to be searched. B$ stands for the substring to be searched for. The result is the position of the substring within the string. If the substring is not found within the target string, the result is zero. The following program should clarify the function.

```
10 A$="THIS IS A SAMPLE STRING"
20 B$="IS"
30 C=INSTR(A$,B$)
40 PRINT C
50 END
```

RUN the program. You'll get the value 6 as the result for variable C.

This function searches for the exact string. This means that the substring is would not have been found, since is contains lowercase letters.

2.5.8   STRING$

This function creates a string which contains a sequence of the same character. For example, enter the following into the computer:

```
A$=STRING$(40,"*"): PRINT A$
```

This prints a line with 40 asterisks as the output. Here again, the upper limit is 255.

2.5.9   SPACE$

The SPACE$ function is similar to the STRING$ function.

```
A$=SPACE$(40)
```

The command line above causes A$ to be filled with 40 spaces. This statement can be used for exact positioning of output, as the following example shows:

```
PRINT SPACE$(12);"IBM PC"
```

This example prints 12 spaces followed by the string "IBM PC".

Exercises

Before we move on to the next chapter, you should solve the following exercises so that you learn to use the new functions.

1.   What difference is there in the output that the following two command sequences produce? Don't enter them in the computer, but try to answer the question.

```
PRINT SPC(5)"TEST 1" TAB(15)"TEST 2"

PRINT TAB(5)"TEST 1" TAB(15)"TEST 2"
```

   a)   The only difference is that the first command sequence will cause the string "TEST 1" to be printed one more character to the right.

   b)   For the first command sequence, five spaces will first be printed followed by the output. After fifteen more spaces the second output appears. For the second command sequence five spaces are first printed but the second output does not occur until 10 more spaces later because the TAB function makes reference to the start of the current line.

   c)   For the first command sequence, five spaces are first printed, then the second output follows 10 spaces later. For the second command sequence, five spaces are also printed, but the second output does not occur until 15 spaces later.

2.   What expression do you get in B$ from the following command sequence if the string A$="DRILL PRESS"?

```
B$=MID$(A$,1,3)+MID$(A$,7,1)+MID$(A$,10,1)
```

3.   What expression does one get with the following command sequence for A$ if A$="ROTOR"?

```
A$=LEFT$(A$,3)+RIGHT$(A$,2)
```

4.   What must the command sequence look like if one wants to get the result B$="MANY" if A$="ELEMENTARY"?

2.6   Editing programs

Before we continue to develop larger programs, we will first look at the commands that make programming somewhat easier. The term editing includes anything having to do with changing a program—whether it's deleting or inserting program lines, or correcting syntax errors. We assume that you know how to insert and delete lines. If you still have difficulty with these, read the corresponding section in your BASIC manual.

We already mentioned that the line numbering should be done in steps of ten. A command that helps you do this is AUTO. If, for example, you enter:

```
AUTO 10,10
```

into the computer and press the <RETURN> key, the computer will automatically provide you with line numbers in increments of 10. The first value passed to the AUTO command specifies the first program line. The second value determines the increments, i.e. the distance between individual program lines.

If you want to turn the automatic line numbering off again, press the keys <CONTROL> + <BREAK>. Be sure to do this on a blank line to insure that all of your previous lines have been stored properly.

If you write programs, sooner or later you'll need:

```
RENUM
```

Lines almost always have to be inserted when developing programs. The numbering could soon look like this:

```
10...
12...
19...
20...
21...
```

Now enter RENUM in direct mode and all program lines will be renumbered in steps of 10, so that the example above would have line numbers from 10 to 60. This command also takes the destinations of GOTO, GOSUB, etc. into account so that jumps still work correctly after the command. You may also specify different line increments as well as a range of lines to be numbered when you renumber your program by entering:

    RENUM X,Y,Z

Here X stands for the line number with which the new numbering is supposed to begin. Y stands for the line number through which the lines will be renumbered, and Z determines the step width. The command:

    RENUM 200,100,5

would renumber the program beginning at the old line number 100 in steps of five, starting with the new line number 200.

It may also occur that you want to delete only certain lines from a program. To do this you would enter:

    DELETE 100-200

into the computer and all lines between 100 and 200 (inclusive) will be erased. You may also delete all lines from the beginning of the program up to a particular line, or from a given line to the end of the program by excluding one of the two line numbers normally specified in this command. For example:

    DELETE -200

will cause all line numbers up to and including line 200 from the program in memory. This command:

    DELETE 200-

will delete line 200 as well as any lines which follow it. Use these commands carefully, however, because you won't get a second chance. Once you press the <RETURN> key, the lines are gone for good.

If you are testing a program and want it to stop at a certain program line, perhaps to check to see if it had run correctly up to that point, you just insert the command:

    STOP

Whenever the interpreter encounters this command in a program, it stops with the message:

```
Break in (line number)
```

This command is very useful for debugging programs, as it will allow you to examine the values held in program variables by printing them with direct mode print statements. With the command:

```
CONT
```

you can cause the program to continue at the same place, while retaining all of the variable contents. In contrast, the command RUN sets all variables to zero, even if you use RUN with a line number. This is an important difference from the CONT command. You can't use CONT if your program stopped because of an error.

Sometimes it is useful to follow the course of a program by means of the line numbers, perhaps to make comparisons to the program flowchart. After entering the command:

```
TRON
```

(TRace ON) each line number is output in square brackets before the line is executed. The command:

```
TROFF
```

(TRace OFF) disables TRACE mode.

The command:

```
NEW
```

erases the program currently in memory. You have already used this command —we mention it again only for the sake of thoroughness. With the command:

```
LIST
```

you can display the program on the screen. You can vary this command in the same manner as the DELETE command. You can output the program to the printer with LLIST.

Two more commands are available for erasing variables. The command:

    CLEAR

clears all variables and arrays. If you are not yet familiar with the term array, don't worry. It will be explained in detail in a later chapter.

If you want to erase only arrays or one array, you must use:

    ERASE (array name)

For example, ERASE A causes the array created with DIM A(20) to be erased. The array can then be redimensioned.

By entering:

    EDIT (line number)

the line you specified for editing is immediately displayed with the cursor resting on the first character.

These editor commands offer you an easy-to-use means of creating and correcting your programs.

2.6.1   Editing keys

The following keys are available for entering and editing program listings. Depending on your particular version of GW-BASIC, these key combinations can produce results different from those listed below, or will have no effect at all.

Effect	Key
Accepts the entered or edited program line and places it in memory.	↵ or Ctrl+M
All input and output is directed to the printer. Pressing these keys again turns this mode off.	Ctrl+P or Ctrl+PrtSc
Clears the screen and places the cursor in the upper left hand corner of the screen.	Ctrl+Home or Ctrl+L
Clears the rest of the program line from the cursor position on.	Ctrl+End or Ctrl+E
Clears the screen line and places the cursor at the start of the line.	Esc

Effect	Key
Clears the screen from the cursor line on.	Ctrl+Z or Ctrl+PgDn
Deletes the character under the cursor.	Del
Deletes the character to the left of the cursor.	Backspace or Ctrl+H
Deletes the contents of the program line from the cursor position to the next colon (:) or the next space.	PgDn
Inserts a blank line within the program line.	Ctrl+↵ or Ctrl+J
Moves the cursor to the next tab position to the right.	Tab or Ctrl+I
Places cursor at the end of the program line.	End or Ctrl+N
Places the cursor in the upper left corner of the screen without clearing the screen.	Home or Ctrl+K
Sets the cursor at the start of the word to the right of the cursor.	Ctrl+→
Sets the cursor at the start of the word to the left of the cursor.	Ctrl+← or Ctrl+B
Stops the output of a listing on the screen. The listing is continued when another key is pressed.	Ctrl+ Num Lock
Terminate the edit mode, causing any changes to be lost. In the program mode, the program is terminated and GW-BASIC is returned to the direct mode.	Ctrl+C or Ctrl+Break
The current screen contents are printed on the printer. Normally only text screens can be printed. The MS-DOS utility GRAPHICS.COM must be loaded for printing graphics hardcopy.	Shift+PrtSc
The listing is scrolled up. The cursor must be on a line with a valid line number.	Ctrl+Y or Ctrl+↓
This listing is scrolled down on the screen. The cursor must be on a line with a valid line number.	Ctrl+X or Ctrl+↑
Toggles between insert and overwrite modes.	Ins or Ctrl+R
Toggles the function key display in the 25th line on and off.	Ctrl+T

Values for parameters, variables and constants can be entered in decimal notation without a prefix, in hexadecimal notation with the prefix &H, and in octal notation with the prefix &O. For some commands the period (.) is used to represent the last line processed. The last line processed is the last line changed or the last line in which an error occurred.

GW-BASIC normally indicates input errors or errors during program execution by halting the execution of the command. It then displays an error message that lists the contents of the line in which the error occurred.

2.6.2   Shortcuts with the Alt key

The most often used commands can be entered in GW-BASIC in "shorthand" with the following key combination:

Alt+*another key*

Hold down the Alt key and then press the appropriate key. When you release the key, the corresponding keyword appears on the screen:

Key	Keyword	Key	Keyword
A	AUTO	N	NEXT
B	BSAVE	O	OPEN
C	COLOR	P	PRINT
D	DELETE	Q	unused
E	ELSE	R	RUN
F	FOR	S	SCREEN
G	GOTO	T	THEN
H	HEX$	U	USING
I	INPUT	V	VAL
J	unused	W	WINDOW
K	KEY	X	XOR
L	LOCATE	Y	unused
M	MERGE	Z	unused

This list is not valid for all versions of GW-BASIC. Your particular version might have some differences. In contrast to the function keys, these assignments cannot be changed.

2.7 Screen control

While many commands are available for controlling output to the screen, most of these fall into the graphics or window command categories. Two commands come to mind as being useful in all modes. The most useful of these two commands, the CLS statement, clears the screen and places the cursor at the first position on the screen. You will notice this command is used often to clean up screen clutter and help give an overall neatness to the appearance of the display. This command may also be entered in direct mode. Enter the command:

    CLS

and press <RETURN>. Notice the effect of this command.

The other command, though less often used, is also important to how the display looks. This is the WIDTH statement. This command is used in a number of different ways, but most important to us is its use in formatting screen output. GW-BASIC normally defaults to a screen width of 80 characters. It is possible to change this value to 40, which means each character becomes twice as wide. This is not an effect you will want to use in all situations. However, if you consider the readability of a program intended for young children, using a 40 column screen would be a definite plus. To change the screen width to 40 columns, enter the following command:

    WIDTH 40

Experiment with this mode by entering a few direct print statements. When you are done, enter:

    WIDTH 80

to return back to 80 column mode. Most of our example programs are written in 80 columns, but if you like the effect, or want to experiment a little, try rewriting some of the routines for 40 columns.

3.   Extended program structures

Up to now we have limited the examples to linear programs which execute the lines consecutively. Now we'll move on to programs containing jumps, or *branches*. Linear programs have the disadvantage that the program runs once, and must then be restarted in order to get a new result. No branches of any kind take place. If there were no commands to perform such program branches, you would be limited to writing only very simple programs in BASIC.

3.1   Unconditional program jumps

The first and simplest type of a program branch is the GOTO command. This command allows the program to deviate from linear execution as determined by the sequence of line numbers. It is called an *unconditional program branch* because it is not tied to any condition—that is, the program performs this jump under all circumstances.

The disadvantage of unconditional program branches is that you can create only "infinite" loops with them. Once the program is started, it can only be stopped by pressing the <CONTROL> and <BREAK> keys at the same time. This stops execution of the program.

We will use this command with an example we've already discussed: the problem where we had to calculate a person's ideal weight.

Let's suppose you're at a gathering and want to use this program as a game. Each of the guests will learn his or her ideal weight. Without the GOTO command, the program would have to be restarted for each guest. Therefore we place a GOTO command before the END command. This tells the computer to jump to the start of the program. Our program would then look like this:

```
10 INPUT"ENTER HEIGHT IN CM";CM
20 REM CALCULATE IDEAL WEIGHT
30 IW=(CM-100)-(CM-100)/100*10
40 REM OUTPUT
50 PRINT"YOUR IDEAL WEIGHT IS";IW;"KG"
60 REM UNCONDITIONAL JUMP WITH GOTO
70 GOTO 10
80 END
```

61

This program calculates a person's ideal weight in one line, line 30. After outputting the result, the program encounters the GOTO command in line 70 and branches to line 10. A new value for the calculation can then be entered. Line 80 does not have to be entered because the program never reaches this line as a result of the GOTO command. The data flowchart is not affected by this command. The figure below shows how it would look.

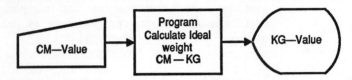

Data flow chart

The program flowchart does change as a result of this command. A symbol is added to it. This is the *connector*. It designates the location at which the program is to continue when the jump connector is reached. The jump connectors stand at the place where the GOTO command is found in the program. The entry connector is located directly after the start symbol. Both connectors are designated with an A, because they form a connector pair. The program flowchart is shown in the following diagram.

The following program lines can be added to convert from metric to English units.

```
10 INPUT "ENTER YOUR HEIGHT IN INCHES";IN
15 CM=IN*2.54:REM CONVERT TO CM
45 IW=IW*2.2:REM CONVERT TO LBS
50 PRINT "YOUR IDEAL WEIGHT IS";IW;"LBS"
```

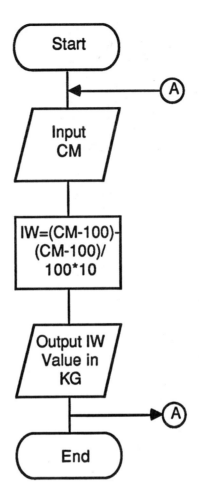

Program flowchart

The end symbol can be omitted, but was included here for the sake of thoroughness. This example shows that only infinite loops can be created with the GOTO command alone—the program can't end without a checking condition. Conditional program jumps remedy this situation.

3.2   Conditional program jumps

One of the strengths of a computer lies in its ability to make logical decisions or comparisons. For example, it can test to see if a variable is greater or less than zero, and then branch within the program depending on whether the result is True or False. The IF...THEN...ELSE command is one that performs a comparison.

3.2.1   IF...THEN...ELSE

The IF, THEN, and ELSE statements are combined to work together in programs. If the computer encounters an IF statement when executing a program, it checks the condition that follows it. If the condition is *true* (fulfilled), it executes the instructions or commands that follow a THEN statement. If the condition after IF is not fulfilled—if it is *false*—the computer continues with the next program line, or the commands following an optional ELSE statement. All instructions or commands following the THEN are ignored until the ELSE statement or next program line are reached.

Logical operators, strings, variables, comparisons, numbers, or their combinations can follow IF. Usually a line number follows a THEN statement to indicate which line the program should branch to. This is considered to be an assumed GOTO statement. Assigning new values to a variable is also possible. We will talk more about this in a later section. Let's first take a look at a simple example of the use of the IF...THEN command.

```
10   INPUT"ENTER A NUMBER";N
20   IF N > 0 THEN 50
30   IF N < 0 THEN 70
40   IF N = 0 THEN 90
50   PRINT"THE NUMBER IS GREATER THAN ZERO"
60   GOTO 100
70   PRINT"THE NUMBER IS LESS THAN ZERO"
80   GOTO 100
90   PRINT"THE NUMBER IS EQUAL TO ZERO"
100  END
```

With this program you can enter a number and the computer will tell you if this number is greater than, less than, or equal to zero. While

this is a trivial program, this simple example will clarify the use of the
IF...THEN command in a program and the computer's reaction to it.

Suppose you enter a number less than zero. The computer comes to
line 20—here a check is made to see if the number is greater than zero.
This condition is not fulfilled, so the computer ignores the following
THEN statement and continues with the execution of the next program
line. There a check is made to see if the number entered is less than
zero. This condition is true, so the computer jumps according to the
instruction following the THEN, to line 70. Line 70 outputs the
message on the screen that the number is less than zero. In line 80, the
computer encounters the unconditional jump command GOTO and
jumps to line 100, where the program ends. If you want the program to
run continuously, you need only replace the END command in line 100
with GOTO 10.

Following this simple example, we want to turn to a more complicated
program. No doubt you're familiar with the game where someone
thinks of a number and someone else has to guess it. After each
question the person guessing is told if the number is larger, smaller, or
equal to the number in mind. We'll recreate this game on the computer.
To do this, enter the following program:

```
10   REM NUMBER GUESSING
20   CLS:PRINT:RANDOMIZE 0
30   PRINT"ENTER TWO NUMBERS FOR"
40   PRINT"THE UPPER AND LOWER BOUNDARIES"
50   PRINT"LOWER LIMIT";L
60   PRINT"UPPER LIMIT";U
70   N=INT((U+1-L)*RND)+L
80   INPUT"YOUR GUESS";NG
90   IF NG < N THEN 120
100  IF NG > N THEN 140
110  IF NG = N THEN 160
120  PRINT"THE NUMBER IS LARGER"
130  GOTO 80
140  PRINT"THE NUMBER IS SMALLER"
150  GOTO 80
160  CLS:PRINT"HURRAY! YOU GUESSED IT!"
170  PRINT"PLAY AGAIN (YES/NO)";
180  INPUT A$
190  IF A$="YES" THEN 20
200  END
```

The first lines of this program consist of a remark and a randomizing function. The interval for the number to be guessed is prompted in lines 30-60. Line 70 determines the number sought with the entered range.

If line 70 gives you difficulty, refer back to Section 2.3.2 on random numbers. Line 80 asks you to enter a number. This number is compared with the random number, stored in the variable N, in lines 90 to 110. According to whether the number is greater, less than, or equal to the intended number, the computer branches to the corresponding line. There it continues with the program. If you guessed the number, the program jumps to line 160. In line 170 you are asked if you want to play again. If you enter YES, the condition in line 190 is fulfilled. The program starts all over again.

In lines 90 to 110 the IF...THEN command is used to make comparisons between the number the player guesses (NG) and the random number (N). In line 190, the IF...THEN command is used to make a comparison to a string variable. Note that in order for the condition to be true, both strings must be exactly the same. You could enter Y in line 180, but the program will end because the branch to line 20 is made only if the characters Y, E, and S are entered—the string YES.

With the IF...THEN command we now have the ability to program controlled loops. Controlled means that the loop will not be executed continuously, but will be executed only as long as a specified condition is fulfilled. The following program shows you how such a controlled loop is programmed. If you want to output the times table for three, you would write a program like this:

```
10 A=3
20 PRINT A
30 A=A+3
40 IF A > 30 THEN 60
50 GOTO 20
60 END
```

In line 10, the variable A is first initialized with the value 3. Line 20 outputs the current value of A on the screen. In line 30, a counter is used. It always adds the value 3 to the current contents of variable A. In line 40 a check is made to see if A has exceeded the value 30. As long as A is less than or equal to 30, the program continues with the GOTO command in line 50. We have created a loop that is executed exactly 10 times. We have now learned a way to create loops that are executed a certain number of times. The above example is well-suited to using ELSE. We can then get rid of line 50. Here is the modified program with ELSE:

```
10 A=3
20 PRINT A
30 A=A+3
40 IF A > 30 THEN 60 ELSE 20
60 END
```

When you start this program, you will see that you get the same results as with the previous example. Since in the first 10 comparisons variable A is not greater than 30, the condition is not fulfilled and the command behind the ELSE is executed. The program then branches to line 20. As soon as A has the value 33, the program is ended at line 60. We retained the line number 60 to emphasize the fact than line 50 is missing.

Exercises

1. Write a program that calculates an income tax of 33 or 51 percent based on the annual income. The dividing line between these tax brackets must be set at an annual income of $50,000. All amounts larger than $50,000 must be taxed at 51 percent. The output of the result should be done with accompanying text.

2. Write a program that calculates the sum of the numbers from 1 to 100.

3. Write a program that outputs 6 random numbers in the range 1 to 49.

4. Which numbers are printed by the following program? Solve the exercise without entering the program.

```
10 A=7
20 A=A+5:Z=Z+1
30 IF Z < 9 THEN 20
40 PRINT A,Z
50 END
```

5. Write a program that searches for a given substring in a given string. As a test use the string A$="INFORMATION" and search for and output the substring B$="FORMAT". The difficulty of this exercise is that you may not use the INSTR function. Now write a program in BASIC that replaces the INSTR function.

3.2.2   FOR...TO...NEXT

Up to now we have created loops with the IF...THEN command. Here a counter is used and its value is incremented or decremented. The value of the counter is checked at certain points in the program, and the program jumps to another line depending on the result of the test (true or false). Creating a loop like this is rather complicated, since the counter and the test are extra programming statements. GW-BASIC offers a simpler solution in the form of FOR...NEXT loops. Examine this example program introducing this method of creating loops:

```
10 REM OUTPUT THE FIRST 10 PERFECT SQUARES
20 CLS:PRINT
30 PRINT "THE FIRST 10 PERFECT SQUARES"
40 FOR I=1 TO 10
50 PRINT "SQUARE OF";I;"=";I*I
60 NEXT I
70 PRINT "DONE"
```

Enter the program into your computer and RUN it. It works similar to that of the IF...THEN command. Programming loops with FOR...NEXT is simply more elegant and also saves memory.

The index variable is called I, and it is assigned an initial value. In our case this is 1. The initial value is then incremented by 1 until the end value is exceeded. Every command appearing between FOR and NEXT will be repeated as often as the loop is executed. The initial and end values can be numbers, variables, or arithmetic expressions.

Some examples:

```
10 A=10:B=20
20 FOR N=A TO B
30 PRINT N;
40 NEXT N
50 END
```

In this example the variables A and B are first initialized. Line 20 begins the loop using these variables. Line 30 outputs the values of N until the index variable is greater than 20. This is comparable to the IF...THEN command:

```
IF N > 20 THEN 50
```

69

The FOR...NEXT loop is executed until N is greater than 20. You can check this by entering the following command in direct mode after the program has been RUN:

```
PRINT N
```

As the result for N, you get the value 21! The next example will show that arithmetic expressions can also be used.

```
10 A=10:B=15:C=5
20 FOR N=A TO A+B-C
30 PRINT N;
40 NEXT N
50 END
```

The only difference from the previous example is that the end value is calculated from the expression A+B-C.

If you want to use an increment other than 1, the step size must be specified with STEP. The following example outputs the even numbers between 2 and 20, using steps of 2.

```
10 REM EVEN NUMBERS FROM 2 TO 20
20 FOR I=2 TO 20 STEP 2
30 PRINT I
40 NEXT I
50 END
```

The starting and ending values may also be negative or fractional numbers, as may be the step width. As an example we will program a countdown.

```
10 REM COUNTDOWN
20 FOR I=20 TO 0 STEP -1
30 PRINT I
40 NEXT I
50 END
```

After you start the program, the output quickly flashes before your eyes. Normally a countdown counts down in increments of thousandths of a second. We can slow down the loop by "nesting" other FOR...NEXT loops within each other. The next example shows what we mean:

```
10 REM COUNTDOWN
20 FOR I=20 TO 0 STEP -1
30 PRINT I
40 FOR Z=0 TO 1000
50 REM DELAY LOOP
60 NEXT Z
70 NEXT I
80END
```

RIGHT!

Enter the program and run it, noting that it now counts down in increments of almost exactly one second. This is taken care of by a *delay loop* in lines 40 to 60. Such delay loops are often used to display text on the screen for specific periods of time.

The delay loop in our program is intended only to clarify the nesting of FOR...NEXT loops. Naturally other BASIC commands could be in this nested loop.

What happens in this program? In line 20 the first loop starts with I=20. Line 20 outputs the current value of I. In line 40 the second loop starts—its NEXT is found in line 50. This second loop is processed completely before the first loop starts through its second pass. The second loop is completed as often as I is printed.

You must make sure that your nesting of FOR...NEXT loops is legal. You may not "cross" loops. That is, the first loop opened must be the last closed, and the last loop opened must be closed first. The program above shows correct nesting of loops. The following example is intended to show how loops may *not* be nested. Trying to run this program will result in the following error:

```
NEXT without FOR in 70
```

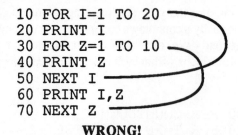

```
10 FOR I=1 TO 20
20 PRINT I
30 FOR Z=1 TO 10
40 PRINT Z
50 NEXT I
60 PRINT I,Z
70 NEXT Z
```

WRONG!

If you have several loops nested within each other and want to close them all at once, you don't need a special NEXT for each FOR. One NEXT suffices. To this NEXT are appended the individual index variables *in the proper order*. The variables must be separated from each other by commas. The following example will clarify this.

```
10 FOR I=1 TO 10
20 FOR Z=1 TO 10
30 PRINT I;Z
40 NEXT Z,I
50 END
```

Enter this program into the computer and RUN it. Only one NEXT is used in line 40 to close both loops. Here again, the loop last opened must be the first closed. This is why the variable Z follows the NEXT first, and then I.

One mistake beginners often make is jumping into a loop. That means a jump is not made to the FOR...TO instruction, but somewhere in between FOR and NEXT. Since a loop usually contains several program lines, sometimes you jump to a line in the loop where everything turns out all right. The error is usually gone unnoticed until the program encounters the NEXT statement. The result is the termination of the program with the following error message:

```
NEXT without FOR in (line #)
```

If you had first made a detailed flowchart, such an error probably wouldn't have occurred. Further, if the starting value is larger than the ending value, the step value must be negative. If you forget to specify the step value, the loop will be exited immediately, as the following example shows:

```
10 FOR A=5 TO 1
20 PRINT A
30 NEXT A
40 END
```

In line 10 there is no specification of the step width, such as STEP -1. Hence, no output is given. Ending a loop prematurely is done by setting the index variable to an ending value. This can be done independently on certain variables, or other conditions that can be tested within the program. Normally the start and end values are placed in variables. If the values of these variables change within the program, different loop lengths are possible.

In conclusion, we'd like to show you a program that interrupts the loop prematurely by setting the index variable to the end value. Then we'll present a program that determines the different loop lengths through variables. The values of the variables are determined with the string functions. Such applications are frequently found in database programs —when searching for character combinations.

```
10 REM PREMATURE LOOP END
20 FOR A=0 TO 20
30 PRINT A
40 IF A=12 THEN A=20
50 NEXT A
60 END
```

The program doesn't make a whole lot of sense, since it's so short. It is intended only to show how a loop can be prematurely ended. Normally the loop would count to 20. However, in line 40, once A reaches 12 it is set to 20. This causes only values up to 12 to be printed. This method of changing the value of the index variable within the loop is seldom used.

More often the start and end values of a loop are placed in variables. This allows the loop to be controlled more easily. The following example illustrates this:

```
10 INPUT "ENTER A WORD";A$
20 FOR A=1 TO LEN(A$)
30 PRINT LEFT$(A$,A)
40 NEXT A
50 FOR A=LEN(A$) TO 1 STEP -1
60 PRINT RIGHT$(A$,A)
70 NEXT A
80 END
```

Start the program, enter your name, and press the <RETURN> key. You see that you get the same results as we got from the program in the section on string functions. But here we used the FOR...NEXT loop and made it dependent on the length of the string entered. This means that the passes through the loop are controlled by the length of the string. Take a close look at the example and try to understand all of it.

Let's summarize the most important points of working with FOR...NEXT loops.

1.   Exactly one NEXT instruction belongs to each FOR instruction. A NEXT instruction can close several nested loops if the index variables follow this NEXT instruction in the proper order, separated by commas.

2.   You may not jump into a loop, because the program will terminate with an error message.

3.   The starting value may not be larger than the ending value if the step width is positive, or the loop will not be executed. The same applies for negative step widths.

4.   Generally, a FOR...NEXT loop is executed until the value of the index variable is greater than the end value.

3.2.3   Loops with WHILE...WEND

The command combination WHILE...WEND offers you another option for constructing loops within a program. This form of loop control is more flexible than the FOR...NEXT loops. You don't have to specify a set increment for WHILE...WEND.

The start of the loop is indicated with WHILE, and the end with WEND. The logical expression following WHILE is tested before each pass through the loop. As long as the expression is true, the loop is executed up to WEND. If the condition behind WHILE is no longer fulfilled, the execution of the program is continued after the WEND. You terminate a loop with this command combination quite randomly, as the following example shows:

```
5   RANDOMIZE 0
10  WHILE A < 100
20  A=INT(101*RND)
30  Z=Z+1
40  IF A=100 THEN EXIT
50  WEND
60  PRINT A,Z
70  END
```

Here the WHILE...WEND loop is executed until the value of A reaches the value 100 by chance. If the statement in line 40 is true, the next command that follows the WEND is executed. In our case this is program line 60. Here A and the counter Z are printed. The counter tells you how many times the loop was executed. This example should make the operation of the WHILE...WEND loop clearer.

We can make the following general rules for the use of loops:

a)   If the number of repetitions of the loop is known from the beginning, we use the FOR...NEXT loop.

b)   If the number of repetitions of the loop is unknown, we construct the loop with IF...THEN or WHILE...WEND.

We have already seen an exception to these rules, in the last example program of Section 3.2.3. These rules are only intended to be guidelines.

So far we have learned about the use of conditional and unconditional program jumps in our programming. We also know about program loops, especially the FOR...NEXT loop.

What is still missing is a way to represent these structures in the program flowchart. The symbol for representing a logical branch in a program flowchart is the diamond. It looks like this:

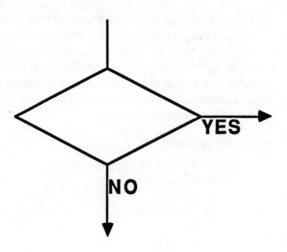

Logical Branch Symbol

First we'll look at a program flowchart for the program that calculates income tax. On the next page you'll see the program flowchart and its explanation.

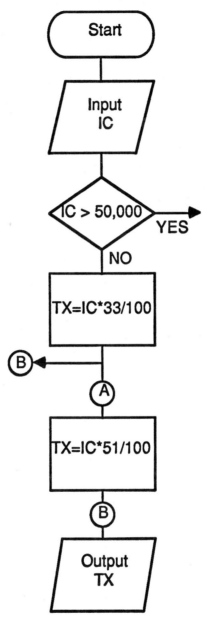

Program flowchart for calculating income tax.

We recognize the *start* and *end* symbols in our program flowchart. The diamond, as we said before, is the symbol for a logical branch. It has a YES branch and a NO branch. If the condition is fulfilled, a branch is made via the jump connector A to the corresponding entry connector A. In our example the branch would take place via the YES branch. This could also be the NO branch, depending on the type of program. The calculation of the tax of 51 percent and output of the value follow the entry connector A.

If the condition is not fulfilled, the 33 percent is calculated. After the calculation comes jump connector B. It designates an unconditional jump to entry connector B. It should be noted that the jump connector B comes before the entry connector A, or the flowchart would contain a logical error.

This program flowchart showed how the IF...THEN command is represented in a flowchart. What we now need to know is how a FOR...NEXT loop is represented.

For this we'll use the program that asks you to input your name, and write a flowchart for it. The next two pages contain the program flowchart and its explanation.

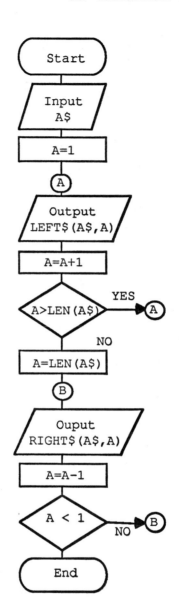

Program flowchart for the program on page 74.

The symbols in this flowchart should be familiar to you. In the first rectangle, the starting value of the loop is set to one. Next we isolate the substring with LEFT$(A$,A). The counter is then incremented by one. In the diamond the counter is tested to see if it is greater than the number of characters in A$. If this is not the case, a branch is made to entry connector A via jump connector A. The loop is thereby created in the program flowchart.

If the counter is greater than LEN(A$), the second loop comes into action. The second loop has the same arrangement of symbols as the first loop. The connectors have the different designations in order to avoid confusion. However, the course is the same as the one described above.

With this information you should be in a position to create program flowcharts for any program on your own. Remember, practice makes perfect.

3.3   Calculated jump commands

The calculated jump commands have the advantage of making the actual program more flexible. Up to now we have seen only jump commands that jump to a specific program line. The line numbers in the GOTO command cannot be changed—GOTO 100 always continues execution at line 100.

But it would be nice if you could enter a value at the start of a program and the program would then branch based on the value. This could be achieved with some IF...THEN comparisons. But this would require a jump command for each program line, for every comparison. A simple example will clarify this:

```
10 REM JUMP TO CERTAIN LINES
20 PRINT "ENTER A NUMBER BETWEEN"
30 PRINT "1 AND 4"
40 PRINT
50 INPUT "WHAT NUMBER";Z
60 IF Z = 1 THEN 100
70 IF Z = 2 THEN 200
80 IF Z = 3 THEN 300
90 IF Z = 4 THEN 400
100 PRINT "JUMPED TO LINE 100"
110 GOTO 410
200 PRINT "JUMPED TO LINE 200"
210 GOTO 410
300 PRINT "JUMPED TO LINE 300"
310 GOTO 410
400 PRINT "JUMPED TO LINE 400"
410 END
```

In this program, a branch is made to program line 100, 200, 300, or 400, depending on the input of a number 1-4. Programming these tests with IF...THEN is rather complicated in such applications, and is relatively slow in execution speed. BASIC offers a more flexible solution for such cases. The command has the following syntax:

ON (*variable*) GOTO (*line number*)

This extended GOTO command with ON allows the program to branch to one or several line numbers or labels following the GOTO. The range of the variables extends from zero to the number of line numbers given.

If the variable does not have an integer value, the non-integer portion is ignored. Negative values are also ignored.

If the variable has a value that is larger than the number of line numbers available following the GOTO, the line following the ON...GOTO command is executed. Here are some simple examples:

a)
```
10 ON Z GOTO 100,200,250,300
20 PRINT
   .
   .
   .
```

If the variable Z in this example has the value 1, the program jumps to line 100. If Z runs through the values 2-4 in a loop, the program jumps to lines 200, 250, and 300 in succession. Z designates the positions of the individual line numbers that follow the GOTO. If Z assumes values larger or smaller than the number of line numbers behind the GOTO, the program continues with the next command following the GOTO. This is the PRINT command in our example. The GOTO command is simply skipped.

b)
```
10 ON Z+3/4 GOTO 100,200,300
20 PRINT
   .
   .
   .
```

You see that an arithmetic expression can be used instead of a variable. The advantage of this ON...GOTO command is that it can replace several IF...THEN commands. This saves programming time, as well as memory space. Our previous short program could have the following form:

```
10 REM JUMP TO CERTAIN LINES
20 PRINT "ENTER A NUMBER BETWEEN"
30 PRINT "1 AND 4"
40 PRINT
50 INPUT "WHAT NUMBER";Z
60 ON Z GOTO 100,200,300,400
100 PRINT "JUMP TO LINE 100"
110 GOTO 410
200 PRINT "JUMP TO LINE 200"
210 GOTO 410
```

```
300 PRINT "JUMP TO LINE 300"
310 GOTO 410
400 PRINT "JUMP TO LINE 400"
410 END
```

We saved three program lines in this short program. With larger programs in which comparisons with IF . . . THEN can occur, you can save even more lines.

This program uses a programming technique that can be very helpful, especially with large programs. If you create a program flowchart for this program, the jumps to the various lines are symbolized with horizontal branches. Since we don't know yet what line numbers these lines will have, we choose extra-large numbers. This is how to make room within the program for other program segments.

The destination line numbers of ON . . . GOTO represent certain program segments within the program in which special tasks are generally performed. It helps to designate these with "smooth" line numbers. This can be done in steps of one hundred, as in our example program. This improves the readability of the individual program segments.

3.3.1   Example program—MATH TUTOR

We have now learned a relatively large number of BASIC commands. This is a good excuse to try a larger project.

Suppose you want to write a math drill program for your children that features the four basic mathematical operators of GW-BASIC. The drill has the following properties:

1. One of the four operators is selected or the program is ended.
2. A given problem must be solved in a maximum of 3 attempts.
3. After the third failed attempt, the correct result is displayed.
4. After each problem, a prompt asks if more problems of the same calculation type are to be solved.

Take a look at the math lesson program listing starting below. Don't worry if individual lines are not always separated from each other by steps of exactly ten. Since the program is relatively long, we'll now give you the commands for saving a program, even though we haven't discussed them yet.

Insert a formatted disk in the drive. Enter the following command into the computer:

```
SAVE "MATH"
```

After pressing return, the program will be saved on the diskette. If you want it again, you need only call it up from the appropriate disk. This is done with the LOAD command. Simply replace SAVE with LOAD at the appropriate time and the program will be loaded into the computer.

Here is the program listing. The ¶ characters in the following listing should not be entered. They only show the actual end of the BASIC line. Formatting the programs for this book split some lines that should not have been split. The ¶ characters show the end of the line.

```
5       REM **** MENU ****¶
10      CLS: F=0¶
20      PRINT¶
30      PRINT TAB(32)"MATH TUTOR"¶
40      PRINT:PRINT¶
50      PRINT TAB(32)"YOUR CHOICES:"¶
60      PRINT¶
70      PRINT TAB(32)"[1] - ADDITION"¶
77      ER=A1-A2¶
80      PRINT¶
90      PRINT TAB(32)"[2] - SUBTRACTION"¶
100     PRINT¶
110     PRINT TAB(32)"[3] - DIVISION"¶
120     PRINT¶
130     PRINT TAB(32)"[4] - MULTIPLICATION"¶
140     PRINT¶
145     PRINT TAB(32)"[5] - END"¶
148     PRINT¶
150     PRINT TAB(32);:INPUT"WHICH NUMBER";Z¶
160     IF Z < 1 OR Z > 5 THEN 10¶
170     ON Z GOTO 200,600,1000,1300,1600¶
200     REM ********¶
210     REM ADDITION¶
220     REM ********¶
230     CLS¶
240     PRINT TAB(10)"INPUT THE LARGEST NUMBER"¶
```

```
250    PRINT¶
260    PRINT TAB(10)"FOR ADDITION"¶
270    PRINT¶
280    PRINT TAB(10);:INPUT"LARGEST";GR¶
299    REM¶
300    REM CREATE RANDOM NUMBERS¶
301    RANDOMIZE TIMER¶
310    A1 = INT (GR*RND)+1¶
320    A2 = INT(GR*RND)+1¶
329    REM¶
330    REM COMPUTE RESULT¶
340    ER = A1 + A2¶
350    CLS¶
360    PRINT¶
370    PRINT "HOW MUCH IS "A1"+" A2 " = ";¶
380    INPUT ES¶
390    IF ES=ER THEN PRINT:PRINT TAB(10)"CORRECT!"
       :F=0:GOTO 470¶
400    PRINT:PRINT TAB(10)"WRONG!"¶
410    FOR I = 1 TO 2000:NEXT I¶
420    F=F+1¶
430    IF F<= 2 THEN 350¶
440    PRINT¶
450    FOR I = 0 TO 2000:NEXT I¶
460    PRINT"THE ANSWER IS "ER¶
470    FOR I = 0 TO 3000:NEXT I¶
480    PRINT TAB(5)"ANOTHER PROBLEM? (Y/N)";¶
490    INPUT A$¶
500    IF A$="Y" THEN F=0:GOTO 300¶
510    GOTO 10¶
600    REM ***********¶
610    REM SUBTRACTION¶
620    REM ***********¶
630    CLS¶
640    PRINT TAB(10)"INPUT THE LARGEST NUMBER"¶
650    PRINT¶
660    PRINT TAB(10)"FOR SUBTRACTION"¶
670    PRINT¶
690    PRINT TAB(10);:INPUT"LARGEST";GR¶
699    REM¶
700    REM CREATE RANDOM NUMBERS¶
701    RANDOMIZE TIMER¶
710    A1 = INT (GR*RND)+1¶
```

```
720    A2 = INT(GR*RND)+1¶
729    REM¶
730    REM COMPUTE RESULT¶
740    IF A1 < A2 THEN I = A1:A1=A2:A2=I¶
750    CLS¶
760    PRINT¶
770    ER=A1-A2¶
780    PRINT "HOW MUCH IS "A1"-" A2 " = ";¶
790    INPUT ES¶
800    IF ES=ER THEN PRINT:PRINT TAB(10) "CORRECT!"
       :F=0:GOTO 880¶
810    PRINT:PRINT TAB(10) "WRONG!"¶
820    FOR I = 1 TO 2000:NEXT I¶
830    F=F+1¶
840    IF F<= 2 THEN 750¶
850    PRINT¶
860    FOR I = 0 TO 2000:NEXT I¶
870    PRINT"THE ANSWER IS "ER¶
880    FOR I = 0 TO 3000:NEXT I¶
890    PRINT TAB(5) "ANOTHER PROBLEM? (Y/N)";¶
900    INPUT A$¶
910    IF A$="Y" THEN F=0:GOTO 710¶
920    GOTO 10¶
1000   REM ********¶
1001   REM DIVISION¶
1002   REM ********¶
1010   CLS¶
1020   PRINT TAB(10)"INPUT THE LARGEST NUMBER"¶
1030   PRINT¶
1040   PRINT TAB(10)"FOR DIVISION"¶
1050   PRINT¶
1060   PRINT TAB(10);:INPUT"LARGEST";GR¶
1070   REM¶
1080   REM CALCULATE RANDOM NUMBER¶
1081   REM¶
1085   RANDOMIZE TIMER¶
1090   A1=INT(GR*RND)+1¶
1100   A2 = INT(GR*RND)+1¶
1109   REM¶
1110   REM CALCULATE DIVISION¶
1111   REM¶
1120   ER =A1*A2¶
1130   CLS¶
```

```
1140    PRINT¶
1150    PRINT "WHAT IS "ER" / " A1 "= ";¶
1160    INPUT ES¶
1170    IF ES=A2 THEN PRINT:PRINT TAB(10) "CORRECT !"
        :F=0:GOTO 1260¶
1180    PRINT :PRINT TAB(10) "WRONG!"¶
1190    FOR I = 0 TO 2000:NEXT¶
1200    F=F+1¶
1210    IF F<=2 THEN 1130¶
1220    PRINT¶
1230    FOR I = 0 TO 2000: NEXT¶
1240    PRINT TAB(5)" THE ANSWER IS "A2¶
1250    FOR I= 0 TO 3000:NEXT¶
1260    PRINT TAB(5)"ANOTHER PROBLEM Y/N";¶
1270    INPUT A$¶
1280    IF A$="Y" THEN F=0: GOTO 1090¶
1290    GOTO 10¶
1300    REM **************¶
1301    REM MULTIPLICATION¶
1302    REM **************¶
1310    CLS¶
1320    PRINT TAB(10) "INPUT THE LARGEST NUMBER"¶
1330    PRINT¶
1340    PRINT TAB(10) "FOR MULTIPLICATION"¶
1350    PRINT¶
1360    PRINT TAB(10);:INPUT"LARGEST";GR¶
1370    REM¶
1380    REM CALCULATE RANDOM NUMBER¶
1381    REM¶
1385    RANDOMIZE TIMER¶
1390    A1=INT(GR*RND)+1¶
1400    A2 = INT(GR*RND)+1¶
1409    REM¶
1410    REM CALCULATE MULTIPLICATION¶
1411    REM¶
1420    ER =A1*A2¶
1430    CLS¶
1440    PRINT¶
1450    PRINT "WHAT IS "A1" * " A2 " =";¶
1460    INPUT ES¶
1470    IF ES=ER THEN PRINT:PRINT TAB(10) "CORRECT !"
        :F=0:GOTO 1550¶
1480    PRINT :PRINT TAB(10) "WRONG!"¶
```

```
1490   FOR I = 0 TO 2000:NEXT¶
1500   F=F+1¶
1510   IF F<=2 THEN 1430¶
1520   PRINT¶
1530   FOR I = 0 TO 2000: NEXT¶
1540   PRINT TAB(5)" THE ANSWER IS "ER¶
1550   FOR I= 0 TO 3000:NEXT¶
1560   PRINT TAB(5)"ANOTHER PROBLEM Y/N";¶
1570   INPUT A$¶
1580   IF A$="Y" THEN F=0: GOTO 1390¶
1590   GOTO 10¶
1600   CLS¶
1610   END¶
```

We will now discuss the most important lines of this program listing. The MENU is displayed by lines 10 to 150. The MENU allows you to select from various choices.

Line 150 requests you enter a number, which represents a menu selection. Line 160 checks to see if a valid number was entered. This line is a good example of the use of a logical operator. If a number is either less than 1 *or* greater than 5, a branch is made to line 10. Only one of these conditions needs to be fulfilled, so the operator OR is used.

Line 170 illustrates the use of the ON...GOTO command. If z has the value 1, a branch is made to line 200. If z has the value 2, the program branches to line 600, and so on. The individual computation operators are selected by entering a number. Here, with the ON...GOTO command we saved 5 IF...THEN comparisons.

Lines 200 to 220 visually separate the program segment for addition. It is also a memory aid for the programmer.

In larger programs you learn to appreciate such REM statements, because they make the program much easier to read. You don't have to search through the entire program when the program needs to be changed.

Line 230 clears the screen. The next lines request a number to set the upper limit of the sums for addition. After this, two random numbers A1 and A2 are generated, from which the addition problem is formed. The problem is printed on the screen in line 370. Semicolons between text and variables are not necessary. In line 380 the result is taken from the user. Line 390 checks to see if the value entered matches the value calculated in line 340. If the value entered is false, a blank line is first created on the screen by line 400. Following this, the message WRONG! is printed on the screen. In line 410 a delay loop is processed so that the user can read the message.

Line 420 sets a counter that checks how many wrong answers the user has already given for this problem. Remember, the program displays the result after three incorrect answers. Line 430 checks to see if three wrong answers have been given. If this is not the case, the program branches to line 350 and redisplays the question again. If three incorrect answers were given, the program continues with the execution of line 440.

If the right answer was given in the meantime, the program jumps from line 390 to line 450. After the delay loop in line 450 runs out, the result is printed in line 460. After another delay loop, line 480 queries if another problem is to be asked. If the user enters Y here, the counter F is first set to zero and then a branch is made to line 300. There the two new random numbers required for the new problem are generated. If the user presses a key other than the Y key, the program jumps back to line 10, where the menu is reconstructed. The counter F must be set back to zero, because the user must be allowed three attempts for the new problem. If we forget this, the old value of F is carried along. Accordingly, the result may be printed after one or two wrong answers. Remember this if you use counters in your own programs.

The other sections of the program—Subtraction, Division, and Multiplication—are constructed on the same principle. They differ only slightly in the creation of their respective problems. Let's take a look at subtraction.

Line 740 is special in its calculation of the result. This line ensures that we get only positive results by subtracting only smaller numbers from larger. If A1 is larger than A2, the problem statement in line 780 is correct. But if the reverse is true, the values in the variables must be exchanged or a larger number will be subtracted from a smaller in line 780. This is the purpose of line 740.

If A1 is smaller than A2, the value of A1 is stored temporarily in I. If we did the following:

```
A1=A2 : A2=A1        < WRONG
```

the value of A1 would be lost. Since A1 is first set equal to A2, variable A1 now contains the value of A2. After this we try to set A2 equal to A1, but A1 already has the value of A2. We don't exchange two variables in this way. First we must "save" one value—that is, store it in another variable.

First the variable I receives the value of A1:

    I=A1

After this the variable A1 is assigned the value of A2:

    A1=A2

Now we need:

    A2=I

since I has the value of A1, and the exchange is complete. This temporary storage technique is very important. Make sure you understand this principle, so you can use it later in your own programs.

GW-BASIC has an easier way of accomplishing this function. This instruction:

    SWAP (X,Y)

exchanges the contents of the variables X and Y. You can replace the corresponding lines in the program with this instruction.

This point was the important one in the subtraction section. In the division segment a little trick was also used in order to get only integer results. In line 1120, as with the multiplication, the result of A1 and A2 is formed. Then in the problem statement the result ER is divided by the value of A1. The result can only be an integer number since the result is generated from two whole numbers, namely A1 and A2.

The section dealing with multiplication has no special features. In structure, it is identical to the program segment for addition.

Before moving on to the programming exercises, here are some guidelines for using ON...GOTO:

1. The value that follows ON (which can be a number, a variable, or an arithmetic expression) determines the position of the line number in the list that follows the GOTO. The first line number is the branch destination for a value of 1, the second line number the branch destination for the value of two, and so on.

2. If this value is greater or less than the number of line numbers in the list, the next command, the one following the GOTO is executed.

3. Several IF...THEN comparisons can be grouped together with ON...GOTO.

3.3.2   Program jumps with ON...ERROR

This special type of the ON...GOTO command is used to automatically manage errors that occur in a program allowing errors to be handled by the program itself. A typical program line could look like this:

```
100 ON ERROR GOTO 1000
```

A small error-handling routine can be located at line 1000 to react to the error accordingly. But how do we know what error has occurred, and in which line number?

GW-BASIC has two system variables that are tested to tell us this information. These are the variables:

```
ERR and ERL
```

With ERR, you can determine the error code of the error. ERL is the line number in which the error occurred. The termination of a error-handling routine is designated by the command:

```
RESUME (line number)
```

With this RESUME command, you determine the program line at which the program is to continue execution after the error message. RESUME

NEXT causes execution to continue with the command following the one that caused the error.

You also have the ability to let the GW-BASIC error messages be printed from within the program. You must use the following command:

```
ON ERROR GOTO 0
```

You can check the ON ERROR function on your computer with the following program:

```
10   ON ERROR GOTO 100
20   GOTO 40
30   FOR I=1 TO 20
40   PRINT I
50   NEXT
60   END
100  PRINT ERL, ERR
110  RESUME NEXT
```

When you RUN the program, it will display the following:

```
0
  50                1
Ok
```

The error number as well as the number of the line containing the error are passed in the two variables ERL and ERR.

After running the program, check the values of these variables by entering the following command in direct mode:

```
PRINT ERR, ERL
```

and you'll notice that although the error number has been cleared from the ERR variable, ERL has retained the error line number. This can be useful in error handling routines.

On the next page are some exercises for you to work through. Remember to keep the five programming rules in mind when working on these problems.

Exercises

1. Write a program that adds up the "harmonic series" $(1 + 1/2 + 1/3 + 1/4 + 1/5 + \dots + 1/n)$ up to a given number. After each 50 additions the number of additions should be printed. In conclusion, the number of required sums should be printed.

2. Write a program that calculates the real zeros of a quadratic equation of the form:

    $AX^2 + BX + C = 0$

    The solutions can be obtained from the following formula:

    ```
    x1 = (-B + SQR(B2+4AC))/2A
    x2 = (-B - SQR(B2+4AC))/2A
    ```

    There is no real solution for $B^2 - 4AC < 0$. Take this into account in your program.

3. What happens in the following program if the value 4 is entered for Z? Solve the problem without entering the program into the computer.

    ```
    10 REM TEST OUTPUT WITH ON...GOTO
    20 INPUT"ENTER A NUMBER";Z
    30 ON Z GOTO 100,150,400:CLS
    40 PRINT"ILLEGAL VALUE"
    50 END
    100 PRINT"LINE 100"
    110 END
    150 PRINT"LINE 150"
    160 END
    400 PRINT"LINE 400"
    410 END
    ```

3.4   Reading the keyboard

GW-BASIC has various options for reading the keyboard. You are already familiar with the simplest option: reading data using INPUT and assigning it to a variable.

The INKEY$ function is also provided. Using INKEY$ allows you to input a single keypress. This can include using <CONTROL> and <ALT> in combination with another key. Most of these key combinations result in a one character string, but some combinations can result in two characters. You may check this using the following program:

```
10 A$=INKEY$ : IF A$="" THEN 10
20 PRINT LEN(A$)
```

Notice that if you hold down the <ALT> key and press the <Z> the program will print the number "2" to indicate that the length of the string produced by this key combination is 2 characters long.

Another option for selecting keys involves the use of INPUT$.

```
10 INPUT$(1)
20 A=ASC(A$)
30 PRINT A
```

The parameter in parentheses specifies how many characters you want to read in. In our example, a character is read and its ASCII value determined. The advantage of this function over the standard INPUT statement is that the <RETURN> key need not be pressed.

This covers all of the major functions for inputting characters from the keyboard. Now let's take a look at some commands and functions not used very often in programs. You should know what you're dealing with when you encounter such a command in a program.

3.5 FRE and POS

GW-BASIC contains a vast number of advanced functions which are seldom used in simple BASIC programs. This has little to do with their importance. Many of these commands are used in programs requiring communications with external devices. Considering the very technical nature of these commands, they do not fall within the scope of this book. Some of the advanced commands are useable in many programming situations such as the FRE and POS functions. You will find the FRE function useful when writing larger programs, or programs which must adjust themselves to the amount of available memory in the computer. The FRE function is most often used to determine the amount of free memory space. The syntax of the function looks like this:

    FRE(x) or FRE(x$)

The argument x or x$ may be any legal variable or string. Using a string as the argument will also cause BASIC to clear out unused strings. This is often called garbage collection, or housecleaning. If you want to know the free memory space in the computer, you can enter:

    PRINT FRE(X)

in the direct mode. If there is no program in memory, you get the maximum free space as the value. If you do not want to print out the amount of free memory, you may assign it to a variable. This is more useful in programs, since you shouldn't concern the user with such matters. Instead, the program should handle memory in a manner which is transparent to the user. Here is an example of assigning the value returned by the FRE function to a variable.

    X=FRE(X)

Using this example, if you were writing a program to store names and each name could be a maximum of 40 characters long, you could divide X by 40 to determine how many phone numbers would fit into memory.

The FRE(X$) form of the FRE function is most useful when writing programs which add strings together, or perform many other string functions. It will clear up memory which was used to perform these string functions, but is no longer needed. Often this function can be time consuming, so you may wish to display a message to warn the user that the computer is busy. This function is also assignable to a variable. Here is an example:

```
X$=FRE (X$)
```

The POSition function is used to determine the current cursor position on the screen. The following examples should explain more about the function. Enter into the computer in the direct mode:

```
PRINT "TEST" POS(X); "TEST A" POS(X)
```

and press the <RETURN> key. As output you get:

```
TEST 5 TEST A 14
```

The number 5 indicates the position of the cursor after the first execution of the print command. Correspondingly, the number 14 shows the cursor position after the second execution of the PRINT command. You can check this by entering the line again without the first POS command. You will then see that TEST A is printed directly after TEST, that the first character begins at the fifth position on the line. With POS you can determine the position in the line, and the next output with PRINT will take place.

3.6   READ, DATA and RESTORE

Up until now we have discussed reading data from the keyboard. The data is stored in variables and then processed further.

If a program requires a large amount of data, numerical values or strings, it is very tedious to have to enter these values each time the program is started. To get around this, you can use the READ and DATA statements.

The DATA statement is composed of a list of data items, where the individual values are separated by commas. The type of data that can be placed in a DATA statement can be either numerical or character.

With READ you can assign the individual data items in the DATA statements to variables. The variable type that follows the READ must correspond to the type of data contained in the DATA statement. You may not read a string into a numerical variable.

The DATA lines are not required to appear at any specific location within the program. They can be at the beginning, in the middle, or at the end. Often programmers place DATA statements at the end of the program, sometimes after the END statement. When the program encounters a READ command, it automatically searches for the DATA statement. Let's take a look at a simple example. First enter NEW — this command should always be used before you start a new program. Then enter the following program:

```
10 READ X
20 PRINT X
30 DATA 50
40 END
```

The program displays the value 50. In line 10 the numerical variable X is assigned the value 50 with a READ command. If the program encounters the READ command, it searches for the corresponding DATA line and reads the first value. This value is assigned to the variable that follows the READ. In line 20 the contents of the variable X are printed. Line 30 has no further influence on the program. Change the program in the following manner:

```
10 READ X,Y,Z
20 PRINT X,Y,Z
30 DATA 10,20,30
40 END
```

After you have started the program you get the following output:

```
10      20      30
```

READ first assigned the first value in the DATA line to the variable X. Then it assigned the second value read to the variable Y, and then the third value to the variable Z.

Upon each READ access to the data in the DATA lines, the next value is always read. A pointer is maintained inside the computer that is always advanced each time an item is read. This pointer always points to the next element to be read. At the start of a program this pointer points to the first element in the DATA line. The next lines should clarify this. The pointer is represented by the ↑ character.

```
30 DATA 10,20,30
        ↑
```

When the program encounters a READ, the pointer is incremented by one, and so points to the second element.

```
30 DATA 10,20,30
           ↑
```

When this element is read, the pointer is again incremented by one. When the pointer reaches the end of a list of DATA instructions, it is **not** automatically set back to the first element, but points after the last element. If you then try to access the list again with READ, the computer outputs the error message:

```
Out of DATA in (line #)
```

What if you want to access the data more than once? There is a command to allow this. It's called:

```
RESTORE
```

The RESTORE command sets the pointer back to the very first element of DATA. This gives you the ability to read the data in the DATA lines as often as you like. Enter the following program in order to see what happens when the program tries to read more data than is available.

```
10 READ A,B,C
20 PRINT A,B,C
30 DATA 10,20,30
40 READ D,E,F
50 PRINT D,E,F
60 END
```

After the values 10, 20, and 30 are printed, the error message:

```
Out of DATA in 40
```

appears. In line 40 an attempt was made to read the fourth element of DATA, an element that does not exist. To eliminate this error, you can either append three more values to the DATA statement or reset the pointer with RESTORE. Try this out once. Enter the following line in the computer and press the <RETURN> key.

```
35 RESTORE
```

Now enter the LIST command. Your program should look like this:

```
10 READ A,B,C
20 PRINT A,B,C
35 RESTORE
30 DATA 10,20,30
40 READ D,E,F
50 PRINT D,E,F
60 END
```

If you start the program now, the error message does not appear and you get the following output:

```
10      20      30
10      20      30
```

The pointer was again set to the first data element with the command RESTORE. Therefore the numerical variables D, E, and F were assigned the values 10, 20, and 30. The command:

```
READ A,B,C
```

causes three values to be read from the DATA line simultaneously. The values can also be read one at a time as the next example shows.

```
10 FOR I=1 TO 3
20 READ X
30 PRINT X
40 NEXT I
50 DATA 10,20,30
60 END
```

In this example, the commands READ X and PRINT X are placed in a FOR...NEXT loop that is executed a total of three times. On each pass through the loop, a new value is read from the DATA line, assigned to X, and printed.

As already mentioned, you can also put strings in the DATA lines. Normally these strings do not have to be placed in quotation marks. As usual, there are exceptions here too. Any string with a comma must be placed in quotes. Remember that a string cannot be assigned to a numerical variable.

If you have a long list of mixed data, a wrong assignment can occur quite quickly. The following example should make the problem clear:

```
10 FOR I=1 TO 3
20 READ A,B,C$
30 PRINT A,B,C$
40 NEXT I
50 DATA 10,20,TEST 1,30,40,TEST 2,50,TEST 3,OK
60 END
```

The program runs correctly through the second pass of the loop. Up to that point, the assignment of data values the variables that follow the READ command. According to READ, two numerical variables and then one string variable are to be READ. The order of the data in line 50 corresponds to the variable assignment behind READ, but only up to the seventh item—to the value 50. After this the program tries to read the string "TEST 3" into the numerical variable B. Since this is not possible, the program stops after two passes through the loop with the error message:

```
Syntax error in 50
```

Be extremely careful when combining different variable types in a READ command.

We've learned a lot about how we can get data into the computer or program. We've also learned how to read in data from the keyboard with INPUT and INPUT$. The second method of inputting data is by statements so that they do not have to be manually input all the time. In this way, the data value contained in the DATA statements are saved as part of the program. To save data entered with INPUT, these values must be saved separately on a disk file.

One common use of this combination of READ and DATA is when a program in machine language is to be generated by BASIC. This is usually done by placing the numerical values of the machine codes in DATA statements, then reading them with a FOR...NEXT loop and writing them into memory with the POKE command. The machine language program is then started with the CALL command. Since these are very advanced commands, we will not discuss these any further.

In the next chapter you will learn about how you write more complex programs in BASIC. The generation of arrays plays an important role in these programs. You will see that the commands READ and DATA will also have important applications.

4. Advanced BASIC applications

4.1 Arrays

The programming and management of arrays is one of the most difficult concepts for the beginning BASIC programmer. The more complex the arrays, the more difficult it is to work with them. Even advanced programmers have problems with array management.

But a beginner <u>can</u> learn how to work with arrays. It's all a matter of practice. We'll begin with very simple examples.

4.1.1 One-dimensional arrays

Imagine that you want to write a program that calculates your average monthly salary. We start with 12 monthly totals. This first example loop is used to read in the amounts for the monthly totals. We can write a program as follows:

```
5    CLS
10   REM AVERAGE MONTHLY INCOME
20   REM CALCULATE FOR 12 MONTHS
30   FOR I = 1 TO 12
40   PRINT "INCOME FOR MONTH" I;
45   INPUT M
50   S=S+M
60   NEXT I
70   D=S/12
80   D=INT(D*100)/100
90   PRINT "AVERAGE INCOME IS ";
100  PRINT "$ ";D
110  END
```

After you have entered this program into the computer, RUN it and enter 12 values. As the results you get the average monthly income, rounded off to two places after the decimal. In this program the individual monthly salaries are read in a FOR...NEXT loop with INPUT. The sum of the salaries is also formed within the loop (line 50). Line 70 calculates the average monthly income and the amount is rounded to 2 places in line 80. The program should be understandable to you.

We've now calculated the average monthly income. But what if we want to know later exactly how much money we made in May? In the last example the individual monthly values are lost.

There's no problem in solving that. We'll use 12 variables instead of one and assign a monthly total to each one. Let's change the program:

```
5    CLS
10   REM AVERAGE MONTHLY INCOME
20   REM SAVE INDIVUDAL MONTHS
30   INPUT "INCOME FOR MONTH 1";M1
40   INPUT "INCOME FOR MONTH 2";M2
50   INPUT "INCOME FOR MONTH 3";M3
60   INPUT "INCOME FOR MONTH 4";M4
70   INPUT "INCOME FOR MONTH 5";M5
80   INPUT "INCOME FOR MONTH 6";M6
90   INPUT "INCOME FOR MONTH 7";M7
100  INPUT "INCOME FOR MONTH 8";M8
110  INPUT "INCOME FOR MONTH 9";M9
120  INPUT "INCOME FOR MONTH 10";M10
130  INPUT "INCOME FOR MONTH 11";M11
140  INPUT "INCOME FOR MONTH 12";M12
150  S=M1+M2+M3+M4+M5+M6+M7+M8+M9+M10+M11+M12
160  D=S/12
170  D=INT(D*100)/100
180  PRINT "AVERAGE INCOME IS ";
190  PRINT "$ ";D
200  END
```

With these changes you have already moved a good deal closer to programming with arrays. If you now want to add to the program, you can refer back to the individual month values at any time. For example, if you want to know your total income for the month of May, you need only read variable M5 and you have your answer—assuming that the month numbers correspond to the numbers behind the variable name.

We now have the month value available in our program, but at the cost of additional program lines. And you've got to admit that it's rather cumbersome having to work with 12 variables. If we had to output these values again, we couldn't do it in a loop since it involves 12 different variables. You would have to use a PRINT command for each individual variable or one PRINT command followed by all 12 variables. It would look like this:

```
145 PRINT M1,M2,M3,M4,M5,M6,M7,M8,M9,M10,M11,M12
```

This is hard to read and inelegant—a quick-n-dirty solution, as we say in the business. It would be nice if we had a variable with a running index, something like this:

```
A(I)
```

This would make it possible to output the monthly values in a loop, and also access them through the specification of I. As you probably guessed, this arrangement is known as an *array*.

What do we mean by the term *array*?

Earlier in the book we compared a variable to a drawer that could hold numerical values or strings, depending on the type of variable. Imagine an array as a chest of drawers, with the drawers stacked on top of each other. Each drawer is designated with a number. This number has nothing to do with the actual contents of this drawer.

This number is called an *index*. This index is placed in parentheses and thereby is separated from the actual variable. We'll show you the notation again:

```
A(1)
```

Such a variable is called an *array variable* or *indexed variable*, since it is more accurately specified through the index. The index is the value in the parentheses.

Do not confuse this notation with the variable A1! There is a great difference between the two. The following picture should clarify the structure of such an array.

A(1)	2334
A(2)	2333
A(3)	2345.65
A(4)	2344.34
.	.
.	.
.	.
.	.
A(12)	3433.20

You see that such an array is very similar to a table (as in table of contents), in that the individual values are written under each other. Our array has 12 individual "drawers," each of which is assigned a value. If we want to know the contents of the third element, we need only use the index 3. This could look like this:

```
PRINT A(3)
```

In our case we would get:

```
2345.65
```

as the output. If we want to use such arrays in our programs, we must first tell the computer how large our array is to be, i.e. how many elements it is to contain. This is the purpose of the DIM instruction in BASIC. It has the following syntax:

```
DIM array name(number of elements)
```

For our array we would have to use the following syntax:

```
DIM A(12)
```

A is the name of the array and 12 is the maximum number of elements. The DIM instruction is usually located at the beginning of a program. Once an array is dimensioned, it may not be redimensioned again in the program with DIM. Otherwise the computer will output the error message:

```
Duplicate Definition in (line #)
```

In our example, an array of single precision floating-point variables was defined. You can also use arrays of string, integer, or double precision variables. Take a look at the following examples:

```
DIM DE$(15)
DIM GZ%(20)
DIM AB!(12)
```

These instructions create arrays of string, integer, and double precision floating-point variables. You can also dimension several arrays at once with one DIM instruction. It looks like this:

```
DIM A(12),B$(16),S%(20)
```

The following facts about arrays should be noted.

1. If you need no more than 11 elements in an array, you don't have to use a DIM instruction. When you access an element, such as A(4), the computer automatically executes a DIM A(10) instruction.

2. Normally, DIM A(10) dimensions 11 elements in the array A(). The indices start with zero, not one, and consequently you have to count A(0) in the total as well. The first element may be changed on all arrays from element 0 to element 1 using the OPTION BASE 1 command, covered later in this section.

The graphic representation of our array has to be expanded by the element A(0). However, will not use this 0th element in our program. If we wanted to add an extra statement to our program, we could do away with the 0th element altogether. This statement:

```
OPTION BASE 1
```

will cause all arrays to be created without a 0th element. The number 1 at the end of the command could be changed to a zero to indicate that we want all arrays to be created *with* a 0th element. OPTION BASE should only be set once in a program. If the program attempts to execute a second OPTION BASE statement the following error is generated:

```
Duplicate Definition in (line #)
```

Remember that dimensioning need not take place when 11 or fewer elements are used. For instance, if you know that you will need only 6 elements, omit the instruction DIM X(5) or DIM X(6) to save memory.

Let's take a look at the program that calculates the average monthly income using an array.

```
5    CLS
10   REM AVERAGE MONTHLY INCOME
20   REM WITH ONE ARRAY
30   DIM M(12)
40   FOR I = 1 TO 12
50   PRINT "INCOME FOR MONTH";I;
55   INPUT M(I)
60   S=S+M(I)
70   NEXT I
80   D=S/12
90   D=INT(D*100)/100
100  PRINT "AVERAGE INCOME IS ";
110  PRINT "$ ";D
120  END
```

Using an array adds only one additional program line when compared to the original example. By adding one additional line, the monthly values are available in the rest of the program. For example, if you want to output the monthly values once more before the output of the average monthly income, you could change the program as follows:

```
     •
     •
90   D=INT(D*100)/100
100  FOR I = 1 TO 12
110  PRINT "INCOME FOR MONTH";I;" $";M(I)
120  NEXT I
130  PRINT "AVERAGE INCOME IS ";
140  PRINT " $";D
150  END
```

By using an array we have made the monthly incomes available throughout the rest of the program—but we haven't made the program more complicated.

Arrays which have the following general syntax:

    A(X)

are called one-dimensional arrays.This is because they have only one index. The index does not have to be a constant. It can be a variable or a numerical expression. Imagine that you want to change our example program so that it will work with a variable number of months. The following modifications to the program would be possible:

```
    .
    .
30  INPUT"HOW MANY MONTHS";N
35  DIM M(N)
40  FOR I=1 TO N
    .
80  D=S/N

100 FOR I=1 TO N
```

The number of months input will determine the size of the array. Using this little trick, you can adapt the program exactly to current requirements, as well as make optimal use of the memory of the computer.

If you try to access an element that lies outside the dimensioned array, the computer displays the following error message:

    Subscript out of range

If you have defined an array with DIM A(15) and try to access the element A(16), this error message would be printed.

We now want to practice working with some examples. We'll use the arrays X and Y$ with 6 elements each. We won't use the 0th element.

4.1.2   Examples of one-dimensional arrays

Normally you can assume that after the DIM statement the individual elements of the array are empty. But within a program you may have to clear an entire array. With numerical arrays you can do this by assigning the individual elements with a zero value. The following program shows how this is done.

```
10 REM CLEAR A NUMERICAL ARRAY
20 DIM X(6)
30 FOR I=1 TO 6
40 X(I)=0
50 NEXT I
60 END
```

We have assumed we are working with an array containing 6 (or 7) elements. The FOR...NEXT loop has the starting value 1 and the ending value equal to the maximum number of elements in the array— 6 in our example. By running through this loop, I takes the value 1, 2, 3, 4, 5, and 6 in succession. This causes all elements of the array to be set to zero, since the index of X is incremented each time. Written out, the assignments would look like this:

```
X(1)=0
X(2)=0
X(3)=0
X(4)=0
X(5)=0
X(6)=0
```

When you clear a variable containing a string, you must remember not to fill the strings with zeros. This is because the zero is treated as a character. You could assign a space to each array element. But if you concatenate strings in your program, the space is included as one of the characters in the string. This can lead to errors in your program, such as when you use the LEN function, for example. Therefore, you should assign the elements of a string with "" (a null string) as shown here:

```
10 REM CLEAR A STRING ARRAY
20 DIM Y$(6)
30 FOR I=1 TO 6
40 Y$(I)=""
50 NEXT I
60 END
```

The method is the same as for clearing a numerical array.

The individual elements are assigned null strings in line 40. Make sure that there are no spaces between the two quotation marks.

Now we come to examples using the index in connection with FOR...NEXT loops. We assume three arrays with 6 elements each. The elements have the following contents:

a)	b)	c)
1	10	2
4	8	4
9	6	8
16	4	16
25	2	32
36	0	64

How can these three arrays be used in a FOR...NEXT loop?

A little study will show that the elements of example a) exactly match the squares of the indices. The program could look like this:

```
10 DIM X(6)
20 FOR I=1 TO 6
30 X(I)=I*I
40 NEXT I
50 END
```

The function of this loop is easier to see if we write down the individual steps:

```
DIM X(6)

I = 1 : X(1) = 1*1 =  1
I = 2 : X(2) = 2*2 =  4
I = 3 : X(3) = 3*3 =  9
I = 4 : X(4) = 4*4 = 16
I = 5 : X(5) = 5*5 = 25
I = 6 : X(6) = 6*6 = 36
```

I is incremented by one each pass through the loop. I is multiplied by itself and the result is assigned to the element whose index is I. This fills the array with the squares of each value from 1 to 6.

The same principle of using the loop variable for calculation is used in example b) as well.

With example b) we decrease the values of the array elements by 2 with every increase of the index. The starting value of the first array is 10. To create this effect, we cannot change the FOR. . .NEXT loop. This is because the elements are accessed via the loop index. We must work out an assignment rule that decreases the value of the elements in steps of two with every increase of the index. The solution to this problem might look like this:

```
10 DIM X(6)
20 FOR I=1 TO 6
30 X(I)=12-2*I
40 NEXT I
50 END
```

In line 30 we have our assignment rule. Again, we've incorporated the index into the calculation. If you run I from 1 to 6 in your mind, you see that it produces exactly the sequence of numbers in example b). You can check this by expanding the program with the following lines. The program will then output the entire array.

```
50 FOR I=1 TO 6
60 PRINT X(I)
70 NEXT I
80 END
```

If you have difficulty understanding these programming solutions, use the method in example a). Try writing the course of the program down on paper.

Now to example c). You probably recognized a pattern here as well. The numbers are the powers of two.

It shouldn't be any problem to find an assignment rule for this example. We use the 2 as a constant and the loop variable or index as the power. The program then looks like this:

```
10 DIM X(6)
20 FOR I=1 TO 6
30 X(I)=2^I
40 NEXT I
50 END
```

Check the accuracy of this assignment by appending the program lines from example b). You can also work the process out on paper to make it clearer. With practice the principle of this technique will become quite familiar. And when you encounter such techniques or applications in more complex programs, you should be able to figure them out.

Up to now we have looked only at numerical arrays. Now we want to turn to string arrays. There is usually no pattern to the layout of the individual elements in string arrays. Assignments for the string arrays are often made by the user via the keyboard. But another possibility is using the commands READ and DATA to initialize an array.

String arrays can be used to store such data as names, addresses, or numbers that exist as strings. First we'll create an array in which we store our friends' first names in the computer.

We'll specify the size of the array at 6, only our close friends. When the capacity of the array is reached, the program will output a message on its own, instead of an error message. Our example will show how such a program is created. Make sure you have your CAPS LOCK on when entering and running this program or it will not operate properly.

```
5    CLS
10   REM LIST OF FIRST NAMES
20   DIM Y$(6)
30   Z=Z+1
40   INPUT "FIRST NAME";Y$(Z)
50   PRINT "MORE INPUT Y/N ?"
60   A$=INKEY$:IF A$="" THEN 60
70   IF A$ <> "Y" THEN 100
80   IF Z < 6 THEN 30
90   PRINT "LIST IS FULL!"
```

```
100 END
```

To make the program easier to read, an array of only 6 (or 7) elements is used here (line 20). Line 30 contains the counter. This counter is incremented by one for each input. Since we don't know the exact number of names, we cannot use a FOR...NEXT loop. Line 40 asks for the entry of a name with INPUT and assigns this to the element with the index of Z. In line 50 you're asked if additional input is yet to be made. The function in line 60 should be familiar to us. Line 70 compares the character entered to Y. This line also contains the reason this program will not work properly if you do not enter and run it with the CAPS LOCK on. If the character is not equal to (capital) Y, the program is ended at line 100. If more input is to take place, line 80 compares the counter to 6 to see if it is smaller. If the counter already has the value 6, the message LIST IS FULL! is printed in line 90, and the program is ended. If we had not incorporated this check, the program would have terminated on a value greater than 6 with the error message:

```
Subscript out of range in 40
```

If Z reaches the value 7, line 40 attempts to access the element Y$(7). Because of the DIM statement, this element does not exist. Unwanted program interruptions such as this should be avoided whenever possible. The same effect could be achieved with ON ERROR GOTO and a corresponding error-handling routine.

The program still doesn't do a whole lot, but the principle should become clear. We could now add a question to see if the user wants to output the whole list. You can make this enhancement yourself by incorporating the appropriate IF...THEN test into the program. You can then display the contents of the array with a FOR...NEXT loop.

Now we'll look at an example where an array is filled with READ and DATA commands. Imagine that you need the days of the week in your program. It would require a lot of work to enter this information each time the program was started. Why not put this data in DATA lines, then read them into an array at the program's start with READ? Take a look at the following example program:

The ¶ characters in the following program are not to be entered, they only show where a BASIC line actually ends. When formatting the listing to fit in the book, some lines may be split that should not be. The ¶ character shows where a line actually ends.

```
5    CLS¶
10   REM DAYS OF THE WEEK¶
20   DIM WD$(7)¶
30   FOR I= 1 TO 7¶
40   READ WD$(I)¶
50   NEXT I¶
60   DATA MONDAY,TUESDAY,WEDNESDAY,THURSDAY,
     FRIDAY,SATURDAY,SUNDAY¶
70   REM OUTPUT YES/NO¶
80   PRINT "OUTPUT THE ARRAY Y/N"¶
90   A$=INKEY$:IF A$="" THEN 90¶
100  IF A$<>"Y" THEN 140¶
110  FOR I = 1 TO 7¶
120  PRINT WD$(I)¶
130  NEXT I¶
140  END¶
```

This program is very similar to the one for the name list. The major difference is found in line 40, where the data is read with READ instead of INPUT. The DATA line is self-explanatory. At the conclusion of the program is an option to output the entire array.

You've now learned how to transfer data to an array with the READ and DATA commands. Before we turn to two-dimensional arrays, brush up on your knowledge of one-dimensional arrays with the exercises on the following page.

Exercises

1) Write a program that reads six names and places them in an array. Furthermore, the program should output the name that would come first in an alphabetical listing. Test the program with the names Jim, Doug, Gene, Julie, Arnie, and Jan. Remember that strings can be compared with each other to see if they are equal, less than, or greater. The result will be the name "Arnie."

2) Write a program that creates 6 random numbers and places these numbers in an array. The largest of these numbers should be printed. The random numbers should occur in the range 50 to 150.

3) Start with the following array X(6):

X(1)	X(2)	X(3)	X(4)	X(5)	X(6)
0	2	6	12	20	30

Write a program and develop an assignment rule that creates this array. Output the array to check yourself. Don't worry that we listed the array elements horizontally this time. This isn't important when you're working with one-dimensional arrays.

4.1.3   Multi-dimensional arrays

Up to now we have used only one-dimensional arrays. We compared these arrays to a drawer in which the data elements were stacked one above the other. These drawers or lists usually don't consist of horizontal or vertical data, but a combination of the two. They are composed of rows and columns. Imagine that you wanted to expand the program that read a person's first name into an array, so that the last names and the birthdates were also available under the same index.

One way to do this is create three arrays in which the data can be stored. Array A$(X) can hold the first names, array B$(X) the last names, and array C$(X) the birthdates. You have created three arrays with different names. These arrays can be easily filled with data, but working with them within the program is rather complicated. Therefore, we have the same problem we had at the introduction to one-dimensional arrays.

Why shouldn't it be possible to use just one array instead of three? The solution to our problem is called a *multi-dimensional array*.

In this particular case, we need a two-dimensional array. That's because we want to store the individual first names in the same row as the data for the last name and birthdate. Therefore, our array requires rows and columns. The structure of such an array looks like this:

	Column 1	Column 2	Column 3
Row 1			
Row 2			
Row 3			
Row 4			
Row 5			

The DIM statement for this array is:

```
DIM A$(5,3)
```

This reserves an array with 5 lines and 3 columns. (This DIM statement actually generates an array of 6 lines and 4 columns. However, we will not use the 0th elements).

If you do not execute the DIM statement and use one of the elements from this array, the computer automatically creates an array of size (10,10). It's wise to use the DIM statement for multi-dimensional arrays, because you can save quite a bit of memory space.

How is such an array used? Imagine that you want to fill the first three columns of the first line of this array with data. You could use the following program line:

```
.
.
40 INPUT"FIRST NAME, LAST NAME, BIRTHDATE";
   A$(1,1),A$(1,2),A$(1,3)
.
.
```

This requires the input of three elements (first name, last name, birthdate), separated from each other by commas. However, this command is rather hard to read within a program. Instead, we should use a total of three INPUT commands written on three separate program lines. These lines look like this:

```
.
.
40 INPUT"FIRST NAME";A$(1,1)
50 INPUT"LAST NAME";A$(1,2)
60 INPUT"BIRTHDATE";A$(1,3)
.
.
```

This assignment is easier to read. It also helps to avoid input errors, because there is a prompt for the input of each element.

Why isn't the input made in a loop—where the first name, last name, and birthdate are read in succession with just one INPUT command? In our example, each INPUT command has its own prompt describing the value to be entered. This is why the three INPUT commands cannot be replaced by a single INPUT, so a loop cannot be used.

We want to read exactly six first names, last names, and birthdates. We can use a FOR...NEXT loop for this, as the following example shows:

```
10  REM READ 6 FIRST & LAST NAMES
20  REM AND BIRTHDATES
30  DIM A$(6,3)
40  FOR I=1 TO 6
50  PRINT"FIRST NAME OF #";I;
55  INPUT A$(I,1)
60  INPUT"LAST NAME";A$(I,2)
70  INPUT"BIRTHDATE";A$(I,3)
80  NEXT I: END
```

You can find program segments similar to this in all small data management programs.

Data for multi-dimensional arrays is not input from the keyboard only. Data from DATA statements read with the READ command can furnish data for a program as well. You are familiar with this technique from the one-dimensional arrays. We can use nested FOR...NEXT loops in programs of this type. The following example shows how a two-dimensional array of size (3,4) would be filled with data from DATA statements:

```
10  REM LOAD ARRAY WITH DATA LINES
20  DIM X(3,4)
30  FOR R=1 TO 3
40  FOR C=1 TO 4
50  READ X(R,C)
60  NEXT C,R
70  DATA 11,12,13,14,21,22,23,24,31,32,33,34
80  REM ARRAY OUTPUT
90  PRINT"DISPLAY ARRAY (Y/N)?"
100 A$=INKEY$:IF A$="" THEN 100
110 IF A$ <> "Y" THEN 170
120 FOR R=1 TO 3
130 PRINT X(R,1);X(R,2);X(R,3);X(R,4)
140 NEXT R
170 END
```

This example has an array with 3 rows and 4 columns which will be filled by two nested FOR...NEXT loops. The inner loop (40 FOR C=1 TO 4) causes all elements in a row to be filled. Once this loop is completed the outer loop (30 FOR R=1 TO 3) fills all three rows in succession. The following figure shows how the array is filled with data.

ARRAY X(3,4)

```
11  *  *  *    11 12  *  *    11 12 13  *    11 12 13 14
 *  *  *  *     *  *  *  *     *  *  *  *     *  *  *  *
 *  *  *  *     *  *  *  *     *  *  *  *     *  *  *  *


11 12 13 14    11 12 13 14    11 12 13 14    11 12 13 14
21  *  *  *    21 22  *  *    21 22 23  *    21 22 23 24
 *  *  *  *     *  *  *  *     *  *  *  *     *  *  *  *


11 12 13 14    11 12 13 14    11 12 13 14    11 12 13 14
21 22 23 24    21 22 23 24    21 22 23 24    21 22 23 24
31  *  *  *    31 32  *  *    31 32 33  *    31 32 33 34
```

If you want to output the array, you need only press the Y key. The array will be printed in the form you see above. This output is accomplished with line 130. All four columns are printed on one line simultaneously. Only the output of the three rows is accomplished by the FOR...NEXT loop.

The next example shows you another way of outputting the array with this technique (the first lines of the program are omitted):

```
     .
     .
80   REM ARRAY OUTPUT
90   PRINT"DISPLAY ARRAY (Y/N)?"
100  A$=INKEY$:IF A$="" THEN 100
110  IF A$ <> "Y" THEN 170
120  FOR R=1 TO 3
130  FOR C=1 TO 4
140  PRINT X(R,C);:ZZ=ZZ+1
150  IF ZZ=4 THEN ZZ=0:PRINT
160  NEXT C,R
170  END
```

You can use two nested FOR...NEXT loops if you modify your program this way. The semicolon in line 140 causes the values of the individual elements to be printed one after the other. In order to construct the structure of the array on the screen, a new line must be started after each four elements are printed. This is the reason for the additional counter ZZ. This counter registers how often an output has been made with PRINT. Line 150 tests to see if this counter has the value 4. If this is the case, the counter is set back to zero and another PRINT command is executed, causing the next element to appear at the start of the next screen line. You can make the output easier to read by using two PRINT commands, as in our example.

We now come back to the first example. We said that similar program segments were found in data management programs. In this example, we assumed that we would record the data of only 6 people. But the total number of people is rarely known ahead of time. Usually we know only the number of data elements for each person to be recorded—the last name, first name, and telephone number.

Say you want to write a program to replace your telephone directory. In most cases, you don't know the number of persons, only the number of data elements. So you can only approximate your dimensions. Let's assume that you want to record about 100 telephone numbers. The DIM statement X$(120,3) should be sufficient in this case. Here's an example:

```
10   REM READ IN DATA
20   DIM X$(120,3)
30   CLS
40   Z=Z+1
50   INPUT "FIRST NAME";X$(Z,1)
60   PRINT
70   INPUT "LAST NAME";X$(Z,2)
80   PRINT
90   INPUT "PHONE NUMBER";X$(Z,3)
100  PRINT
110  PRINT "DO YOU WANT TO"
120  PRINT "INPUT MORE DATA (Y/N)?"
130  A$=INKEY$:IF A$="" THEN 130
140  IF A$="Y" THEN 30
150  END
```

The preceding program could be solved more elegantly. We just want you to understand the principle used here.

Since we don't use a FOR...NEXT loop, the counter in line 40 must be inserted to increment the index by 1 for each new input. The data is then read with INPUT commands that assign the data to the appropriate elements. If additional data is to be entered, the program branches to line 30. Otherwise the program is ended. This is where a jump to a main menu in a data management program might occur—the place where the user could then select additional options.

A comparison is made in line 140 with IF . . . THEN to see if more data is to be entered. This is different from the first program, where this task was assumed by a FOR . . . NEXT loop.

We use IF . . . THEN when the exact number of data is *not* known ahead of time.

These examples show how to use multi-dimensional arrays. GW-BASIC will allow arrays with up to 13 indices. This means that not only two, three, or four-dimensional arrays can be created, but arrays with as many as thirteen dimensions. Arrays beyond three dimensions become more difficult to picture graphically, but this does not mean that they can't be used in solving certain problems.

Let's take a look at an example of a three-dimensional array. We will define the indices as follows:

> **x** = Row
> **y** = Column
> **z** = Depth

We will now create a three-dimensional array that we'll represent with 3 stacked planes. This three-dimensional array can best be imagined as three two-dimensional arrays, one after the other. The following illustration should clarify this concept:

(1,1,3)	(1,2,3)	(1,3,3)	A(X,Y,Z)

X = row
Y = column
Z = plane

| (2,1,3) | (1,1,2) | (1,2,2) | (1,3,2) |

| (3,1,3) | | | |

Plane 3

| (2,1,2) | (1,1,1) | (1,2,1) | (1,3,1) |

| (3,1,2) | (2,1,1) | (2,2,1) | (2,3,1) |

Plane 2

| (3,1,1) | (3,2,1) | (3,3,1) |

Plane 1

To create this array, the DIM statement looks like this:

    DIM C(X,Y,Z)

or, as in our example:

    DIM A(3,3,3)

This array has a total of 27 individual elements (3*3*3=27). Actually, this array has 64 elements if we count the zero elements (4*4*4=64).

Your problem now is writing a program to fill this array with data. The number of data is known. Assume that, in this 3D array, first the column values of a row will be filled, then the rows themselves (as for a two-dimensional array), and finally the individual "planes". Write the program to create the array shown in the illustration above. The value assignments of the individual planes is intended. You don't have to create the spatial effect in the output.

Our solution follows. The ¶ characters in the following program are not to be entered, they only show where a BASIC line actually ends.

123

When formatting the listing to fit in the book, some lines may be split that should not be. The ¶ character shows where a line actually ends.

```
10   REM 3-D ARRAY¶
20   DIM W(3,3,3)¶
30   FOR Z=1 TO 3¶
40   FOR Y=1 TO 3¶
50   FOR X=1 TO 3¶
60   READ W(X,Y,Z)¶
70   NEXT X,Y,Z¶
80   DATA 1,1,1,1,1,1,1,1,1,2,2,2,2,2,2,2,2,2,3,3,
     3,3,3,3,3,3,3¶
90   REM ARRAY OUTPUT¶
100  FOR Z=1 TO 3¶
110  FOR Y=1 TO 3¶
120  FOR X=1 TO 3¶
130  PRINT W(X,Y,Z);:ZZ=ZZ+1¶
140  IF ZZ=3 THEN ZZ=0:PRINT¶
150  NEXT X,Y,Z¶
160  END¶
```

You've got to remember the initial DIM statement, as in line 20. What applies to a two-dimensional array also holds true for a three-dimensional array. If you forget the DIM statement, the computer will create an array of 10*10*10=1000 elements, or 11*11*11=1331 elements! That would be an enormous waste of memory space—you only need 27 elements.

Take a look at the three FOR...NEXT loops, opened in lines 30 through 50. The outer loop causes the individual planes of the cube to be filled. The other two loops fill a two-dimensional slice of the array. Line 70 closes all three loops at once. Make sure that the loop variables are placed after the NEXT in the proper order. The array is not printed in a spatial representation, but the "planes" should be recognizable.

This concludes the section on multi-dimensional arrays. You should now be able to use either one-dimensional or multi-dimensional arrays in your programs. One and two-dimensional arrays are the ones most often used in programs. The predominant application of arrays is data management.

4.2   Subroutines

A *subroutine* is a program segment that replaces several often-used, similar program sections. A subroutine is an independent segment of a program, and is usually located at the start or end of the main program. Using a subroutine is made with the command:

    GOSUB (line number)

GOSUB is an abbreviation for GOto SUBroutine. The line number indicates the location where the subroutine begins. When the computer encounters this program command, it makes note of the line number from where it's branching. Then it branches to the line number of the subroutine. The computer continues with program execution until it encounters the return command:

    RETURN

Program execution then returns to and continues with the statements following the GOSUB command. If the program encounters the RETURN command without first having received the GOSUB command, the program stops with the error message:

    RETURN without GOSUB in (line #)

Whenever you call a subroutine you must use the GOSUB command. A common error is branching to a subroutine with the GOTO command. This is often done with IF . . . THEN, as in the following:

```
110 IF A < 1 THEN GOTO 130          <!! ERROR !!
120 GOTO 90
130 REM SUBROUTINE
140 A=A+1
150 RETURN
```

In this example, a branch is made to a subroutine with a GOTO in line 110 (if A is less than 1). When GOTO is improperly used in such a subroutine, the program would terminate with the error message:

    RETURN without GOSUB in 150

The proper syntax of line 110 must be:

```
110 IF A < 1 THEN GOSUB 130          < CORRECT
```

The following example shows another error. This error is difficult to recognize in larger programs using subroutines:

```
10  REM ERROR IN SUBROUTINE
20  PRINT
30  PRINT Z
40  GOSUB 70
50  Z=Z+1:GOTO 20
60  END
70  REM SUBROUTINE
80  FOR I=1 TO 25
90  PRINT I;
100 IF I>=15 THEN 50
110 NEXT I
120 RETURN
```

Enter this program and start it. After the 8th execution of the subroutine, the program will terminate with the error message:

```
Out of memory in 90
```

The error lies in the call to the subroutine. The program creates a blank line after the start (line 20). Then the current value of the variable is printed—Z serves as a counter for the number of times the subroutine is executed.

Line 40 makes the call to the subroutine with GOSUB 70. The program jumps to the subroutine in line 70, and starts execution of the FOR...NEXT loop. Line 90 outputs the value of the loop variable I.

Line 100 breaks two rules at once. First, you should never exit a FOR...NEXT loop with GOTO. This can lead to problems with the internal management of this loop. The second error is the more serious error of the two: you *cannot* exit a subroutine without using the RETURN command. Line 100 requires a jump out of the subroutine, for the case in which I is greater than or equal to 15. Instead of THEN 50, we should write THEN RETURN.

You can branch back and forth *within* a subroutine with GOTO as with normal programs. However, you cannot simply *exit* a subroutine with GOTO. In our example, the program stops after the 8th execution of the subroutine.

If you make an error like this in any of your programs, it may appear to run correctly at first. Then, under certain conditions it suddenly will crash. For this reason you should always check your subroutines for this error. A program carefully thought out and well planned will help you avoid such errors.

Now we come to a practical application of subroutines. You might recall the program MATH TUTOR. Look through this program listing for program segments that are repeated in the program. You will probably discover that some program segments could be combined into subroutines. The lines that are often repeated are listed again here.

The ¶ characters in the following listing should not be entered. They only show the actual end of the BASIC line. Formatting the programs for this book split some lines that should not have been split. The ¶ characters show the end of the line.

```
10   REM THIS LINE IS NEEDED TO BE ABLE TO RUN¶
230  CLS¶
240  PRINT TAB(10)"INPUT THE LARGEST"¶
250  PRINT¶
260  PRINT TAB(10)"NUMBER FOR ADDITION."¶
270  PRINT¶
290  PRINT TAB(10);:INPUT"LARGEST";GR¶
299  REM¶
300  REM RANDOM NUMBERS¶
301  REM¶
310  A1=INT(GR*RND(1))+1¶
320  A2=INT(GR*RND(1))+1¶
329  REM¶
330  REM COMPUTE RESULT¶
331  REM¶
340  ER=A1+A2¶
350  CLS¶
360  PRINT¶
370  PRINT "HOW MUCH IS" A1 "+" A2 "= ";¶
380  INPUT ES¶
390  IF ES=ER THEN PRINT:PRINT TAB(10)"CORRECT!"
     :F=0:GOTO 470¶
400  PRINT:PRINT TAB(10)"WRONG."¶
410  FOR I=0 TO 2000:NEXT I¶
420  F=F+1¶
430  IF F<=2 THEN 350¶
440  PRINT¶
450  FOR I=0 TO 2000:NEXT I¶
460  PRINT TAB(5)"THE CORRECT ANSWER IS" ER¶
```

127

```
470 FOR I=0 TO 3000:NEXT I¶
480 PRINT TAB(5)"ANOTHER PROBLEM Y/N";¶
490 INPUT A$¶
500 IF A$="Y" THEN F=0:GOTO 300¶
510 GOTO 10¶
```

These repeated program lines can be grouped into specific blocks. The first block is the lines from 230 to 290, which requires the input of the largest number for the calculation type. The problem with this segment is that each calculation type for which the largest number is read must be named. The output:

```
INPUT THE LARGEST

NUMBER FOR ADDITION
```

must be made more flexible in the subroutine, specifically regarding the type of calculation.

We access the individual program segments such as addition, subtraction, etc. with ON X GOTO in the menu. Therefore, it's advisable to use X as an index. We'll see why we do this shortly.

At the start of the program we can create an array that contains the terms addition, subtraction, division, and multiplication in the order in which these terms appear in the menu. We can also output the menu itself with the contents of this array. Let's look at the modified program start:

```
10   REM ****************¶
20   REM * PROGRAM START *¶
30   REM ****************¶
50   DIM RA$(4),BE$(4)¶
60   FOR I=1 TO 4¶
70   READ RA$(I),BE$(I)¶
80   NEXT I¶
90   DATA ADDITION,+,SUBTRACTION,-,DIVISION,/,
     MULTIPLICATION,*¶
100  GOTO 580¶
.¶
.¶
.¶
```

In line 50 the two arrays RA$ and BE$ are generated. The two arrays are loaded with the FOR...NEXT loop in line 60. The array RA$ is initialized with the terms addition, subtraction, etc. The array BE$ is initialized with the corresponding characters of the calculation types. After the program is started, the arrays are filled with this data.

Let's take a look at lines 570 to 790 of the modified program to see how the array RA$ is used to construct the menu.

```
.
.
.
570    REM **********
580    REM *  MENU  *
590    REM **********
600    CLS:F=0
610    PRINT
620    PRINT TAB(32)"MATH TUTOR"
630    PRINT:PRINT
640    PRINT TAB(32)"CHOOSE:"
650    PRINT
660    PRINT TAB(32)"1 FOR "RA$(1)
670    PRINT
680    PRINT TAB(32)"2 FOR "RA$(2)
690    PRINT
700    PRINT TAB(32)"3 FOR "RA$(3)
710    PRINT
720    PRINT TAB(32)"4 FOR "RA$(4)
730    PRINT
740    PRINT TAB(32)"5 TO END"
750    PRINT
760    PRINT TAB(132)"WHICH NUMBER?"
770    E$=INKEY$:IF E$="" THEN 770
780    P=VAL(E$):IF P < 1 OR P > 5 THEN 770
790    ON P GOTO 800,890,990,1090,1180
.
.
.
```

In contrast to the previous version of the program, the menu selections addition, subtraction, etc. are not mentioned individually, but are read from the array RA$ in lines 660 to 720. The array elements were accessed individually here for the sake of readability. You could also achieve this with a FOR...NEXT loop. The following example illustrates this:

```
        .
        .
660     FOR I=1 TO 4
670     PRINT TAB(31)I" FOR "RA$(I)
680     PRINT
690     NEXT I
700     REM *** DELETE LINES 700 - 730 ***
        .
        .
```

When a character is read in line 770, it is first checked in line 780 to see if it is a valid character (a digit between 1 and 5). If this is the case, the numerical value is determined with VAL(E$) and assigned to the variable P. Branches are made to the appropriate lines based on P. If addition is selected, P has the value 1. This causes a branch to line 800. There begins the program segment for addition. Let's take a look at the program lines for this:

```
        .
        .
800 REM ************
810 REM * ADDITION *
820 REM ************
830 GOSUB 110
840 GOSUB 310
850 ER=A1+A2
860 GOSUB 390
870 IF A$="Y" THEN 840
880 GOTO 580
        .
        .
```

In line 830 the first subroutine is called. This is the segment in which the highest number to be used in the calculations is entered. The next lines constitute this first subroutine:

```
        .
        .
110 REM **************
120 REM * SUBROUTINE *
130 REM **************
140 REM ************************
150 REM * INPUT LARGEST NUMBER *
160 REM ************************
```

```
170 CLS:A$="":B$=""
180 PRINT TAB(10)"INPUT THE LARGEST NUMBER"
190 PRINT
200 PRINT TAB(10)"FOR "RA$(P)"."
210 PRINT
220 PRINT TAB(10)"LARGEST NUMBER?   ";
230 FOR I=1 TO 3
240 A$=INKEY$:IF A$="" THEN 240
250 IF ASC(A$)<48 OR ASC(A$)>57 THEN 240
260 B$=B$+A$:PRINT A$;
270 NEXT I
280 GR=VAL(B$)
290 RETURN
     .

     .
```

The first part of line 170 should be familiar. But why are the variables A$ and B$ set to null in the second half? Since B$ is combined with A$ in line 260, it always "drags" its contents along. If the calculation type was changed and this subroutine called again, the old contents of the variable would be appended to the newly-read values. This would give a six-digit number for the calculation of the random numbers. This is why the two variables are set to null at the start of the subroutine.

The input of the three digits is done with INKEY$ (see the section on data input with INKEY$). In our current example, a couple of changes are necessary. For one, only digits between 0 and 9 can be entered (line 250). The digits entered are displayed in line 260 with PRINT A$. If you want to use just a two-digit number, you must first enter a zero and then the remaining digits.

Line 200 is quite interesting. Here the value of P is used as an index. This index enables the computer to read the suitable calculation type from the array RA$. You can see that it makes a lot of sense to use indexed variables.

We assume that the data was placed in the array in the proper order. If we selected addition, P has the value of 1. The term "addition" is located in RA$(1). For this reason, the character for calculation type is also placed in a different array with the same index. With this little trick we have made our subroutine match each of the four calculation types.

The next program line for addition, line 840, calls the subroutine for the creation of the random numbers. This is the smallest and simplest subroutine:

```
       .
       .
300 REM *************************
310 REM * CREATE RANDOM NUMBERS *
320 REM *************************
325 RANDOMIZE TIMER
330 A1=INT(GR*RND(1))+1
340 A2=INT(GR*RND(1))+1
350 RETURN
       .
       .
```

In line 325 the random number generator is seeded with the value from TIMER, a system variable containing the content of the system clock. No further explanation should be needed for this subroutine.

More important is the next subroutine, PROBLEM SET-UP. Here are the lines for the following subroutine (note the ¶ characters that show the end of the BASIC line):

```
  .¶
  .¶
360 REM ******************¶
370 REM * PROBLEM SET-UP *¶
380 REM ******************¶
390 CLS¶
400 PRINT¶
410 PRINT "HOW MUCH IS";A1;BE$(P);A2;"= ";¶
420 INPUT ES¶
430 IF ES=ER THEN PRINT:PRINT TAB(10) "RIGHT!"
      :F=0:GOTO 500¶
440 PRINT:PRINT TAB(10) "WRONG!!"¶
450 FOR I=1 TO 2000: NEXT I¶
460 F=F+1¶
470 IF F<=2 THEN 390¶
480 PRINT¶
490 FOR I=1 TO 2000: NEXT I¶
500 PRINT:PRINT TAB(5) "THE ANSWER IS"ER¶
510 F=0¶
520 FOR I=1 TO 3000:NEXT I¶
```

```
530 PRINT¶
540 PRINT TAB(5)"ANOTHER PROBLEM Y/N";¶
550 INPUT A$¶
560 RETURN¶
.¶
.¶
```

Lines 390 and 400 need no explanation. Line 410 of this subroutine is interesting. Here the statement of the problem is formulated. First the three words:

```
HOW MUCH IS
```

are printed. Then the values of the variables A1, BE$(P), and A2 are printed. These variables are followed by an equal (=) sign. We could formulate the general form of this screen output like this:

```
HOW MUCH IS A1 + (or -,*,/) A2 = ?
```

The proper calculation character BE$(P) is printed, depending on the calculation type selected via the index P.

We must ensure that A1 and A2 always contain the *correct* values independent of the calculation type. By *correct* values we mean that the answer is always a positive whole number. We must prepare the values of the variables A1 and A2 in the individual program selections of addition, subtraction, etc., so that our subroutine remains valid for all calculation types.

The remaining program lines to line 540 should be familiar to you from the original MATH TUTOR program. In line 550, A$ accepts the answer from the question in line 540. Line 560 ends the subroutine with the RETURN command. The contents of variable A$ are processed in the program segments corresponding to the individual calculation types.

This concludes the program segment containing the subroutines. You've no doubt noticed that we placed the subroutines at the start of the program. Many books advise you to place the subroutines at the end of the main program. Our decision was made in consideration of a program library. This example sorts subroutines according to line numbers. This is so the subroutine for rounding a number is a line 50000, and so on. If you write a new program, you can load these routines with a special command and append them to the program. The MERGE instruction is used to perform this.

Why is it advantageous to give the subroutines low line numbers, thereby placing them at the start of the program? It doesn't matter whether a subroutine is appended to a program or the program is appended to the subroutines. The results are equivalent.

A subroutine causes the computer to branch to the start of a program. There it begins searching for the line number at which the subroutine starts. If the subroutines are located at the start of the program, the execution time of the program is reduced. For small programs this will hardly be noticeable, if at all. But once the program has reached a moderate length, this trick will make the program several seconds faster.

We said that the variables A1 and A2 for the subroutine PROBLEM SET-UP must be prepared in the individual program segments for the calculation type. This applies only to subtraction and division, since the values for the variables from addition ER=A1+A2 and multiplication ER=A1*A2 can be passed directly to the subroutine.

For subtraction, you must make sure that A1 is always larger than A2, to ensure that no negative values arise. This is accomplished with the program line 940. If A1 is smaller than A2, the two values are exchanged in temporary storage.

When division takes place, we want only integer results. For this reason, the result ER is first calculated by multiplying the variables A1 and A2. In the original program MATH TUTOR, we could state the problem as follows:

```
HOW MUCH IS ER / A1 = ?
```

The previously-calculated result ER is divided by the variable A1. This must lead to an integer value, namely the variable A2.

Our subroutine cannot use this method directly, since it is generalized for all four arithmetical computations. This must be done in the Division program section. The following program lines are used:

```
   .
   .
   .
1040 ER=A1*A2
1050 I=ER:ER=A1:A1=I
   .
   .
```

Here too the result is first calculated with the multiplication. Line 1050 assigns the correct values for the subroutine PROBLEM SET-UP. Since we can't switch the variable designations when the variable is output, we must reassign the values of the variables.

To accomplish this, the technique of temporary storage is used. The variable I initially contains the value of the variable ER. ER is then assigned the value of A1. Finally, A1 contains the value of I—that is, the old content of ER. The contents of the two variables are exchanged in this manner. This is how we get the proper assignments in the problem statement subroutine.

Now we'll list the complete program. The ¶ characters in the following program are not to be entered, they only show where a BASIC line actually ends. When formatting the listing to fit in the book, some lines may be split that should not be. The ¶ character shows where a line actually ends.

```
10   REM ****************¶
20   REM * PROGRAM START *¶
30   REM ****************¶
50   DIM RA$(4),BE$(4)¶
60   FOR I=1 TO 4¶
70   READ RA$(I),BE$(I)¶
80   NEXT I¶
90   DATA ADDITION,+,SUBTRACTION,-,DIVISION,/,
     MULTIPLICATION,*¶
100  GOTO 580¶
110  REM **************¶
120  REM * SUBROUTINE *¶
130  REM **************¶
140  REM **********************¶
150  REM * INPUT LARGEST NUMBER *¶
160  REM **********************¶
170  CLS:A$="":B$=""¶
180  PRINT TAB(10)"INPUT THE LARGEST NUMBER"¶
190  PRINT¶
200  PRINT TAB(10)"FOR "RA$(P)"."¶
210  PRINT¶
220  PRINT TAB (10)"LARGEST NUMBER?  ";¶
230  FOR I=1 TO 3¶
240  A$=INKEY$:IF A$="" THEN 240¶
250  IF ASC(A$)<48 OR ASC(A$)>57 THEN 240¶
260  B$=B$+A$:PRINT A$;¶
```

```
270 NEXT I¶
280 GR=VAL(B$)¶
290 RETURN¶
300 REM *************************¶
310 REM * CREATE RANDOM NUMBERS *¶
320 REM *************************¶
325 RANDOMIZE TIMER¶
330 A1=INT(GR*RND(1))+1¶
340 A2=INT(GR*RND(1))+1¶
350 RETURN¶
360 REM ******************¶
370 REM * PROBLEM SET-UP *¶
380 REM ******************¶
390 CLS¶
400 PRINT¶
410 PRINT "HOW MUCH IS";A1;BE$(P);A2;"= ";¶
420 INPUT ES¶
430 IF ES=ER THEN PRINT:PRINT TAB(10)"RIGHT!"
    :F=0:GOTO 500¶
440 PRINT:PRINT TAB(10)"WRONG!!"¶
450 FOR I=1 TO 2000: NEXT I¶
460 F=F+1¶
470 IF F<=2 THEN 390¶
480 PRINT¶
490 FOR I=1 TO 2000: NEXT I¶
500 PRINT:PRINT TAB(5)"THE ANSWER IS"ER¶
510 F=0¶
520 FOR I=1 TO 3000:NEXT I¶
530 PRINT¶
540 PRINT TAB(5)"ANOTHER PROBLEM Y/N";¶
550 INPUT A$¶
560 RETURN¶
570 REM **********¶
580 REM *  MENU  *¶
590 REM **********¶
600 CLS:F=0¶
610 PRINT¶
620 PRINT TAB(32)"MATH TUTOR"¶
630 PRINT:PRINT¶
640 PRINT TAB(32)"CHOOSE:"¶
650 PRINT¶
660 FOR I=1 TO 4¶
670 PRINT TAB(31)I" FOR "RA$(I)¶
```

```
680 PRINT¶
690 NEXT I¶
740 PRINT TAB(32)"5 TO END"¶
750 PRINT¶
760 PRINT TAB(32)"WHICH NUMBER?"¶
770 E$=INKEY$:IF E$="" THEN 770¶
780 P=VAL(E$):IF P < 1 OR P > 5 THEN 770¶
790 ON P GOTO 800,890,990,1180¶
800 REM ***********¶
810 REM * ADDITION *¶
820 REM ***********¶
830 GOSUB 110¶
840 GOSUB 310¶
850 ER=A1+A2¶
860 GOSUB 390¶
870 IF A$="Y" THEN 840¶
880 GOTO 580¶
890 REM **************¶
900 REM * SUBTRACTION *¶
910 REM **************¶
920 GOSUB 110¶
930 GOSUB 310¶
940 IF A1 < A2 THEN I=A1:A1=A2:A2=I¶
950 ER=A1-A2¶
960 GOSUB 390¶
970 IF A$="Y" THEN 930¶
980 GOTO 580¶
990 REM   ***********¶
1000 REM * DIVISION *¶
1010 REM ***********¶
1020 GOSUB 110¶
1030 GOSUB 310¶
1040 ER=A1*A2¶
1050 I=ER:ER=A1:A1=I¶
1060 GOSUB 390¶
1070 IF A$="Y" THEN 1030¶
1080 GOTO 580¶
1190 REM *****************¶
1100 REM * MULTIPLICATION *¶
1110 REM *****************¶
1120 GOSUB 110¶
1130 GOSUB 310¶
1140 ER=A1*A2¶
```

```
1150 GOSUB 390¶
1160 IF A$="Y" THEN 1130¶
1170 GOTO 580¶
1180 REM *******¶
1190 REM * END *¶
1200 REM *******¶
1210 CLS¶
1220 END¶
```

By using three subroutines we saved 43 program lines—despite our using more REM statements! You can see that it's not only *easier* to use subroutines, but it also helps save memory space. Also, you've no doubt recognized the purpose of line 100. The subroutines are skipped and a branch is made directly to the menu.

Not only is it possible to call the subroutines from the main program, it is also possible to call them from a subroutine. Graphically this would look as follows:

Main Program

```
30 GOSUB 100                100 .....          200 .....
                            110 .....          210 .....
                             . GOSUB 200
                             . RETURN           RETURN

900 END
```

Subroutine 1

Subroutine 2

When the program is run, this routine works as follows:

The program encounters the GOSUB command in line 30. It then jumps to Subroutine 1 at line 100. While in Subroutine 1, a GOSUB 200 calls Subroutine 2. Subroutine 2 is executed until the RETURN command.

The RETURN jumps the program back to Subroutine 1, where it continues execution with the instruction following the GOSUB. The Subroutine 1 is then executed through the RETURN command. From

there, execution returns to the main program, i.e. the instruction
following the GOSUB (line 40).

You can "nest" subroutines in much the same way as you nest
FOR...NEXT loops.

Furthermore, we have already learned the ON X GOTO command. This
command sequence also works with GOSUB. Here is an example of the
notation:

```
ON P GOSUB 800,890,990
```

Remember that after the jump to the subroutine, the program continues
on at the line after this statement.

We hope that the examples given have clarified the technique of using
subroutines. To see how well you have understood all this, try solving
the following:

There's another way of using subroutines in the new version of MATH
TUTOR—the ON GOSUB command. Your goal is to modify the program
in this form. You don't have to rewrite the program for this. First
consider which program segments must be changed. You don't have to
place the new subroutines at the beginning of the main program this
time. Again we have placed the solution to this problem following so
that we can discuss the solution now.

Here is the program listing. The ¶ characters in the following listing
should not be entered. They only show the actual end of the BASIC
line. Formatting the programs for this book split some lines that
should not have been split. The ¶ characters show the end of the line.

```
10    REM ****************¶
20    REM * PROGRAM START *¶
30    REM ****************¶
50    DIM RA$(4),BE$(4) ¶
60    FOR I=1 TO 4¶
70    READ RA$(I),BE$(I) ¶
80    NEXT I¶
90    DATA ADDITION,+,SUBTRACTION,-,DIVISION,/,
      MULTIPLICATION,*¶
100   GOTO 580¶
110   REM *************¶
120   REM * SUBROUTINE *¶
130   REM *************¶
```

```
140    REM ************************¶
150    REM * INPUT LARGEST NUMBER *¶
160    REM ************************¶
170    CLS:A$="":B$=""¶
180    PRINT TAB(10)"INPUT THE LARGEST NUMBER"¶
190    PRINT¶
200    PRINT TAB(10)"FOR "RA$(P)"."¶
210    PRINT¶
220    PRINT TAB (10)"LARGEST NUMBER?   ";¶
230    FOR I=1 TO 3¶
240    A$=INKEY$:IF A$="" THEN 240¶
250    IF ASC(A$)<48 OR ASC(A$)>57 THEN 240¶
260    B$=B$+A$:PRINT A$;¶
270    NEXT I¶
280    GR=VAL(B$)¶
290    RETURN¶
300    REM *************************¶
310    REM * CREATE RANDOM NUMBERS *¶
320    REM *************************¶
325    RANDOMIZE TIMER¶
330    A1=INT(GR*RND(1))+1¶
340    A2=INT(GR*RND(1))+1¶
350    RETURN¶
360    REM ******************¶
370    REM * PROBLEM SET-UP *¶
380    REM ******************¶
390    CLS¶
400    PRINT¶
410    PRINT "HOW MUCH IS";A1;BE$(P);A2;"= ";¶
420    INPUT ES¶
430    IF ES=ER THEN PRINT:PRINT TAB(10)"RIGHT!"
       :F=0:GOTO 510¶
440    PRINT:PRINT TAB(10)"WRONG!!"¶
450    FOR I=1 TO 2000: NEXT I¶
460    F=F+1¶
470    IF F<=2 THEN 390¶
480    PRINT¶
490    FOR I=1 TO 2000: NEXT I¶
500    PRINT:PRINT TAB(5)"THE ANSWER IS"ER¶
510    F=0¶
520    FOR I=1 TO 3000:NEXT I¶
530    PRINT¶
540    PRINT TAB(5)"ANOTHER PROBLEM Y/N";¶
```

```
550     INPUT A$¶
560     RETURN¶
570     REM **********¶
580     REM *  MENU  *¶
590     REM **********¶
600     CLS:F=0¶
610     PRINT¶
620     PRINT TAB(32)"MATH TUTOR"¶
630     PRINT:PRINT¶
640     PRINT TAB(32)"CHOOSE:"¶
650     PRINT¶
660     FOR I=1 TO 4¶
670     PRINT TAB(31)I" FOR "RA$(I)¶
680     PRINT¶
690     NEXT I¶
740     PRINT TAB(32)"5 TO END"¶
750     PRINT¶
760     PRINT TAB(32)"WHICH NUMBER?"¶
770     E$=INKEY$:IF E$="" THEN 770¶
780     P=VAL(E$)¶
790     IF P < 1 OR P > 5 THEN 770¶
800     IF P=5 THEN 1100¶
810     GOSUB 110¶
820     GOSUB 310¶
830     ON P GOSUB 880,930,990,1050¶
840     GOSUB 390¶
850     IF A$="Y" THEN 820¶
860     GOTO 580¶
870     REM ************¶
880     REM * ADDITION *¶
890     REM ************¶
900     ER=A1+A2¶
910     RETURN¶
920     REM ***************¶
930     REM * SUBTRACTION *¶
940     REM ***************¶
950     IF A1 < A2 THEN I=A1:A1=A2:A2=I¶
960     ER=A1-A2¶
970     RETURN¶
980     REM ************¶
990     REM * DIVISION *¶
1000    REM ************¶
1010    ER=A1*A2¶
```

```
1020   I=ER:ER=A1:A1=I¶
1030   RETURN¶
1040   REM *******************¶
1050   REM * MULTIPLICATION *¶
1060   REM *******************¶
1070   ER=A1*A2¶
1080   RETURN¶
1090   REM *******¶
1100   REM * END *¶
1110   REM *******¶
1120   CLS¶
1130   END¶
```

You probably found the solution quickly. A total of five program lines always appear in the program lines listing the four calculation types. For example, the following lines are for addition:

```
830 GOSUB 110
840 GOSUB 310
860 GOSUB 390
870 IFA$="Y" THEN 840
880 GOTO 580
```

The only difference in the individual program sections lies in the calculation itself. This is why lines 830, 840, 860, 870, and 880 are placed after the menu. The test of P=5 is made separately, since the end of the program does not involve a subroutine.

This way we can write the calculations for addition, subtraction, etc. as subroutines and call them with the command:

```
ON P GOSUB
```

We save nine program lines in this manner.

This solution concludes the section on subroutines.

Here is a summary of important things to remember when working with subroutines:

1. Subroutines combine several repetitive sections of a program.

2. Subroutines are called with GOSUB and terminated with RETURN. They may never be called or exited with GOTO. The GOTO command may be used *within* the subroutine, however.

3. Subroutines may be "nested," in the sense that one subroutine may call another. Since the return addresses are stored in the computer, the total number of nested subroutines is limited. Be sure that each GOSUB command has a corresponding RETURN.

4. Subroutines may also be called with ON X GOSUB.

In the next section we will take a look at the structure and use of menus.

4.3 Menu techniques

Once you have become proficient in BASIC programming, you will probably want to write larger programs on your own. You may want to write sizable programs for fun—or even profit. If you do write a program intended for sale in the highly competitive software market, it's a real advantage if your program is *user-friendly*. What do we mean by this?

A program is written to perform certain tasks, like calculate formulas or draw charts. But the user must know exactly how to use the program—what keys to press to recalculate a column of numbers, or change a bar graph's fill pattern. *User-friendly* means that someone who isn't familiar with the program will still be able to use it without a great deal of explanation or training. Naturally, no large program is complete without a user's manual. But good programmers try to write programs so that the user won't have to refer to the manual for every minor function.

Don't worry. We don't expect you to write any instruction manuals. For now it's sufficient for you to master the principles of menu techniques.

We've already mentioned the term *menu* in connection with the program MATH TUTOR; in fact, you worked with a menu in that program. For our purposes, we'll define the term menu as follows:

Menu is a list of the individual points in the program that the user can choose from by pressing a letter or number key on the keyboard.

What a menu looks like is up to you. But a menu should always be as clear and readable as possible. Separating the different program functions should be as concise and easy to understand as possible, not overwhelming. And you should always try to make your menus aesthetically pleasing.

Next we'll show you how to construct a menu step-by-step. As a working example we'll create a mathematical table of commonly-used computations.

First we clearly determine the purpose of the program. Our mathematical table will require the following computational functions:

```
Square root
Sine
Cosine
Natural logarithm
Base 10 logarithm
```

The user will select one of these five functions to be performed.

This initial menu lacks something—the program end option. You should write your programs so that they can be ended with such an option, not just with <Control> <C> or the on/off switch. This gives our menu six options.

We also need a statement in our program that will prompt the user to enter a number or a letter, something like:

```
ENTER YOUR SELECTION (1-6)
```

The planning for our menu is now almost complete. We want to add a heading and a border as aesthetic improvements. We will write the program so the title will be on the screen during execution of each program segment. A subroutine is a good way to create a title. This illustrates how the menu will later appear on the screen.

```
****************************************
*                                      *
*          MATHEMATICAL TABLE          *
*                                      *
****************************************


1 SQUARE ROOT
2 SINE
3 COSINE
4 NATURAL LOGARITHM
5 LOGARITHM BASE 10
6 END PROGRAM

INPUT THE NUMBER OF YOUR CHOICE (1-6)
```

We'll need to read the number in the last line, as well. At first we'll use the INPUT command for the input. Later we'll see how to use the INKEY$ command in this position. Here's a listing of a program to create this menu:

Here is the program listing. The ¶ characters in the following listing should not be entered. They only show the actual end of the BASIC line. Formatting the programs for this book split some lines that should not have been split. The ¶ characters show the end of the line.

```
10    REM ****************¶
20    REM * PROGRAM START *¶
30    REM ****************¶
40    REM¶
50    CLS¶
60    DIM M$(6)¶
70    FOR I=1 TO 6¶
80    READ M$(I):NEXT I¶
90    DATA "1 SQUARE ROOT"¶
100   DATA "2 SINE"¶
110   DATA "3 COSINE"¶
120   DATA "4 NATURAL LOGARITHM"¶
130   DATA "5 LOGARITHM BASE 10"¶
140   DATA "6 END PROGRAM"¶
150   GOTO 330¶
160   REM ***************¶
170   REM * SUBROUTINES *¶
180   REM ***************¶
190   REM¶
200   REM ***********¶
210   REM * HEADLINE *¶
220   REM ***********¶
230   CLS¶
240   PRINT TAB(20);:FOR I=1 TO 40:PRINT"*";:NEXT
      I:PRINT¶
250   PRINT TAB(20);"*";SPC(38);"*"¶
260   PRINT TAB(20);"*";SPC(10);"MATHEMATICAL TABLE";
      SPC(10);"*"¶
270   PRINT TAB(20);"*";SPC(38);"*"¶
280   PRINT TAB(20);:FOR I=1 TO 40:PRINT"*";:NEXT
      I:PRINT¶
290   RETURN¶
300   REM ********¶
310   REM * MENU *¶
320   REM ********¶
330   GOSUB 230¶
390   FOR I=1 TO 2:PRINT:NEXT I¶
400   FOR I=1 TO 6¶
410   PRINT TAB(31);M$(I)¶
```

```
420   NEXT I¶
430   PRINT¶
450   PRINT TAB(21);"INPUT THE NUMBER OF YOUR CHOICE
      (1-6)";¶
460   W$=INKEY$:IF W$="" THEN 460¶
```

First we will explain the individual program lines. Line 50 clears the screen. In lines 60 through 80, the array M$ is initialized with the data from the DATA statements from lines 90 to 140. The program then branches past the subroutines and continues execution with line 330. From there the program branches to line 230, where the menu heading is created. After leaving the subroutine, program execution continues with line 340. Line 390 outputs three blank lines so that the menu options don't appear right below the heading. Lines 400 to 420 display the array with the individual menu options. Line 450 displays the prompt for the user to enter a value. Since the PRINT command in this line is terminated with a semicolon, the input is expected directly behind the parentheses (1-6).

These are all fundamentals of creating a menu. We'll skip the variable input and program branch, as we have already covered these subjects in previous sections. The principle is the same as for the MATH TUTOR program. Since we are working with INPUT$, remember to check the entered values for validity.

Note the subroutine HEADLINE. You can call this subroutine whenever you want to reconstruct the screen. When you branch to the program segment for square root calculation, the first call there should be:

```
GOSUB 230
```

You can then ask for the input of the value to be calculated.

Finish writing this program for the practice—but first we want to explain about cursor positioning.

4.3.1   Cursor positioning using LOCATE

LOCATE sets the cursor to a specific position on the screen.

The notation of LOCATE is:

```
LOCATE Y,X
```

The parameters are:

Y = line number (1-25)
X = column number (1-80)

The positioning is usually followed by output with PRINT. The following example should clarify this:

```
10 CLS
20 LOCATE 19,12
30 PRINT "OUTPUT WITH LOCATE"
40 END
```

This gives us an easy-to-use method for outputting text at arbitrary locations on the screen. This can prove quite useful as used in the following section.

4.3.2   Using input routines in the menu

The input operations we previously used with INKEY$ were very primitive. If you entered three characters or numbers, they were automatically accepted without discrimination. Also, three characters of input were always required, forcing the user to enter the digit sequence 054 for the number 54. Furthermore, it wasn't possible to enter a number larger than 999. We had to resort to the INPUT command.

We should mention again that the INPUT command is usually sufficient for your own applications. But if you want to eliminate error conditions in your program, eventually you'll have to use the INKEY$ instruction.

Now we'll deal with the development of our own input routine. Once completed, it can be adapted for use in your own programs. The first line should look familiar:

```
10 A$=INKEY$:IF A$="" THEN 10
```

With this you can read any character from the keyboard and assign it to
A$. In this example we want to read numbers only. Therefore, input
other than numbers must be disregarded. We accomplish this with an
IF...THEN test:

```
10 A$=INKEY$:IF A$="" THEN 10
20 IF ASC(A$) < 48 OR ASC(A$) > 57 THEN 10
```

The ASCII values 48 through 57 represent the numbers from 0 to 9. If
the ASCII value entered is less than 48 or greater than 57, the input is
ignored and the program branches back to line 10. To limit the number
to a certain number of digits, we must count valid characters. If the
largest number is to be 4 digits, we must test the counter to see if it's
larger than 4. We need two additional lines—one in which the counter
is incremented, and one in which the counter is checked for the value 4.

```
10 A$=INKEY$:IF A$="" THEN 10
20 IF ASC(A$) < 48 OR ASC(A$) > 57 THEN 10
30 Z=Z+1
40 IF Z>4 THEN 10
```

The counter Z in line 30 is incremented only when a valid value is
entered. If Z already has a value of 4, no more values are accepted and
the program jumps back to line 10.

We now tell our routine that the entered value is acceptable. As with
the INPUT command, we will use the <RETURN> key. What ASCII
code does the <RETURN> key have? From the table in the Appendix,
we learn it has the value 13. We need only test ASC(A$) for the value
13. But where do we put this test? Since 13 is less than 48, we can't
put this test *after* line 20. Otherwise the <RETURN> key will be
ignored. This test must have a line number less than 20. Let's use the
number 15.

Where should the routine branch when the <RETURN> key is pressed?
We really don't know yet. However, we can see that the routine
probably won't get very large, so we'll branch to line 100.

```
10 A$=INKEY$:IF A$="" THEN 10
15 IF ASC(A$) = 13 THEN 100
20 IF ASC(A$) < 48 OR ASC(A$) > 57 THEN 10
30 Z=Z+1
40 IF Z>4 THEN 10
```

What we need now is a line that chains the entered characters together into a string. This is done in line 50. Furthermore, we want to be able to see our input on the screen. Line 60 prints the characters at the current cursor position, one after the other (as a result of the semicolon):

```
10 A$=INKEY$:IF A$="" THEN 10
15 IF ASC(A$) = 13 THEN 100
20 IF ASC(A$) < 48 OR ASC(A$) > 57 THEN 10
30 Z=Z+1
40 IF Z>4 THEN 10
50 B$=B$+A$
60 PRINT A$;
70 GOTO 10
```

Now we only need to convert the string we have assembled in B$ into a numeric value, and assign it to a numeric variable. This can be done after the <RETURN> key is pressed. Also, we must remember to set counter Z back to zero after the <RETURN> key. Otherwise the old value will be retained the next time the routine is called, and you won't be able to enter a four-digit number.

If the routine is to be a subroutine, the last line must contain a RETURN command. First we'll take a look at the complete routine. After you have entered it, you can experiment with it a little. Maybe, in the last line, you want to output the numerical value assigned to the variable:

```
10 A$=INKEY$:IF A$="" THEN 10
15 IF ASC(A$) = 13 THEN 100
20 IF ASC(A$) < 48 OR ASC(A$) > 57 THEN 10
30 Z=Z+1
40 IF Z>4 THEN 10
50 B$=B$+A$
60 PRINT A$;
70 GOTO 10
100 B=VAL(B$):Z=0
110 PRINT B
120 END
```

Now we have a GET routine that will read a number of up to four digits and display it. If you want to be able to enter larger numbers, change the value in line 40.

This routine is already easier to use than the one in MATH TUTOR. We are still missing the function that allows us to delete values already entered. This function is one of the more complicated features of such a GET routine. The following routine listing contains this function:

```
10   REM GET-ROUTINE
12   LN=16 : REM LINE NUMBER LOCATION
15   LOCATE LN,1
20   A$=INKEY$:IF A$="" THEN 20
30   IF ASC(A$) = 13 THEN 130
40   IF ASC(A$) <> 8 THEN 70
50   IF LEN(B$) < 1 THEN 20
55   LOCATE LN,1:FOR I=1 TO LEN(B$):?" ";:NEXT
60   B$=LEFT$(B$,LEN(B$)-1):Z=Z-1:LOCATE LN,1
65   PRINT B$; :GOTO 20
70   IF ASC(A$) < 48 OR ASC(A$) > 57 THEN 20
80   Z=Z+1
90   IF Z > 4 THEN Z=4:GOTO 20
100  B$=B$+A$
110  PRINT A$;
120  GOTO 20
130  B=VAL(B$):Z=0
140  PRINT B
150  END
```

We'll discuss the program's new lines. Line 40 checks to see if the <BACKSPACE> key was pressed. The ASCII value of this key is 8. If this key was not pressed, the program branches to line 70. If <BACKSPACE> key was pressed, line 50 checks to see if the string B$ still contains characters.

If the string is empty, the <BACKSPACE> key is ignored and the program branches back to line 20.

Line 55 sets the cursor position to one on our input line—designated in line 12. Then it erases the input by replacing it with spaces.

Deleting the character takes place in line 60. The string in B$ is shortened by one character by the command sequence:

B$=LEFT$(B$,LEN(B$)-1)

The function LEFT$(B$,X) creates a string consisting of the X leftmost characters of B$. In most cases, a number takes the place of X. Here we use the LEN function instead of X. The calculation

LEN (B$) −1 is first executed. This means a value exactly one less than the current length of B$ is used. Substring of B$ is assigned this new value. This substring is exactly once character shorter than the original string B$. This substring is then assigned to B$. This process is something similar to the following operation for numerical variables:

```
A=A-1
```

Here the value 1 is subtracted from the variable A and the result is again assigned to A. This command sequence deletes the last character of the string B$.

In addition, the counter Z must be decremented by 1 in line 60 since the number of digits in the entire number has been decreased. We want to enter a maximum number of four digits. Therefore, Z is used as a counter to count valid characters already entered. If we delete a character, not only must the string B$ be shortened by one character, but 1 must also be subtracted from the value of Z. If you forget to decrement the counter, it would no longer be possible to enter anything after four valid characters. The string B$ would be shortened by one character each time the <BACKSPACE> key was pressed, but since the counter had reached the value four, the program would branch in line 90 back to line 20 again.

The last command in line 60 sets the cursor back to the beginning of the line. Line 60 prints the new contents of B$—shortened a character. Then it branches to the character input.

We now have a routine that lets us input short or long strings, depending on the setting of the variable Z. The routine is quite similar to the INPUT command, but we can edit characters and limit the length.

You are now in the position to adapt this routine to your programs. That is, you can determine yourself which keys will be allowed through the corresponding IF . . . THEN tests.

4.4 Sorting procedures

Many programs require data sorted according to various ordering criteria: size, alphabetical order, etc. There are a variety of different procedures for sorting. All differ from each other in performance and degree of difficulty. We will become familiar with a simple procedure that will at least give you an introduction into this subject. The more complicated sorting techniques can be more frightening than exciting to a beginner. However, if you're interested in advanced sorting procedures, there are many books available on the subject.

We'll use what's known as the *bubble sort*. Bubble sorts are so named because individual elements to be sorted "bubble up" to the top according to size. The principle of the bubble sort procedure involves comparing two neighboring elements. If one element is larger than the other, an exchange is made. All elements are compared with each other in succession.

To demonstrate the bubble sort, we'll fill an array with random numbers, and then sort and print it. We will use an array of 6 elements. The first program lines dimension the array and fill it with values:

```
10    REM GENERATE ARRAY
20    DIM F(6):RANDOMIZE TIMER:CLS
30    FOR I=1 TO 6
40    A=INT(50*RND)+1
50    F(I)=A
60    NEXT I
      .
      .
```

The comparisons and exchanges will be accomplished with IF...THEN tests. This could also be done with a FOR...NEXT loop, but the procedure wouldn't be so clear. Once you understand the procedure, you'll be able to perform it with a FOR...NEXT loop.

Now the program lines for the sort procedure:

```
      .
      .
100   REM BUBLE SORT
110   Z=0
120   IF F(6) >= F(5) THEN 140
130   F(0)=F(6):F(6)=F(5):F(5)=F(0):Z=1
```

```
140   IF F(5) >= F(4) THEN 160
150   F(0)=F(5):F(5)=F(4):F(4)=F(0):Z=1
160   IF F(4) >= F(3) THEN 180
170   F(0)=F(4):F(4)=F(3):F(3)=F(0):Z=1
180   IF F(3) >= F(2) THEN 200
190   F(0)=F(3):F(3)=F(2):F(2)=F(0):Z=1
200   IF F(2) >= F(1) THEN 220
210   F(0)=F(2):F(2)=F(1):F(1)=F(0):Z=1
220   IF Z=1 THEN 110
230   FOR I=1 TO 6
240   PRINT F(I);
250   NEXT I
260   PRINT
270   END
```

Line 110 first sets Z to zero. You will see why this is done later on in the program. Line 120 performs the first comparison. If the contents of the element F(6) are already greater than or equal to F(5), no exchange need be made and a branch is made directly to line 140. If F(6) is smaller than F(5), an exchange is performed in line 130.

The principle of the exchange should already be familiar to you. We use the element F(0) for temporary storage of a variable value. Next the value of the element F(5) is assigned to element F(6). Finally, F(5) is assigned the value of F(0)—that is, the old value of F(6). This principle is used in the other program lines as well.

Z is then set to one because an exchange does occur. We can learn from Z whether or not an exchange took place. If Z has the value 1, an exchange was made. Conversely, if Z has the value 0, no exchanges were made. This is a common programming technique to check if specific processes occurred or not. Variables like Z are known as *flags*.

If the flag Z retains the value of zero throughout a pass, we know that no exchanges taken place. Therefore the array is sorted. The advantage flags have under these conditions is that they terminate sorting after one pass—*if* the elements of the array happen to be in the right order already. This procedure is also called a *bubble sort with switch*. Its difference from a standard bubble sort is that it terminates the sorting process as soon as the array is sorted.

The last lines of the sort routine outputs the sorted array. If you want to see how the sorting takes place in the individual steps, change the last program lines as follows:

```
        •
        •
220    FOR I=1 TO 6
230    PRINT F(I);
240    NEXT I
250    PRINT
260    IF Z=1 THEN 110
270    END
```

The bubble sort procedure works well for use with up to about 100 elements. Try to gain a solid understanding of bubble sorts. This knowledge will come in handy when you later work with more complicated, efficient sort procedures. This concludes our discussion of sorting routines.

5   Working with the Disk Drive

5.1   Program management

The internal memory of your computer, like the memory of all computers, is only temporary. If it isn't supplied with electrical current, its contents are lost. For this reason it's necessary to store programs on an external storage medium. For this purpose, your computer is equipped with a disk drive.

The disk drive allows you to store large amounts of data on each disk, either programs or other files, and retrieve this data. GW-BASIC has all the commands needed to save and load programs.

5.1.1   Saving programs

The SAVE command stores a program on the diskette, provided there's no other file on the disk by that name:

```
SAVE " (filespec) "
```

The parameter *filespec* is not optional and must be enclosed in quotes. For example, to save the current program in memory using the filename TEST, you would enter:

```
SAVE "TEST"
```

The actual filename may consist of a maximum of 8 characters. An *extension* of up to 3 characters may be added to the filename as long as you separate the two with a period. Files are classified and easily identified with an extension. If no extension is entered BAS is automatically appended.

A filename may also be preceded by a path in GW-BASIC version 2.0 and later releases. A path may include any legal drive identifier, such as A or B followed by a colon (:), followed by any legal path identifiers, and finally the filename. For example, to save the program TEST in the subdirectory named SAMPLE on drive B, you would enter:

```
SAVE "B:\SAMPLE\TEST"
```

If you don't understand how paths are constructed, check your DOS manual for information on paths, or filespecs.

157

You should also be very careful when saving files. If you attempt to save a file using a name which already exists in that directory, the old file will be replaced by the file being saved. This can be a useful feature when used intentionally, allowing you to periodically update your work while entering long programs.

5.1.2   Loading programs

GW-BASIC also has a command available for loading programs. The `LOAD` command is very similar to the `SAVE` command. The syntax for the `LOAD` command is the same as was shown for the `SAVE` command:

```
LOAD "(filespec)"
```

As with the `SAVE` command, the drive identifier, path, and file extension may be specified along with the filename. If no filename extension is entered, the extension `.BAS` is automatically supplied. If the specified program is not found, the following error message will be printed:

```
File not found
```

Here is an example of loading the file we saved above:

```
LOAD "B:\SAMPLE\TEST"
```

5.1.3   Displaying the disk contents

The GW-BASIC command to display the contents of the diskette is `FILES`. The syntax is as follows:

```
FILES "(filespec)"
```

In the case of this command, the filespec is optional. If the command is entered without a filespec, the entire contents of the current directory are displayed. Supplying the filespec allows you to see only files which match that filespec. The asterisk (*) and question mark (?) wildcard characters may be used in the filespec. An asterisk signifies that all characters from that position on should be ignored. In other words, the asterisk substitutes for groups of characters. Some examples:

```
FILES "A:*.BAS"
```
shows all BASIC programs on drive A.

```
FILES "B:TEST.*"
```
lists all files with name TEST. Extension is ignored.

FILES "A:A*.B*"   lists all files with names beginning with A and
extensions beginning with B.

A question mark designates the individual characters that will be
ignored in the listed filenames. For example:

FILES "?FILE.BAS"

would list the files AFILE.BAS, BFILE.BAS, CFILE.BAS, etc.

5.1.4   Erasing files

Once a disk gets so full that no more programs can be saved on it, you
may want to do some "cleaning up". Sometimes the disk contains old
versions of programs that are no longer required.

The following command is used to erase files:

KILL " *(filespec)* "

The command:

KILL "A:TEST.BAS"

erases the program TEST.BAS from the diskette in drive A, for
instance. The filespec may also contain wildcards to allow erasing
many files at once.

KILL "A:*.*"

deletes <u>all</u> files from drive A.

5.1.5   Renaming files

GW-BASIC also has the ability to rename files. The corresponding
command for this is:

NAME " *(current filespec)* " AS " *(new filespec)* "

The parameters are fairly self-explanatory. For example, if we want to
change the name of the program TEXT05.BAS to TEXTPRO.BAS,
the following command will do it:

NAME "TEST05.BAS" AS "TEXTPRO.BAS"

5.2 Sequential file management

In previous sections, you've learned to handle different types of data, like names, numbers, and equations. This data has always been an integral part of the program, in the form of DATA statements. However, it should be clear that this is an awkward way of handling data. You can't expect the user of your program to modify the program lines when entering or editing data. Doing so in programming languages other than BASIC would require complete program recompilation. Obviously, we have to find a different means of managing data.

The most common way to manage the data is to form an independent file on the disk, reserved for data only. In this section we'll learn to use the best-known form of file organization for data management—*sequential files*.

In a sequential file, the data records are organized one after the other, separated from each other by the ASCII character <RETURN>. This <RETURN> is required because the corresponding command to read an entry in the sequential file reads up to this <RETURN>. The ASCII value for <RETURN> is CHR$(13).

We will explain sequential file management with a few example programs.

Let's assume that we want to store a telephone directory as a two-dimensional table on diskette. Each record consists of three fields:

A$(n,1)	Last name
A$(n,2)	First name
A$(n,3)	Telephone number

The whole list will have 200 entries. Managing such a file requires a continuous *record counter*. The record counter, or RC, always points to the last record. This RC is required for the new name entry, since the next free table location can be determined from RC+1.

We could use a subroutine like the following one to print this table on the screen:

```
1000   REM LIST PHONE
1010   FOR X=1 TO RC
1020   PRINT "ENTRY #";X
1030   PRINT "LAST NAME : ";A$(X,1)
1040   PRINT "FIRST NAME: ";A$(X,2)
1050   PRINT "TELEPHONE : ";A$(X,3)
1060   PRINT
1070   PRINT "PRESS RETURN TO CONTINUE"
1080   K$=INKEY$:IF K$<>CHR$(13) THEN 1080
1090   NEXT X
1100   RETURN
```

This subroutine is fairly easy to read and understand, so we won't explain it any further. It's more important that we should learn how to write these data records on the diskette.

A subroutine to store the data records must first open a file in which the addresses will be written. The command to open a sequential file for writing is the following:

```
OPEN "O",#file number,"filename"
```

If the address file is to be called PHONE.DAT, the OPEN command is:

```
OPEN "O",#1,"PHONE.DAT"
```

The file number is required to distinguish between several open files. Here is a subroutine for writing the addresses:

```
2000   REM SAVE PHONE
2010   OPEN "O",#1,"PHONE.DAT"
2020   PRINT #1,RC
2030   FOR X=1 TO RC
2040   FOR Y=1 TO 3
2050   PRINT #1,A$(X,Y)
2060   NEXT Y,X
2070   CLOSE #1
2080   PRINT "PHONE NUMBERS STORED."
2090   PRINT "CONTINUE WITH RETURN"
2100   K$=INKEY$:IF K$<>CHR$(13) THEN 2100
2110   RETURN
```

After opening the file, first the record counter is saved. It will be required later for loading the address records. The individual elements of the table are stored in a nested loop, in the following order: last name, first name, and telephone number of the first entry; then the last name, first name, and phone number of second entry; and so on. The PRINT #1 command has a file number and is used for writing to the sequential file. Here is the subroutine for entering data into this file:

```
3000   REM LOAD PHONE
3010   OPEN "I",#1,"PHONE.DAT"
3020   INPUT #1,RC
3030   FOR X=1 TO RC
3040   FOR Y=1 TO 3
3050   INPUT #1,A$(X,Y)
3060   NEXT Y,X
3070   CLOSE #1
3080   PRINT "FILE IS LOADED."
3090   PRINT "CONTINUE WITH RETURN"
3100   K$=INKEY$:IF K$<>CHR$(13) THEN 3100
3110   RETURN
```

The mode in the OPEN command is I (input), when reading a file. After the record counter is read, it is used as the argument for the outer loop. The subroutine "knows" by the record counter how far it must read.

The following subroutine allows you to enter the data.

```
4000   REM ENTER RECORD
4010   RC=RC+1
4020   PRINT "ENTRY #";RC
4030   INPUT "LAST NAME : ";A$(RC,1)
4040   INPUT "FIRST NAME: ";A$(RC,2)
4050   INPUT "TELEPHONE : ";A$(RC,3)
4060   PRINT
4070   PRINT "CONTINUE WITH RETURN"
4080   K$=INKEY$:IF K$<>CHR$(13) THEN 4080
4090   RETURN
```

And finally, our main program that pulls it all together. The ¶ characters in the following listing should not be entered. They only show the actual end of the BASIC line. Formatting the programs for this book split some lines that should not have been split. The ¶ characters show the end of the line.

```
100     REM MAIN PROGRAM¶
110     DIM A$(100,3)¶
120     CLS:REM MENU¶
130     PRINT "***********************"¶
140     PRINT "* TELEPHONE DIRECTORY *"¶
150     PRINT "***********************"¶
160     PRINT¶
170     PRINT " 1  ENTER DATA"¶
180     PRINT " 2  LIST DATA"¶
190     PRINT " 3  SAVE DATA"¶
200     PRINT " 4  LOAD DATA"¶
210     PRINT " 5  END"¶
220     PRINT¶
230     PRINT "SELECT ITEM ";¶
240     A$=INKEY$:IF A$<"1" AND A$>"5" OR A$=""
        THEN 240¶
245     PRINT A$: A=VAL(A$)¶
250     ON A GOSUB 4000,1000,2000,3000,300¶
260     GOTO 120¶
300     REM FINISH:¶
310     END¶
```

One command that we should mention when using subroutines is:

```
MERGE "(filespec)"
```

By using this command, you can save all your subroutines individually and then later MERGE them together to create one total program. This way you can keep your much needed subroutines in a library on disk and later incorporate them into your programs.

These subroutines can be easily adapted to your own requirements. Using sequential files, you're now ready to create your own data management programs.

6.   Sound and Graphics

6.1   Sound

Most PC compatible computers have some form of sound output. Some have advanced 3 voice sound chips. GW-BASIC offers commands which are compatible with most of these computers. Sound can play an important role in many BASIC programs. One of the most obvious reasons to use sound in a program, is to warn the user of an incorrect keypress or input. This can be handled simply using the BEEP statement. This statement sends an 800 Hz (cycles per second) signal to the speaker for approximately one quarter of a second. Enter the following command:

```
BEEP
```

After pressing <RETURN> you should have heard a quick tone. You may also perform this same function with the following command:

```
PRINT CHR$(7)
```

The ASCII value of seven is called the BEL function, and when printed causes the bell, or BEEP tone to be sounded.

6.1.1   The SOUND statement

The simple tone created by the BEEP statement can find many uses in programs, as mentioned above. But many programs require more sophisticated sounds, to play a series of notes or even full songs. GW-BASIC provides two commands for this type of sound generation. The SOUND statement is the simpler of these to use, and requires less programming. Two parameters are specified when using the SOUND statement, as follows:

```
SOUND frequency, duration
```

The frequency value determines the actual note to be played. The legal range for frequency is from 37 Hz to 32767 Hz. The duration value controls how long the note will be played. This value is specified in clock ticks which occur 18.2 times per second. The legal range for duration is .027 to 65535 in most versions of BASIC and extends down to .015 in some other versions. Here is an example of using the SOUND statement:

```
FOR I=100 TO 3500 STEP 100:SOUND I,1:NEXT I
```

This command will cause frequency to rise quickly from 100 Hz to 3500 Hz in intervals of 100 Hz. Each note will be played for a duration of approximately .054 seconds. You may reverse the effect by using:

```
FOR I=3500 TO 100 STEP -100:SOUND I,1:NEXT I
```

Here is a chart of frequencies for use with the SOUND statement:

NOTE	FREQ	NOTE	FREQ	NOTE	FREQ	NOTE	FREQ
$D\#_1$	38.89	B_2	123.47	G_4	392.00	$D\#_6$	1244.51
E_1	41.20	C_3	130.81	$G\#_4$	415.30	E_6	1328.51
F_1	43.65	$C\#_3$	138.59	A_4	440.00	F_6	1396.91
$F\#_1$	46.25	D_3	146.83	$A\#_4$	466.16	$F\#_6$	1479.98
G_1	49.00	$D\#_3$	155.56	B_4	493.88	G_6	1567.98
$G\#_1$	51.91	E_3	164.81	C_5	523.25	$G\#_6$	1661.22
A_1	55.00	F_3	174.61	$C\#_5$	554.37	A_6	1760.00
$A\#_1$	58.27	$F\#_3$	185.00	D_5	587.33	$A\#_6$	1864.66
B_1	61.74	G_3	196.00	$D\#_5$	622.25	B_6	1975.53
C_2	65.41	$G\#_3$	207.65	E_5	659.26	C_7	2093.00
$C\#_2$	69.30	A_3	220.00	F_5	698.46	$C\#_7$	2217.46
D_2	73.42	$A\#_3$	233.08	$F\#_5$	739.99	D_7	2349.32
$D\#_2$	77.78	B_3	246.94	G_5	783.99	$D\#_7$	2489.02
E_2	82.41	C_4	261.63	$G\#_5$	830.61	E_7	2637.02
F_2	87.31	$C\#_4$	277.18	A_5	880.00	F_7	2793.83
$F\#_2$	92.50	D_4	293.66	$A\#_5$	932.33	$F\#_7$	2959.96
G_2	98.00	$D\#_4$	311.13	B_5	987.77	G_7	3135.96
$G\#_2$	103.83	E_4	329.63	C_6	1046.50	$G\#_7$	3322.44
A_2	110.00	F_4	349.23	$C\#_6$	1108.73	A_7	3520.00
$A\#_2$	116.54	$F\#_4$	369.99	D_6	1174.66	$A\#_7$	3729.00

Here is an example program using the SOUND statement. This program converts your computer keyboard into a musical keyboard. The keys which may be pressed to produce musical notes are displayed on the screen. You may end the program by pressing the <RETURN> key.

```
10    KEY OFF
20    CLS
30    WIDTH 40
40    DIM TONE(256)
50    TONE$="Q2W3ER5T6Y7UI900P"
60    FOR I=1 TO LEN(TONE$)
```

```
70    READ TONE(ASC(MID$(TONE$,I,1)))
80    NEXT I
90    LOCATE 4,16
100   PRINT "PC MUSIC"
110   LOCATE 8,10
120   PRINT " 2 3   5 6 7   9 0"
130   LOCATE 10,10
140   PRINT "Q W E R T Y U I O P"
150   NOTE$=INKEY$
160   IF NOTE$="" THEN 150
170   IF NOTE$=CHR$(13) THEN END
180   SOUND TONE(ASC(NOTE$)),2
190   GOTO 150
200   DATA 261.63,277.18,293.66,311.13
210   DATA 329.63,349.23,369.99,392
220   DATA 415.3,440,466.16,493.88
230   DATA 523.25,554.37,587.33,622.25
240   DATA 659.26
```

6.1.2   The PLAY statement

The SOUND statement will fill a lot of your sound effects needs, but
when it comes to actually playing a tune, the PLAY statement is better
suited. PLAY will allow you to indicate notes and durations in a way
that makes converting music to data much easier. It will also allow you
to define large amounts of musical information in each line, making
your program much more efficient. The syntax for PLAY is:

    PLAY " (string)"

The string used by the PLAY statement may contain any of the
parameters given below. Parameters need not be separated, though you
may separate them by semicolons. Extra spaces in the string are
ignored. Here are the possible parameters:

X variable
    An "X" should begin the string when you wish to use another
    string with the PLAY statement.

O n The O parameter is used to specify the octave. There are 7
     octaves in all, numbered from 0 to 6. Middle C (C just below A-
     440) starts off octave 3. Each octave number starts with C and
     continues through B. Octave 4 is the default when no octave has
     been specified.

`< n   or   > n`

It is also possible to change octaves by preceding a note with a greater-than (>) symbol which will increase the octave by one. The less-than (<) symbol works in a similar manner, decreasing the octave by one.

`L n`   This parameter is used to indicate the length of the note or notes to follow. The legal range for this parameter is from 1 to 64, and produces a note length of 1/n. Therefore, a length of 1 is equal to a whole note, and a length of 64 is equal to a sixty-fourth note.

`. (period)`

A period or dot may be used after a note or note value to indicate a dotted note. Dotted notes play for one and a half times the current length. A dotted sixteenth note plays for one sixteenth plus one thirty-second.

`T n`   This is used to set the overall tempo (speed) of the notes to be played. The range begins at 32 and extends to 255, with a default value of 120. This value is equal to the number of beats per minute.

`A through G`

This indicates the value of the note to be played. Sharps may be indicated by following the note with the number/pound symbol (#) or plus sign (+). Flats are indicated with the minus sign (-). It is important to note that sharps and flat are only legal if they are not equal to some other note value. For example, C flat is not legal since it is equal to B.

`N n`   This is an alternative means of indicating the note to be played. There are 84 notes in the 7 octaves covered by the PLAY command. Using the N parameter will allow you to specify the particular note to be played without specifying the octave separately. The legal range is from 0 to 84 with 0 being equal to a rest.

`P n`   The P parameter indicates a pause or rest. The values used with P are the same as are used with the L (length) parameter, and will cause the PLAY statement to wait the specified period of time before playing the next note.

`M parameter`

The parameter following M is used to indicate one of 5 MUSIC commands. Three of these specify how long the note will be sounded during the note length. These are:

L (legato)   Each note sounds for the full length of the note length.

N (normal)   Each note sounds seven eighths of the note length.

S (staccato)   Each note sounds for three quarters of the note length.

If none of these are specified in the PLAY statement, the default is MN or Music Normal. The other two parameters useable with M are for setting the mode of the PLAY and SOUND commands. These are:

F (foreground) All PLAY and SOUND commands are processed by BASIC, which waits for completion of the last note before processing the next note.

B (background) Notes from the PLAY and SOUND commands are placed into a buffer and processed by the computers interrupts. This allows program execution to continue while notes are being played.

If no mode is specified in the PLAY statement, MF or Music Foreground is the default. The MB command is best avoided until you become somewhat more proficient at programming. The M commands may not be followed with a semicolon (;) in PLAY strings.

The values indicated in the parameters for N, may be a constant or may be substituted by using an equal sign followed by a variable. When using a variable instead of a constant, a semicolon following the variable is required. This means that both of these statements are legal:

```
PLAY "L4G#"
PLAY "L=LENGTH;G#"
```

If the variable LENGTH above is set to a value of 4 prior to the execution of the PLAY statement, then both of these statements will result in the same note and duration.

You may also define a string with the proper values before using the PLAY command. In this case, you must use an X as the first character in the PLAY statement's string followed by the name of the string to be played. Unlike most uses of strings, the PLAY statement requires the name of the string followed by a semicolon to appear within the quotes after PLAY. For example, to play the following string:

```
SONG$="CDEFGAB>C"
```

the proper syntax would be:

```
PLAY "XSONG$;"
```

Only you can decide which form of the PLAY command is best for your program. The following example program uses the PLAY and SOUND commands. This program shows you how you may store a song in strings.

```
10 REM BUGS PLAYS PIANO
20 BUG1$="T200O3L8F#EL4D.L8EDP8L4DF#AGB>D#D#P1"
30 BUG2$= "T200O3L8F#EL4D.L8EDP8L4DF#AGB>C#C#P2L4D#D#P1"
40 BUGSRIGHT$="T200O3L8F#EL4D.L8EDP8L4DF#AGB>DD"
50 PLAY "XBUG1$;"
60 PLAY "XBUG2$;"
70 PLAY "XBUGSRIGHT$;"
75 SOUND 37,10
80 END
```

6.2   GRAPHICS

GW-BASIC contains many commands to allow you to perform
extensive graphics with your computer. Some computers will be
unable to access all the graphics commands due to the type of display
or video controller card installed in the computer. GW-BASIC helps
you handle different displays with SCREEN modes. A SCREEN
statement is used to instruct BASIC which display mode to use. This
statement:

        SCREEN 0,0

places the display into text mode and turns off color on color monitors.
Our first few examples will use this mode. The first parameter controls
the display *resolution*. You may already be aware that the display is
made up small dots. These dots, or *pixels* as they are called, are lined
up into rows and columns on the screen. Screen resolution is most
often referred to in terms of the number of pixels wide by the number
of pixels high. Since screen mode 0 is a text only mode, the resolution
is measured in characters instead of dots. The resolution of screen mode
0 can be either 80x25 or 40x25, depending on the screen width.

The second parameter shown in the SCREEN statement controls the
color signal on a CGA (Color Graphics Adapter) equipped computer. It
is ignored if there is only a monochrome display adapter (MDA)
installed. There are other parameters available with the SCREEN
statement, but the two covered here are the only ones required for most
programs.

The graphics examples in this chapter will be limited to using screen
modes 0 through 2. The following diagram should simplify
understanding of the SCREEN statement parameters:

Syntax: SCREEN *mode,burst*						
mode	Display	Resolution	Colors	Palette	*burst* ON	*burst* OFF
0	MDA	80x25 text	2	2	1	0
		40x25 text				
1	CGA	320x200	16	4	0	1
2	CGA	640x200	2	2	n/a	n/a

171

6.2.1   Text mode graphics

PC compatible computers have an extended character set which not only includes the standard letters, numbers, and symbols, but a number of graphic characters as well. All video controllers are capable of displaying these characters. This means that forming display screens using these characters is the most universal method of graphic programming. The characters in the range of character string 127 through 255 are the most useful for this purpose. The following values can be used to make up almost any size or type of box:

```
CHR$(179)="|"
CHR$(180)="┤"
CHR$(191)="┐"
CHR$(192)="└"
CHR$(193)="┴"
CHR$(194)="┬"
CHR$(195)="├"
CHR$(196)="─"
CHR$(197)="┼"
CHR$(217)="┘"
CHR$(218)="┌"
```

The following programming example shows how to use these character codes for graphic programming.

```
10   SCREEN 0,0
20   CLS
30   HLINE$=""
40   FOR I=1 TO 76
50   HLINE$=HLINE$+CHR$(196)
60   NEXT I
70   LOCATE 2,2
80   PRINT CHR$(218);
90   PRINT HLINE$;
100  PRINT CHR$(191)
110  FOR I=1 TO 3
120  LOCATE 2+I,2
130  PRINT CHR$(179)
140  LOCATE 2+I,79
150  PRINT CHR$(179)
160  NEXT I
```

```
170 LOCATE 6,2
180 PRINT CHR$(192);
190 PRINT HLINE$;
200 PRINT CHR$(217)
210 MESSAGE$="THIS IS A GOOD WAY TO MAKE MENUS"
220 LOCATE 4,40-(LEN(MESSAGE$)/2)
230 PRINT MESSAGE$
240 K$=INKEY$:IF K$="" THEN 240
250 END
```

This program prints a large box on the screen and then displays the text stored in MESSAGE$ centered within the box. As you can see, it is easy to program graphics using the character string codes. Using commands you learned earlier, such as LOCATE and PRINT, you can position the graphics where you want them on the screen. Make the following changes to the previous program:

```
40  FOR I=1 TO 21
110 FOR I=1 TO 14
140 LOCATE 2+I,24
170 LOCATE 17,2
210 FOR J=1 TO 10
220 READ VALUE(J)
230 NEXT J
240 FOR I=90 TO 0 STEP -5
250 FOR J=1 TO 10
260 LOCATE 16-(I/10),2+(J*2)
270 IF VALUE(J)>I+5 THEN PRINT CHR$(219):GOTO 290
280 IF VALUE(J)>I THEN PRINT CHR$(220)
290 NEXT J,I
300 K$=INKEY$:IF K$="" THEN 300
310 END
320 DATA 10,20,27,35,39,47,58,72,84,96
```

After running the program with these modifications, you should see a square box displayed with a vertical bar graph printed inside of it. With simple BASIC programming, you can create programs which will display nearly any type of data.

6.2.2   CGA GRAPHICS

There are so many graphic commands in GW-BASIC that it would take an entire book to teach them all. This section will instead explain the principles on which the graphic commands operate, providing some common example programs. To achieve the full power of BASIC's graphic commands, it will be necessary for you to continue to experiment on your own. In this way, you will discover new and more efficient routines for performing graphics. As we mentioned earlier, if you do not have a CGA (Color Graphics adapter) or EGA (Extended Graphics Adapter) compatible video board installed in your computer, you will not be able to access most screen modes. This is true of the modes used in this section. If you only have a Monochrome display adapter, an MDA, then skip this section.

The screen is made up of a number of dots or pixels. Some graphic commands in GW-BASIC will access these dots individually, while others use a special coordinate method which will allow you more flexibility in your programming. We also mentioned that the number of pixels which make up the screen is determined by the SCREEN mode selected. You may wish to refer back to the screen mode chart in Section 6.2 to refresh your knowledge of these modes.

Modes 1 and 2 are of the most importance to anyone programming for a CGA system. As you can see from the chart, the resolution for these modes are 320x200, and 640x200. The advantages of mode 1 over mode 2 is that mode 1 allows for the use of 4 colors of 16 total colors. Mode 1 offers a much higher resolution, however, only 2 colors may be used. The following diagram shows the coordinate system of the pixels and how they are referenced on the screen:

```
(0,0) Modes 1 & 2                              Mode 1 (319,0)
                                               Mode 2 (639,0)












                                               Mode 1 (319,199)
(0,199) Modes 1 & 2                            Mode 2 (639,199)
```

As you can see, the upper left hand corner has a value of zero for both the X (horizontal) and Y (vertical) parameters. Since zero is used in specifying these screen locations, the maximum values for X and Y are one less than the actual resolution.

As long as you understand the way in which the screen is formatted, you can use the graphic commands effectively. One of the most important commands available for graphics is the PSET statement. PSET is used to set a starting point on the screen for use with other commands. Here is the syntax for PSET:

```
PSET [STEP] (X,Y) [, drawing color]
```

The STEP part of this statement is optional. If used, the X and Y values will be used as offsets from the current position. This means that if the last pixel accessed by your program was at 200,100, and the program then issued this statement:

```
PSET STEP (20,20)
```

the new pixel position would be located at 220,120. Using this same command without STEP included, would cause the new pixel position to be located at 20,20. PSET is usually used prior to the DRAW statement. DRAW is by far the most extensive graphic command available in GW-BASIC. The following is a detailed break down of the DRAW statement syntax and parameters.

```
DRAW "string"
```

string

Can be a constant, variable, or the result of a string expression. The current position that DRAW will start at, is either the center of the screen or the last position used by a graphics command. Any other positions must be set before using DRAW; with a command such as PSET. The following parameters can be part of the string:

U num Draws num points up.
D num Draws num points down.
L num Draws num points to the left.
R num Draws num points to the right.
E num Draws num points diagonally to the upper right.
H num Draws num points diagonally to the upper left.
F num Draws num points diagonally to the lower right.
G num Draws num points diagonally to the lower left.

If the number is not a constant, the numerical value must first be converted to a string. Otherwise, DRAW must be told that a variable is being used with the equal sign (=) in front of the variable and a semicolon after it, as in the PLAY statement.

B *dir* Moves the "pen" one pixel in the given direction without drawing any points. The dir contains the characters U, D, L, R, E, F, G or H (see above).

N *dir* Moves the "pen" one pixel in the given direction, setting that point. The dir contains the characters U, D, L, R, E, F, G or H (see above).

M *X,Y*

If X,Y is specified without a preceding plus or minus sign, then a line is drawn from the current point to the point specified by X,Y (absolute coordinates). If X,Y is preceded by + or -, then X,Y is viewed as the relative coordinates.

C *color*

Sets the drawing color, based on the available palettes 0 to 3.

P *F,B*

Fills a region enclosed by border color B with a fill color F. The current position must be inside the enclosed area. P does not have default values, so both parameters must be specified. Both values can range from 0 to 3.

A *angle*

Sets the angle for subsequent movement. Possible values: 0 = 0 degrees, 1 = 90 degrees, 2 = 180 degrees, 3 = 270 degrees. This specification takes precedence over the direction of movement. For example, if you specify the command A3, then L goes right instead of left.

TA *angle*

Specifies the angle of the movement to follow. Unlike A, TA can have values ranging from -360 to +360.

S *factor*

Returns the value from the formula *factor/4*, that should be multiplied with all the numerical parameters for movement to follow. This allows objects to be drawn to scale with one another. Legal values for *factor* range from 0 to 255.

X *string*

Allows often-repeated procedures to be executed from a string. The instructions contained in *string* are inserted at the current position and executed. Remember to include the semicolon following the variable name.

Here is a short example program which uses the PSET and DRAW statements:

```
10 CLS
20 SCREEN 2
30 PSET (160,100),1
40 DRAW "U25R25D25L25E25L25F25BHBLP1,1"
```

This program will draw a small box, divide it into four parts diagonally, and finally fill the bottom quarter. If you wish to see the same routine in color, try changing it to the following:

```
10 CLS
20 SCREEN 1
25 COLOR 7,1
30 PSET (160,100),1
40 DRAW "U25R25D25L25E25L25F25BHBLP2,1"
```

After running this program, or any program which places the display in 40 column mode, you may type:

```
WIDTH 80
```

in direct mode to return to 80 column mode.

The color statement used above has the following syntax:

```
COLOR background,palette
```

The *background* color refers to the screen color. This is specified using a value from 0 to 15. The colors which correspond with these numbers are listed below:

```
0 - Black      5 - Magenta       11 - Light Cyan
1 - Blue       6 - Brown         12 - Light Red
2 - Green      7 - White         13 - Light Magenta
3 - Cyan       8 - Gray          14 - Yellow
4 - Red        9 - Light Blue    15 - High Intensity White
              10 - Light Green
```

177

The palette is usually specified by 0 or 1. Each of these two palettes contain 3 colors. A palette is actually made up of 4 colors, however, one of the colors is always the background color specified above. Here are the palette colors:

Color	Palette 0	Palette 1
0	*background*	*background*
1	Green	Cyan
2	Red	Magenta
3	Brown	White

The CIRCLE statement can be used to draw circles and ellipses on the screen. The syntax for this command is:

    CIRCLE (X, Y), radius, color, start, end, aspect

The values for *X* and *Y* determine the center of the circle or ellipse to be drawn. The value for *radius* is specified in pixels. The values allowable for *color* vary with the screen mode. Mode 1 will allow values from 0 to 3, but only 0 and 1 are legal in mode 2. The *start* and *end* values determine the beginning and ending points of the circle, allowing this command to be used to draw arcs as well. The values allowable for this parameter must be in the range of -6.28 to +6.28. The aspect value can be used to adjust the roundness of the circle. Values of less than 1 cause elongation in the horizontal direction. Values greater than 1 cause elongation in the vertical direction.

The PAINT statement allows you to fill areas with color and/or patterns. Creating patterns for use with the PAINT statement requires a good working knowledge of binary codes, and is beyond the scope of a beginners book. Filling with solid colors, however, is easy to accomplish using the following syntax:

    PAINT (X, Y), paint color, boundary color

X and *Y* must fall within the boundary of the object to be filled. The *paint color* must be a legal value from the current palette. The *boundary color* should be a number which identifies the color of the boundary lines of the object to be painted or filled. Often it is possible to skip specification of the boundary color, as shown in this example of using the PAINT and CIRCLE statements:

```
10   CLS
20   SCREEN 2
30   CIRCLE (320,100),10
40   CIRCLE (320,100),20
50   CIRCLE (320,100),30
60   CIRCLE (320,100),40
70   CIRCLE (320,100),50
80   PAINT (320,100),1
90   PAINT (320,110),1
100  PAINT (320,120),1
```

The LINE statement can be used to form lines and boxes. It also gives you the option of filling the box The syntax looks as follows:

```
LINE (X1,Y1)-(X2,Y2),color,BF,style
```

X1,Y1 signify the starting point of the line, or upper left corner of a box. *X2,Y2* gives the ending point of the line, or lower right corner of a box. The value for *color* can be any legal value from your color palette. B is used to inform the program that you wish to form a box, or BF if you wish to form a box filled with the color specified with *color*. The value for style is a 16 bit integer used to determine the line pattern to be used. If a filled box is requested in the line, style must be left off or it will cause a syntax error.

This program will draw large box on the screen filled with the drawing color:

```
10  CLS
20  SCREEN 2
30  LINE (10,10)-(630,190),1,BF
40  END
```

There are other graphic commands in GW-BASIC, but before learning these or trying to understand some of the attributes of the commands we have covered in this section, you should study Appendix F, Number Systems. This section will help you to gain a fuller understanding of some of the more advanced commands and functions in GW-BASIC. Most importantly, you should never be afraid to experiment and try new things. Remember, as long as you keep backups of important programs and data, there is nothing for you to damage.

Appendix A - Commands, Functions and Statements

This section lists each command, function and statement of GW-BASIC in alphabetical order. You'll find a letter in parentheses at the end of each keyword heading. This letter tells you whether the current item is a command (**C**), function (**F**), statement (**S**) or operator (**O**).

Certain characters and notation used in the syntax and explanations for the keywords have the following meanings:

[ ]   Parameters enclosed in square brackets are optional. These parameters are not necessary for the execution of the command. They generally control special functions of the command.

abc   Parameters are indicated in lowercase letters and *italicized*. This lets you easily distinguish between keywords and their parameters.

| Alternative parameters are separated by a vertical bar. Only one of the parameters in a list separated by this character can be used.

filespec
Filenames can be specified as a *mask*. The mask follows the MS-DOS conventions for drive, path, name and extension. For example:

     a:\dos*.com

Numerical values are entered as decimal numbers. You can also enter a numeric value as a hexadecimal number by preceding the value with &H, or as an octal number by preceding the value with &O.

If a parameter is not specified, GW-BASIC assumes that the most recently used value is the default value. You must enter a comma in place of any required parameter for this default value to be used.

=   **compare data (O)**

IF *expression_1* = *expression_2* THEN *statement*

Tests two expressions for equality.

expression_1, *expression_2*
> The expressions to be compared. These can be constants, variables, or the results of calculations or functions. The expressions are of the same data type.

The relational operator = can be combined with the relational operators < and > in order to test if *expression_1* is less than, greater than, or equal to *expression_2*.

<>   **compare data (O)**

IF *expression_1* <> *expression_2* THEN *statement*

Tests two expressions for inequality.

expression_1, *expression_2*
> The expressions to be compared. These can be constants, variables, or the results of calculations or functions. The expressions are of the same data type.

The relational operator <> can be combined with the relational operator = to test if *expression_1* is less than, equal to, or greater than *expression_2*.

<   **compare data (O)**

IF *expression_1* < *expression_2* THEN *statement*

Tests two expressions to see if the first expression has a lesser value than the second.

expression_1, expression_2
> The expressions to be compared. These can be constants, variables, or the results of calculations or functions. The expressions must be of the same data type.

The relational operator < can be combined with the relational operator = to test if *expression_1* is less than or equal to *expression_2*.

>   **compare data (O)**

IF *expression_1* > *expression_2* THEN *statement*

Tests two expressions to see if the first expression has a greater value than the second.

expression_1, expression_2
> The expressions to be compared. These can be constants, variables, or the results of calculations or functions. The expressions are of the same data type.

The relational operator > can be combined with the relational operator = to test if *expression_1* is greater than or equal to *expression_2*.

+   **concatenate strings (F)**

X$ = *string_1* + *string_2* + *string* ...

Concatenates strings.

string_x
> String constant, variable, or the result of a string function.

The total length of the string cannot exceed 255 characters. Spaces are not inserted before or after the string.

AND   combine comparisons (O)

IF *condition_1* AND *condition_2* THEN *statement*

Combines multiple comparisons. The statement is executed if *condition_1* and *condition_2* are both true.

condition_1, condition_2
> Comparisons using the relational operators =, <>, <=, =>, <, or >.

ASC   ASCII character→decimal (F)

ASC (*expression*)

Returns the decimal value of an ASCII character.

expression
> *expression* can be a string constant, variable, or the result of a string function. Only the first character of *expression* is converted, regardless of how many characters are in the string.

AUTO   automatic line numbering (C)

AUTO [*starting_line*|.] [,*increment*]

Displays the next line number as new program lines are entered. AUTO is disabled when you press Ctrl+Break.

starting_line
> Specifies the first line number displayed. To start with line number 10, type AUTO 10. The default value is 0.

> The current line number can be abbreviated as a period.

increment
> Specifies the interval between successive line numbers. The default value is 10.

184

An asterisk is displayed next to a line number if that line number already exists in the program. Press Enter to retain the old program line. Otherwise, type in the replacement program line.

BEEP   output simple tone (S)

BEEP

Outputs a simple tone, same as PRINT CHR$(7).

BLOAD   load data into RAM

BLOAD *filespec, offset*

Loads a file into a given area of memory.

filespec
> The file specification of the file to be loaded.

offset   Specifies the address of the segment last set with DEF SEG, into which the file is loaded. Data is read from the file until an EOF character (&H1A) is read.

BSAVE   save data from a RAM area (C)

BSAVE *filespec, offset, num_bytes*

Saves a given area of memory to diskette.

filespec
> A file specification corresponding to the MS-DOS conventions, consisting of drive, path, and filename.

offset   Specifies the address of the data to be saved, set by DEF SEG.

num_bytes
> Specifies the number of bytes to be saved from *offset*.

CALL
CALLS
call a machine language routine (S)

CALL[S] *offset_var* [,*data_var*]

Calls a machine language routine previously loaded with BLOAD or placed in memory with POKEs.

[S]   CALLS is a variant of the CALL statement. CALLS places the current segment on the stack in low byte/high byte form before the 2-byte offset pointer. Special compilers are required to pass the segmented address like this.

offset_var
        The offset address at which the routine begins is assigned to an integer variable. The proper segment must be set with DEF SEG before CALL.

data_var
        The data or values to be processed are passed to the routine by variables. One 2-byte offset pointer to the contents of the variable is placed on the stack in low/high format and can be processed from there.

CDBL
→double-precision (F)

CDBL(*expression*)

Converts a numerical expression to a double-precision value.

expression
        expression can be a constant, the result of a calculation, or the result of a numerical function.

CHAIN

```
CHAIN [MERGE] filespec [,start_line]
[,ALL] [,DELETE from_line - to_line]
```

Loads overlays or additional sections of a program.

MERGE   MERGE was introduced earlier. It has the same effect when
         used with CHAIN: the program loaded with MERGE is
         combined with the program in memory so that existing lines
         are replaced, or lines are inserted or appended, depending on
         their line numbers. Execution begins at start_line.

filespec
         A file specification corresponding to MS-DOS conventions,
         consisting of drive, path, and filename.

start_line
         The line at which execution is to start after CHAIN.

,ALL   Tells GW-BASIC to preserve all existing variable values.
         Without ALL, CHAIN erases all of the variables and frees up
         memory. If only certain variables are passed, use COMMON.

DELETE from_line - to_line
         DELETE can only be used together with MERGE. DELETE
         removes the range of lines specified by from_line and
         to_line before the program is loaded with MERGE.

The program to be chained must be saved in ASCII format. This is
done using SAVE filespec,A.

If you use MERGE without ALL, all open files are closed, all variables
are cleared, and all open GOSUB...RETURN, FOR...NEXT, and
WHILE...WEND structures are terminated. CHAIN without MERGE
leaves all files open. Merged programs cannot contain any functions
defined with DEF FN, because functions are defined in the main
program. CHAIN executes a RESTORE before loading. This means that
the DATA pointer in the chained program must be reset to READ. The
value set for arrays by OPTION BASE is unchanged.

RENUM does not change a specified start line, so this must be corrected
by the user.

CHDIR
MKDIR   directory access (C)
RMDIR

```
CHDIR path
MKDIR directory_name
RMDIR directory_name
```

These commands operate like their MS-DOS counterparts.

directory_name, path
> These parameters must be enclosed in quotation marks, unlike MS-DOS, where quotation marks are not required for the system equivalents of these keywords. String variables can be used, but no string operations are allowed.

The abbreviations MD, CD, and RD are allowed by MS-DOS, but are not allowed under GW-BASIC.

CHR$ decimal→ASCII character (F)

```
CHR$ (number)
```

Converts a numerical value to an ASCII character.

number This can be a constant, the result of a calculation, a numerical variable, or the result of a numerical function. *number* is an integer value in the range from 0 to 255.

CINT   →integer value (F)

```
CINT (expression)
```

Converts a numerical expression to an integer value.

expression
> Specifies a constant, the result of a calculation, a numerical variable, or the result of a numerical function. The result is in the range from -32768 to +32767.

CIRCLE   draw circles and ellipses (S)

```
CIRCLE[STEP] (origin_X,origin_Y), radius
[,drawing_color][,arc_start,arc_end]
[,axes_ratio]
```

Draws a circle or an ellipse on the graphic screen at the given coordinates.

origin_X,origin_Y
> Specifies the origin of the circle or ellipse. (*origin_X,origin_Y*) without STEP specifies the absolute coordinates of the point. S T E P (*origin_X,origin_Y*) specifies the position relative to the last position addressed on the screen. *Y* can range from 0 to 199. *X* can range from 0 to 319 or 0 to 639, depending on the resolution selected.

radius Specifies the radius of the circle or ellipse in pixels. If *radius* results in values that lie outside the resolution specified with SCREEN, only the visible portions are drawn.

arc_start,arc_end
> Specify the starting and ending points of a circle or an ellipse. The values are angles in radians. Values from -2π to +2π are valid. If the values are negative, the origin is a connected arc.

CLEAR   initialize variable storage (C)

```
CLEAR [,data_space][,stack_space]
```

Initializes numeric and string variables and resets the dimensions of array variables. Numeric variables are initialized to zero. String variables are initialized to a null string. Array variables are initially undefined.

data_space
> Specifies the maximum number of bytes reserved for data variables. The default is 65535. By decreasing this value, you can reserve an area of memory above the variable area for machine language routines.

stack_space
> Specifies the number of bytes reserved for memory on the stack. The default size is 512 bytes.

CLOSE   close a file (S)

CLOSE [# file_number, ...]

Writes the data buffer to disk and closes the file.

file_number
> The reference number used when the file was opened.

After a file has been closed properly, all attempts to write to the file, read from it, or apply a function to it will result in the error message Bad file number or Bad file mode.

CLS   clear screen (S)

CLS

Clears the screen and moves the cursor to the upper left corner.

COLOR   set text/background color (S)

COLOR [text_color] [,background_color]

Sets the screen's text and background colors.

text_color
> Sets the color in which the letters and characters are displayed on the screen. Enter an integer value between 0 and 15 according to the color table on the following page.

background_color

Sets the color of the background on which the text is displayed. Enter an integer value from the 0 to 7 according to the color table on the following page.

Color monitor

If you are using a color monitor and a normal CGA card, the background colors are limited to 0 through 7. If you are using an EGA card with a suitable monitor, you can select a background color between 0 and 15.

Composite monitor

Here the selected colors are displayed as raster patterns or grey-levels, depending on the quality of the monitor. Some colors are therefore unreadable.

Monochrome monitor

Here there are no colors, only the attributes:

Intensity	Attribute
Normal	(COLOR 7,0)
Double intensity	(COLOR 15,0)
Underline	(COLOR 1,0)
Reverse video	(COLOR 0,7)
Flashing	(COLOR 31,0)

Color table

Color value	Color	Color value	Color
0	Black	8	Dark grey
1	Blue	9	Light blue
2	Green	10	Light green
3	Cyan	11	Light cyan
4	Red	12	Light red
5	Magenta	13	Light magenta
6	Brown	14	Yellow
7	Light grey	15	White

Adding the value 16 to *text_color* causes the text to flash on and off.

COLOR   select high res. graphic colors (S)

COLOR[foreground] [,background] [,text_color]

Sets the colors for high-resolution graphics mode (640x200 points).

foreground
>
> Specifies both graphic and text colors. Values range from 0 to 15.

background
>
> Defaults to black in this mode. Graphic commands that give a drawing color as a parameter refer to the foreground and background values set with COLOR. Because high-resolution mode is monochrome and not color, some conversion is necessary. The palette color values are taken and adjusted for the monochrome screen, according to the following table:

value:	color:
0	black
1	white
2	black
3	white

COLOR   select medium res. graphic colors (S)

COLOR [background] [,palette] [,graf_back]
[,graf_fore] [,text_color]

Sets colors for medium-resolution graphics mode (320x200 points).

background
>
> Sets the border and background color of the entire screen. Values can range from 0 to 15.

palette
>
> Specifies which of the two palettes are used for drawing colors in graphic commands:

Palette 0   Color 0 = background color
Palette 0   Color 1 = green
Palette 1   Color 0 = background color

`graf_back,graf_fore`

Specifies the standard values for the drawing colors used in graphic commands, dependent upon the palette previously selected.

`text_color`

Specifies the text color based on the palette used. Please note that 0 cannot be used for `text_color`.

COMMON   overlay variables (S)

COMMON `variable,...`

Defines the variables that are passed to a program loaded with CHAIN.

`variable`

Specifies a variable. All available types of variables, including arrays, can be used.

A chained program requires the COMMON statement only if it is loading additional overlays to which data is passed. A variable defined as COMMON must be given a value in the calling program. If necessary, assign a 0 to the null string. When arrays are being passed, the DIM command must precede COMMON.

CONT   continue program execution (C)

CONT

Restarts program execution that was interrupted by a STOP or END statement, or when you pressed Crtl+Break. The program is restarted at the point of interruption.

A program cannot be restarted if the program has been changed following the interruption.

CSNG

→single-precision (F)

CSNG (*expression*)

Converts a numerical expression to a single-precision value.

expression
> This can be a constant, the result of a calculation, a numerical variable, or the result of a numerical function.

CSRLIN

determine cursor location (F)

X=CSRLIN

Returns the current cursor location.

If the screen boundaries are altered with VIEW PRINT, CSRLIN returns the current line within the window.

CVD
CVI
CVS

decompress random-access (F)

X = CVD (*FIELD_var*)
X = CVI (*FIELD_var*)
X = CVS (*FIELD_var*)

Converts data that was compressed with MKD$, MKI$ or MKS$ to normal numerical format.

FIELD_var
> The name of a FIELD variable that was assigned a string created with MKD$, MKI$, or MKS$.

CVD Returns a double-precision result.

CVI Returns an integer result.

CVS Returns a single-precision result.

These functions are effective only if used on strings preprocessed using the MKD$, MKI$, or MKS$ functions. If other strings are used, their contents are viewed as compressed numerical data, and are improperly converted.

DATE$ system date (F,S)

X$ = DATE$ or DATE$ = X$

Returns or sets the MS-DOS system date.

Depending on the setup of the operating system, DATE$ has one of the following formats:

> 10 DATE$ = "month–day–year"
> (or)
> 10 DATE$ = "day–month–year"

DEF FN   (S)
FN   user-defined string functions (F)

DEF FN *string_name (parameter...) = function*
FN *string_name (parameter...)*

DEF FN allows the user to define a function for string operations. FN calls this user-defined function.

string_name

> Specifies the function name that is used when called with FN. This must be a valid string variable name. Arrays cannot be used.

parameter

> Specifies one or more string variable names. These variables are defined locally, meaning that they apply only for this function. The number of variables here must match the number of parameters in the call.

function

> The operations performed on the parameters. All GW-BASIC-supported string functions can be used.

A function defined in this manner cannot call itself. The function must be defined with DEF FN before the first call. The function cannot be longer than one program line. Definitions are not allowed in the direct mode.

DEF FN   user-defined math functions (S)

```
DEF FN var_name (parameter, ...) = function
FN var_name (parameter, ...)
```

Defines/calls a user-defined mathematical function.

var_name

> Specifies the function name that is used when calling with FN. This is a valid name for a numerical variable.

parameter

> Specifies one or more numerical variables. These variables are defined locally, meaning that they are valid only for this function. The number of variables in the definition must match the number of parameters passed in the call.

function

> Determines how the variables are processed. All of the mathematical functions supported by GW-BASIC can be used.

The function cannot call itself. The function must be defined with DEF FN before it is called. The function definition cannot exceed one program line in length. Definitions are not allowed in direct mode.

DEF SEG   set segment address (S)

```
DEF SEG = segment_addr
```

Sets the segment address used for BSAVE, BLOAD, PEEK, POKE, VARPTR, and VARPTR$.

segment_addr

> Specifies the segment referring to the commands and functions. Possible values range between 0 and 65535. If you do not specify this parameter, the data segment (DS)

currently occupied by GW-BASIC is set as the default segment.

GW-BASIC does not check to see if the selected segment is occupied by itself or other programs or data.

DEFXXX   global type definition (S)

DEFINT	*from – to*
DEFSNG	*from – to*
DEFDBL	*from – to*
DEFSTR	*from – to*

A global data type definition allows several variables to be assigned a given data type. The variables are grouped by the first letter of their names.

DEFINT   Defines the data type as integer.

DEFSNG   Defines the data type as single-precision real.

DEFDBL   Defines the data type as double-precision real.

DEFSTR   Defines the data type as string.

from   Specifies the first letter of the range to which the global definition applies.

to   Specifies the last letter of the range to which the global definition applies.

DEF USR   (S)
USR   machine language call (F)

DEF USR *number = offset*
USR *number* [*data_var*]

DEF USR sets the offset variable. USR calls a machine language routine loaded with BLOAD or placed into memory with POKE.

number   A value between 0 and 9. The previous definition is valid, so USR(3), for example, can be used to call various routines.

offset   The offset address that the routine begins. The segment must be previously defined with DEF SEG.

data_var

The variables whose contents are to be processed. The value is not passed by way of the stack, but the information is loaded into the CPU registers:

AL contains:

&H02, for integer variables
&H03, for string variables
&H04, for single-precision variables
&H08, for double-precision variables

BX contains:

An offset pointer to the FAC where the value is stored (for numerical values).

DX contains:

An offset pointer to a 3-byte area that contains the length of the string in the first byte and the offset address to the string text in the two following bytes in low/high order (for string variables).

DELETE   delete program lines (C)

DELETE [*from_line*|.] [-[*to_line*|.]

Deletes a single line or a range of lines in a program.

from_line

Specifies the first line to be deleted in the range.

to_line

Specifies the last line to be deleted in the range.

-          Separates *from_line* and *to_line* when both parameters are specified. If *to_line* is omitted, the lines from *from_line* to the end of the program are deleted. If *from_line* is omitted, all lines from the beginning of the program to *to_line* are deleted.

.   The current line number can be abbreviated to a period.

DIM   dimension arrays (S)

```
DIM var_name(subscripts)
[, var_name(subscripts)]
```

Reserves memory for one-dimensional arrays or multi-dimensional arrays with indexes greater than 10.

var_name

> The name of the array to be dimensioned. For numerical arrays, a type identifier (%, !, or #) can be appended to the variable name. For string arrays, the identifier $ must follow the variable name (assuming that the variable name is not globally defined as a string by DEFSTR).

subscripts

> One or more numeric expressions, separated by commas, that specify the number of elements per dimension of the array. The maximum number of elements per dimension is 255. The total allowable number of elements is limited by available memory.

DRAW   draw variable graphics (S)

```
DRAW string
```

Draws a graphic as described by *string*.

string Can be a constant, variable, or the result of a string expression. The current position at which DRAW will start is either the center of the screen or the last position used by a graphics command. Other positions must be set before DRAW with a command such as PSET. The following parameters can be part of the *string*:

U *num*   Draws *num* points up.

D *num*   Draws *num* points down.

L *num*   Draws *num* points to the left.

R *num*   Draws *num* points to the right.

E *num*   Draws *num* points diagonally to the upper right.

H *num*   Draws *num* points diagonally to the upper left.

F *num*   Draws *num* points diagonally to the lower right.

G *num*   Draws *num* points diagonally to the lower left.

If the number is not to be a constant, the numerical value must first be converted to a string. Otherwise DRAW must be told that a variable is being used with the equal sign (=) in front of the variable and a semicolon after it:

B *dir*   Moves the "pen" one pixel in the given direction without drawing any points. *dir* uses the characters U, D, L, R, E, F, G or H (see above).

N *dir*   Moves the "pen" one pixel in the given direction, setting that point. *dir* uses the characters U, D, L, R, E, F, G or H (see above).

M *X, Y*   If *X, Y* is specified without a preceding plus or minus sign, then a line is drawn from the current point to the point specified by *X, Y* (absolute coordinates). If *X, Y* is preceded by + or -, then *X, Y* is viewed as the relative coordinates.

C *color* Sets the drawing color, based on the available palettes 0 to 3.

P *F, B*   Fills a region enclosed by border color *B* with a fill color *F*. The current position must be inside the enclosed area. P does not have default values, so both parameters must be specified. Both values can range from 0 to 3.

A *angle* Sets the angle for subsequent movement. Possible values: 0 = 0 degrees, 1 = 90 degrees, 2 = 180 degrees, 3 = 270 degrees. This specification takes precedence over the direction of movement. For example, if you specify the command A3, then L goes right instead of left.

TA *angle*
           Specifies the angle of the movement to follow. Unlike A, TA can have values ranging from -360 to +360.

S *factor*
> Returns the value from the *formula factor/4* that should be multiplied with all the numerical parameters for movement to follow. This allows objects to be drawn to scale with one another. *factor* can range from 0 to 255.

X *string_var;*
> Stores often-repeated procedures for later inclusion as needed. The instructions contained in *string_var* are inserted at the current position and executed. Remember to include the semicolon following the variable name.

EDIT   edit lines (C)

EDIT [*line_number|.*]

Displays a program line for changes or corrections. All screen editing commands can be used to edit the program line.

line_number
> Specifies the program line being changed or corrected.

.
> The current line number can be abbreviated to a period.

ENVIRON   access to environment table (S)

ENVIRON *entry = assignment*

MS-DOS stores information about the system environment, such as the search path or command prompt, in the environment table. This table can be accessed from GW-BASIC.

entry   This is a legal entry in the table like PATH or COMSPEC or a parameter specified by SET.

assignment
> This is the new parameter assigned to *entry:*

```
ENVIRON "PATH = C:\WORDSTAR"
ENVIRON "PROMPT = $p$_$n:"
```

The new assignment cannot occupy more characters than the current entry.

ENVIRON$ access to environment table (F)

ENVIRON$ ("*entry*") or (*number*)

MS-DOS stores information about the system environment (like the search path or command prompt) in an environment table that can be accessed from GW-BASIC.

entry   Must be a legal variable entry such as PATH, PROMPT, or COMSPEC. ENVIRON$ returns the current assignment of this entry:

> PRINT ENVIRON$ ("PATH")
> C:\WORDSTAR

ENVIRON$ can also be used to access a certain entry by its number in the table:

> PRINT ENVIRON$ (1)
> C:\WORDSTAR

EOF   test for end of file (F)

EOF (*file_number*)

Tests to see if the end of the file was reached while reading a file.

file_number
        The file number used when the file was opened.

For random-access files, EOF returns the value -1 if a GET# is attempted after the last record in the file, so use of this function is not necessary. EOF is ignored if it is part of a record.

ERASE   erase dimensionsing (S)

ERASE *variable* [,*variable*...]

Erases one or more previously dimensioned arrays.

variable
> Specifies the name(s) of the array(s) from which dimensioning will be removed.

ERDEV   determine error number (F)

X= ERDEV

Returns the error number set from MS-DOS through interrupt 24 in the low byte. The high byte contains information (in the form of a bit pattern) about the device driver that caused the error.

ERDEV$ determine error device name (F)

X$= ERDEV$

Returns the name of the error-causing device:

PRN	Printer error
A:,B:,C:	Disk error
other	Driver error

ERL   determine error line (F)

X= ERL

Returns the line number at which the error occured.

ERL cannot be assigned a value.

ERR   determine error number (F)

X= ERR

Returns the code number of an error.

ERR cannot be assigned a value.

ERROR   generate an error (S)

ERROR *error_num*

Simulates an error. This can be used to test error-trapping routines, or to have such routines trap custom errors.

error_num
>   The error number in integer form. The error number range is 1 to 155.

You cannot generate your own error message texts. An error with the number specified is generated and ERL is assigned the line number of the ERROR instruction.

FIELD#   define random-access file buffer (S)

FIELD# *file_number,length* AS *string_var ,...*

Defines the buffer variables of the buffer used for read/write access to a random-access file.

file_number
>   The file number used when the file was opened.

length AS *string_var*
>   Specifies the individual fields of the buffer. *length* is the field length of *string_var*. All fields must be defined in a single program line.

The contents of a FIELD# variable are not assigned like normal strings. Instead, LSET and RSET are used before they are written to the file with PUT#.

Similarly, after data has been read from the file using GET#, the FIELDed variables can be assigned to other variables.

The sum of the individual field lengths cannot exceed the record length specified in the OPEN command for that file, otherwise the error message FIELD overflow is returned. The sum of the field lengths can be less than the record length specified in the OPEN command for that file.

FILES   display directory (C)

FILES [*filespec*]

Displays the directory filenames in MS-DOS dir/w format.

filespec
> Specifies the filenames to be displayed. *filespec* must appear between quotes (" "). If omitted, all filenames in the current directory are displayed.

FOR...NEXT   program loop (S)

FOR *index_var* = *start_value* TO *end_value*
[STEP *step_width*] *statement*(*s*)
NEXT [*index_var*]

Execute statements within the range (loop) delimited by FOR and NEXT. The specified statements are executed until the index variable reaches the end value.

index_var
> The (integer) loop index variable.

start_value, end_value
> Determine the starting and ending values of the loop index. Can be constants, variables, the results of calculations, or of functions. The result is of type integer.

step_width
> The index value is normally incremented by a value of +1 This can be changed to any desired integer step width by adding STEP to the statement. If *step_width* is negative, FOR...NEXT counts backwards from the starting value.

statement
> Can include any of the commands and functions supported by GW-BASIC, and can consist of as many program lines as required.

NEXT [*index_var*]
> Designates the end of the loop. GW-BASIC recognizes all statements between FOR and NEXT as being part of this loop. The index variable need be specified only in nested FOR...NEXT loops.

FOR...NEXT loops cannot be nested unless their elements are in proper order. The innermost FOR must be concluded with a NEXT before the other loops, followed by a NEXT corresponding to the second most recently defined loop, etc. If this is not done correctly, GW-BASIC will return the error message NEXT without FOR. The loop index value can be changed within the loop. However, this could cause an infinite loop. The loop can be exited at any time with GOTO. To be safe, set the index variable to the ending value so that the NEXT statement properly terminates the loop. However, this can result in the error message Out of memory.

FRE (0)
FRE (" ")   determine free memory (F)

FRE(0)|FRE("")

Returns the amount of free memory. FRE("") also performs garbage collection that removes unused string variables from variable memory. The CLEAR command changes variable memory, thereby affecting the amount of memory available.

GET

`GET[STEP] (X1,Y1)-[STEP] (X2,Y2), array`

Stores graphics in an array, so they can be stored on diskette or moved on the screen.

`STEP(X1,Y1),STEP(X2,Y2)`

> `(X1,Y1)` are the absolute coordinates of the lower left corner. `(X2,Y2)` are the absolute coordinates of the upper right corner of the area to be stored. `Y` can range from 0 to 199. `X` can range from 0 to 319 or from 0 to 639, depending on the resolution selected.

array   The name of the `array` in which the graphic is stored. `array` must have previously been dimensioned to the appropriate size with `DIM`. The size can be calculated with the following formula:

$$X = 4 + INT((pointX*B+7)/8) * pointY$$
> B=1 for 640x200 resolution
> B=2 for 320x200 resolution
> pointX = width of graphic in pixels
> pointY = height of graphic in pixels

The number of bytes an `array` element can store depends on the data type of the array:

Integer:	2 bytes
Single-precision:	4 bytes
Double-precision:	8 bytes

Remember to take this into account in the calculation.

The `X` dimension is stored in the first element of the `array` (0), and the `Y` dimension is stored in the second element (1). If the base of `array` is set to 1 with `OPTION BASE 1`, then the first element is 1 and the second element is 2. Following this is the bit map for the graphic. The bit map is read and stored line by line along the `X` axis. If the last points read from the graphic do not fill a byte, the rest of the element is filled with 0-bits. You should use an integer array for storing the graphic, because the data stored in such an array can be manipulated more easily.

Before the GET command is used, the coordinate field first must be defined with WINDOW.

GET#   read data in COM buffer (S)

GET# *file_num, num_chars*

Reads a specified number of characters from the serial interface into the communication buffer.

file_num
> Refers to the file number used in OPEN COM.

num_chars
> The number of characters to be read from interface into the buffer. Number of characters cannot be longer than the record length given in OPEN COM.

After data has been read from the serial interface into the buffer, the commands INPUT#, LINE INPUT#, and INPUT$ can be used for further processing.

GET#   read data from a random-access file (S)

GET# *file_num* [*, rec_num*]

Reads a record defined with FIELD from disk to buffer.

file_num
> The file number used when the file was opened.

rec_num
> The number of the record to be read. Without *rec_num*, GET# reads the record at which the file pointer is currently set. *rec_num* can have a value from 1 to 16,777,215.

GET# reads as many characters from a file as are defined by the record length in the OPEN statement, and stores the data in the variables defined by FIELD. If the sum of the field lengths are less than the record length, the extra characters are lost.

GOSUB...RETURN   subroutine (S)

GOSUB *line_number* RETURN [*line_number*]

Calls and executes a subroutine, and returns to the statement following the GOSUB.

line_number
> The program line that the subroutine begins, or the line to jump to at the completion of the subroutine.

A subroutine called with GOSUB can also be exited with GOTO. However, this can result in the error message Out of memory.

GOTO   unconditional jump (S)

GOTO *line_number*

Executes the program in memory beginning at *line_number*.

line_number
> The line number in the program to be jumped to.

Program loops (FOR...NEXT, WHILE...WEND) and subroutines called by GOSUB should not be exited using GOTO, because the data stored on the stack is not properly removed.

HEX$ decimal→hexadecimal (F)

HEX$ (*number*)

Converts a decimal value to a string of hexadecimal characters.

number This can be a constant, the result of a calculation, a numerical variable, or the result of a numerical function. *number* is representable as a 16-bit value in the range from -32768 to +65535.

IF...THEN...ELSE   conditional jump (S)

IF *condition* THEN *statement_1* [ELSE *statement_2*]

Branches in the program or executes statements based on the results of a condition or set of conditions.

condition
> A condition or comparison supported by GW-BASIC.

statement_1, statement_2
> Any commands and functions supported by GW-BASIC can be used here. Multiple statements can be separated by colons, but the combined length cannot exceed one program line.

The ELSE branch is optional. If ELSE is omitted and the condition is not fulfilled, execution continues with the next line. If ELSE is specified, it must be in the same line as IF and THEN. For absolute branches with GOTO, the statement GOTO does not have to be specified following THEN and ELSE. GOSUB, on the other hand, must always be specified.

INKEY$ keyboard input (F)

X$=INKEY$

Returns the ASCII character of the last key pressed.

INKEY$ returns a two-byte string for function and control keys. The first byte has the value 0. The second byte contains the ASCII value of the key pressed. The string length must be determined with LEN, and the string then handled appropriately.

INP   read data from a port (F)

X=INP(*port*)

This function returns the current value of a data or control port.

port   Can be a value between 0 and 65535.

INPUT   keyboard input (S)

INPUT [;] ["*message*"];|,*variables*,...

Reads data from the keyboard. A prompt to the user can be displayed. Quotation marks and commas cannot be read.

;   If a semicolon follows INPUT, the linefeed is suppressed when input is ended with the Enter key.

"*message*"
         Text can be specified as a string constant that prompts the user for the expected input.

;|,   The semicolon suppresses a linefeed after printing the message (not implemented in all versions). The comma suppresses the question mark.

variables
         Assigns variables to which the values are stored. The input must correspond to the variable types. Several variables can be used, separated by commas. Also, any data entered must be separated by commas.

INPUT$ read single characters (F)

X$=INPUT$(*num_chars*)

Reads a specified number of characters from the keyboard.

num_chars
         The number of characters to be read.

INPUT#   read data from a file (S)

INPUT# *file_number,variable,...*

Reads file data into a variable.

file_number
> The file number used when the file was opened.

variable
> One or more variables in which the file data is stored. Array elements can be specified.

INPUT reads complete records from the file and assigns them to the variable(s). CR/LF (&H0D/&H0A) is used as a separator between records. If PRINT# with the separators " or , (quotation mark or comma) were written in the file, these also serve as record separators, and therefore cannot be part of a string. Use the LINE INPUT# statement to read these characters. When reading numerical data, spaces are used as separators. INPUT# returns the error message Type mismatch if you try to read data that does not correspond to the variable types.

INPUT$ read characters from a file (F)

X$ = INPUT$(*num_chars* [,#*file_number*])

Reads the specified number of characters from a file.

num_chars
> The number of characters to be read from the file. Since the destination is a string, a value between 1 and 255 can be specified.

file_number
> The file number used when the file was opened.

INSTR   search for character in string (F)

INSTR ([*from_pos*], *string*, *search_char*)

Returns the position of a character in a string.

from_pos
Specifies the character position in *string* at which the search starts. If omitted, the search will start at the first character.

string The search string. This can also be an element of a string array.

search_char
>The character to be found in the string. This can be a constant, a variable, or the result of a string function.

The search character can also be a string, but INSTR will only look for the first character, not the entire string.

IOCTL   access to MS-DOS drivers (S)

IOCTL # *file_num, control_string*

Sends a control string to a device driver previously opened with OPEN. For example, it can be used, to pass format data or initialization values. The standard MS-DOS drivers do not accept IOCTL strings.

file_num
>The reference number used when the file was opened.

control_string
>This string contains the data to be evaluated by the driver. It can contain a maximum of 255 characters.

IOCTL$ access to MS-DOS drivers (F)

X$ = IOCTL$ (# *file_num*)

Returns a device driver's answer to a control string sent by IOCTL.

file_num
>The reference number used when the file was opened.

The standard MS-DOS drivers do not accept IOCTL strings.

KEY   display function key settings (S)

KEY ON | OFF | LIST

Turns the function key display on or off, or lists the function key settings.

ON   Displays the function key settings on the 25th line of the screen.

OFF   Clears the function key settings on the 25th line of the screen.

LIST   Lists the function key settings to the screen.

KEY   define function keys (S)

KEY *key_number, string*

Changes the function key assignments.

key_number
        Specifies the function key number that is assigned *string*. The *key_number* can be from 1 to 10.

string The characters displayed when *key_number* is pressed. If *string* is "", then *key_number* is disabled. *string* can have a maximum length of 15 characters. *string* can contain a control character, e.g. CHR$(13), which replaces the Enter key:

        KEY 1,"FILES A:*.BAS"+CHR$(13)

KEY   interrupt programming (S)

KEY *key_num*, CHR$ (*toggle/shift*) + CHR$ (*scan_code*)

Defines a key or key combination for interrupt checking using ON KEY.

key_num

A value from 15 to 20.

toggle/shift

The following values can be used to specify specific keys:

Ctrl key pressed	04 or &H04
Alt key pressed	08 or &H08
NumLock down	32 or &H20
Shift key pressed	64 or &H40

The values listed above depend on the keyboard and keyboard driver used.

scan_code

The scan codes are not the same as the ASCII characters that represent the keys. A *scan_code* is sent by the keyboard that depends on whether the key was pressed or released. This value is processed by the keyboard driver and converted into an ASCII value. Consult you Computer Operations Manual for the scan code.

When the KEY () STOP is used, the subroutine is not executed. Instead a flag is set for the next KEY () ON statement to indicate the condition is true. When KEY () ON is subsequently encountered, the subroutine is then executed.

KEY () STOP is then reset to prevent an infinite loop. RETURN at the end of the routine re-enables key interrupt checking.

If ON ERROR GOTO is active, a branch to the error-handling routine suspends key interrupt checking. RESUME re-enables key interrupt checking. To suppress the re-enabling of key interrupt checking, issue a KEY () OFF command in the appropriate routine.

KILL   delete a file (C)

KILL *filespec*

Deletes a file.

filespec
> A file specification corresponding to the MS-DOS conventions, consisting of drive, path, and filename.

The file specification must be enclosed in quotation marks if *filespec* is given as a constant. String functions cannot be used after KILL, although the file specification can be entered as a simple string variable. The file to be deleted must be closed, or the error message File already open is returned.

LCOPY   create a hardcopy (C)

LCOPY (*number*)

Prints the current screen contents to the printer. Not included in all versions of GW-BASIC.

number   This number depends on the version of GW-BASIC you have (usually 0, which prints the text screen).

Note: With most versions of GW-BASIC, LCOPY works in text mode only. Some PC system disks are equipped with a program called GRAPHICS.COM. After calling this program you can print a graphic hardcopy by pressing Shift+PrtSc.

LEFT$ dissect a string (F)

X$ = LEFT$ (*string, num_chars*)

Returns the leftmost number of characters of a string.

string   The string to be dissected. Elements of arrays can be specified.

num_chars
> The number of characters (starting at the first position) to be returned from *string*.

LEN
determine length of a string (F)

`X = LEN (string)`

Returns the length of a string.

`string`   The string whose length is to be determined. Elements of arrays can be specified.

LET
initialize variables (S)

`LET variable = value`

Assigns a value to a variable.

`variable`
Any type of variable, including an array element.

`value`   The value assigned to the variable. This must be of the same type as `variable`.

`LET` can be omitted from value assignments in GW-BASIC.

LINE
draw lines and rectangles (S)

```
LINE [STEP] [(from_X, from_Y)] - [STEP]
(to_X, to_Y) [, drawing_color] [,B[F]] [, raster]
```

Draws lines and rectangles.

`from_X, from_Y`
Specifies the starting coordinates of the line to be drawn. For a rectangle, they specify the lower left corner. If these coordinates are omitted, the coordinates from the previous command are applied. If `STEP` is not specified, `from_X, from_Y` specifies the absolute coordinates of the point.

`STEP from_X, from_Y` specifies the position relative to the last position addressed on the screen. `Y` can range from 0 to 199. *X* can range from 0 to 319 or 0 to 639, depending on the resolution.

to_X, to_Y

Specifies the end point of the line. For a rectangle these specify the upper right corner. Both values must be given. If STEP is not specified, then *to_X, to_Y* specifies the absolute coordinates of the point. STEP *to_X, to_Y* specifies the position relative to the last position addressed on the screen. *Y* can range from 0 to 199. *X* can range from 0 to 319 or 0 to 639, depending on the resolution.

drawing_color

The color of the line. Values range from 0 to 3.

B   Draws a rectangle.

F   An F following the B fills in the rectangle with the color specified in COLOR.

raster Specifies the appearance of the line. Normally the line is solid. A 16-bit mask can be used to change the line's appearance.

LINE converts coordinates that lie outside the maximum resolution defined with SCREEN to allowable values to prevent the program from terminating with an error message.

LINE INPUT   keyboard input (S)

LINE INPUT [;] ["*message*"] ; |, *string_var*

Reads one line of input from the keyboard. The separators used in normal INPUT (" and ,) are allowed as input.

;   If a semicolon immediately follows LINE INPUT, no linefeed is printed when the input is terminated with the Enter key.

"*message*"

Text specified as a string constant that prompts the user for the expected input.

; | ,   The second semicolon within the statement suppresses the
                 output of a linefeed after printing the message. Automatic
                 sending of the linefeed is not implemented in all versions.
                 The comma suppresses output of the question mark.

string_var
                 The string variable that input is stored. It is not possible to
                 read in more than one string variable.

LINE INPUT#   read data from a file (S)

LINE INPUT# *file_number*, *string_var*

Reads data, including separators, from a file.

file_number
                 The reference number used when the file was opened.

string_var
                 The name of a string variable in which the data is stored.
                 This can be an element of a string array.

LINE INPUT# reads characters from the file until a CR/LF
(&H0D/&H0A) is encountered, or until 255 characters are read.

LIST   list a program (C)

LIST[*from_line*|.][-[*to_line*|.]] [,*dev*|*filespec*]

Displays program lines on the screen or sends the program lines to a
file or device.

from_line
                 Specifies the first line of the program to be listed.

to_line
                 Specifies the last line of the program to be listed.

-                A dash separates *from_line* and *to_line* if both
                 parameters are specified. If *to_line* is omitted, the
                 program is listed starting at *from_line* to the end of the

program. If *from_line* is omitted, the program is listed from the beginning of the program to *to_line*.

dev Specifies the device to which the program is listed.

filespec
  Specifies the filename of the listed program.

. The current line can be abbreviated to a period.

If both line parameters are omitted, the entire program is listed.

LLIST   list a program (C)

LLIST [*from_line*|.] [-[.*to_line*]]

Lists the current program to the line printer.

from_line
  Specifies the first line of the program to be listed.

to_line
  Specifies the last line of the program to be listed.

- A dash separates *from_line* and *to_line* if both parameters are specified. If *to_line* is omitted, the program is listed starting at *from_line* to the end of the program. If *from_line* is omitted, the program is listed from the beginning of the program to *to_line*.

. The current line can be abbreviated to a period.

If both line parameters are omitted, the entire program is listed.

LOAD   load a program (C)

LOAD *filespec*[,R]

Executes a NEW command and loads a program from disk.

filespec

Specifies the name of the BASIC program to be loaded from disk. *filespec* can specify a drive, path and an extension. *filespec* must be entered between quotation marks ("").

If the drive is omitted, the current drive is the default. If the path is omitted, the current directory is the default. If the extension is omitted, a .BAS extension is assumed.

,R   Immediately executes the program after loading.

LOC
LOF   OPEN COM functions (F)

X=LOC(*file_num*)
X=LOF(*file_num*)

LOC returns the number of characters in the transfer buffer that have been read.

LOF returns the total number of characters remaining in the transfer buffer.

file_num   The file number used in OPEN COM.

LOCATE   position cursor (S)

LOCATE [*line*] [,*column*] [,*on_off*] [,*from_line*]
[,*to_line*]

Positions the cursor on the screen, turns it on or off, and sets the cursor shape.

line, column
> The line on the screen and the column within that line where the cursor is positioned. *line* can have a value between 1 and 25. The value of *column* depends on the limit set with WIDTH and can range from 1 to 80, or 1 to 40.

on_off   This parameter determines whether the cursor will be on (1) or off (0).

from_line, to_line
> The cursor can be displayed in a variety of ways. Depending on the video card used, the cursor is composed of a number of raster lines. The top line is 0, and the maximum lower line is 31. The deciding factor here is the matrix the video card uses to display the characters:

Color and composite monitor: 0 to 7; matrix = 8x8.

Monochrome monitor: 0 to 31; matrix varies with the card.

LOC   determine file position (F)

X = LOC(*file_number*)

Returns the position of the file pointer. For sequential files, the value returned is the number of 128-byte blocks that were read or written.

file_number
> The file number used when the file was opened.

LOF   determine file size (F)

X = LOF (*file_number*)

Determines the size in bytes of a previously opened file. The number returned is a multiple of 128.

file_number
> The file number used when the file was opened.

LPOS   determine position in printer buffer (F)

X=LPOS(*printer_number*)

Returns the position of the buffer pointer in the printer buffer.

printer_number
> The number of the interface connected to the printer. Can be 1, 2, or 3. The default is usually 1.

LPRINT   output data to the printer (S)

LPRINT [TAB (*column*)] [SPC (*number*)]
[*expression*...] [; | ,]

Outputs data to printer.

column   Sets the printhead at a given tab. Printer tab positions must be preset to effectively use this option.

number   Specifies the number of spaces to be printed.

expression
> The data to be printed. *expression* can be constants, variables, or the results of functions or calculations. The data can be of any type, and different types can be combined. The data is separated with one of the following characters:

;   A semicolon suppresses a linefeed after the output. This allows multiple expressions to be printed on the same line.

,   A comma forces a tab during printer output. Tabs are set
           every 8 characters.

The printer can also be opened as a file for output:

```
OPEN "LPTx:" FOR OUTPUT AS #1
PRINT#1,A$
```

X specifies the device number that is the output's destination. Possible
values are 1, 2, or 3. PRINT#, PRINT# USING, and WRITE# can be
used as output statements. The file must be closed when finished with
output.

LPRINT USING   print formatted data (S)

LPRINT USING "mask"; *expression*

Formats output of data to the printer.

"mask"   Sets formatting characteristics for *expression*. A detailed
           description can be found in the PRINT USING description
           in the **Output-Screen** section below.

expression
           Specifies the data to be printed. These can be constants,
           variables, or the results of functions or calculations. The data
           can be of any type. They can be of different types, but
           "mask" must be able to accommodate them.

LSET
RSET   format random-access file data (S)

LSET *FIELD_var* = *string_var*
RSET *FIELD_var* = *string_var*

Formats FIELD variables for storage in a random-access file. LSET
left-justifies the data, and RSET right-justifies the data.

FIELD_var
           The name of a string variable defined in the FIELD
           statement.

string_var
> The name of a string variable whose contents are to be assigned to *FIELD_var*.

LSET and RSET can also format normal string variables.

MERGE   combine program modules (C)

MERGE *filespec*

Combines the program in memory with an ASCII file from disk.

filespec
> Specifies the name of the BASIC program on disk to be combined with the current program in memory. *filespec* can specify a drive, path and extension. *filespec* must be entered between quotation marks ("").

> If the drive is omitted, the current drive is the default. If the path is omitted, the current path is the default. If the extension is omitted, a .BAS extension is assumed.

> *filespec* must be a BASIC program in ASCII format. To create such a file, use the SAVE command with ,A (for example, SAVE *filespec*,A).

> If *filespec* contains line numbers identical to these of the program in memory, the program line from *filespec* replaces the program line in memory.

MID$ dissect string (F)

X$ = MID$(*string, first_char* [,*num_chars*])

Returns the specified number of characters beginning at a given position within a string.

string The string to be dissected. Array elements can be used.

first_char
> The string position at which the operation is to begin.

num_chars
> The number of characters to be returned. If this parameter is not specified, the remainder of the string is returned.

MID$ change parts of strings (S)

```
MID$(dest_string, first_char
[,num_chars]) = src_string
```

Replace one section of a string with another.

dest_string
> Specifies the string to be replaced. Elements of arrays can be specified.

first_char
> States the character in the destination string at which the source string is to be inserted.

num_chars
> Specifies the number of characters in the destination string to be replaced. If this parameter is not given, all characters after first_char are replaced.

src_string
> Specifies the string to replace source string characters starting at first_char. Elements of arrays can be specified.

MKD$
MKI$ number conversion (F)
MKS$

```
X$ = MKD$(expression)
X$ = MKI$(expression)
X$ = MKS$(expression)
```

Converts a numerical expression into a string for compressed storage in random-access files.

expression

>   Can be a constant, a numerical variable, or the result of a
>   function or calculation.

MKD$

>   The result of the numerical expression must be of type
>   double-precision, and is converted into an 8-byte string.

MKI$

>   The result of the expression must be of type integer, and is
>   converted into a 2-byte string.

MKS$

>   The result of the numerical expression must be of type
>   single-precision, and is converted into a 4-byte string.

Note:

>   Data compressed with MKD$, MKI$, and MKS$ cannot be
>   stored in sequential files because the bit pattern of a byte
>   could correspond to a separator, or even the EOF marker.

NAME   rename a file (C)

NAME *old_filespec* TO *new_filespec*

Renames a file.

old_filespec

>   The drive, path, and filename of the file to be renamed. Drive
>   and path are optional, but the filename must be given with
>   its extension. The specification can be a constant or a
>   variable.

new_filespec

>   The new filename, given with its extension.
>   *New_filespec* can be a string constant or variable.

When constants are used for the file specifications, they must be
enclosed in quotation marks. String functions are not allowed. If the
filename specified by *new_filespec* already exists, the error
message File already exists is returned. The error message
RENAME across disks is returned if different drives are specified.
File already open is returned if you try to rename an open file.

NEW — erase BASIC memory (C)

NEW

Erases the program in memory and initializes all variables.

NOT — invert comparison result (O)

IF NOT *condition* THEN *statement*

Inverts the result of a comparison.

condition
      Comparison using operators =, <>, <=, =>, <, or >.

OCT$ — decimal→octal (F)

OCT$ (*number*)

Converts a decimal value to a string of octal digits.

number Specifies a constant, the result of a calculation, a numerical variable, or the result of a numerical function. *number* is representable as a 16-bit value.

ON COM — interrupt programming (S)

ON COM *channel* GOSUB *line_num* COM *channel*
ON | OFF | STOP

The serial interface is read during the system interrupt. If a byte is received, a subroutine is executed.

channel Specifies the number of the serial interface to be read. Values can range from 1 to 4, depending on the number of interfaces installed.

line_num
> Specifies the line number of the subroutine to be executed if a byte is received from the serial interface.

COM *channel* ON
> Enables interrupt checking.

COM *channel* OFF
> Ends interrupt checking.

COM *channel* STOP
> Stops interrupt checking until the next COM *channel* ON.

When STOP is used, the subroutine is not executed if the condition is true. Instead, a flag is set for the next ON option to indicate condition is true. When COM ON is subsequently encountered, the subroutine is then executed. COM STOP is then reset to prevent an infinite loop. RETURN at the end of the routine re-enables interrupt checking. If ON ERROR GOTO is active, a branch to the error-handling routine suspends interrupt checking. RESUME re-enables interrupt checking. To suppress the re-enabling of interrupt checking caused by RETURN or RESUME, issue a COM OFF command in the appropriate routine.

ON ERROR GOTO   trap error (S)

ON ERROR GOTO *line_num*

Suspends the usual error message on an error, branches to *line_num* and executes the error-handling routine you've written.

line_num
> The program line at which the error-handling routine starts. If *line_num* is 0, error trapping is turned off and GW-BASIC displays the usual error messages.

ON KEY   interrupt programming (S)

ON KEY (*key_num*) GOSUB *line_num* KEY (X) ON | OFF | STOP

Read the function and control keys during the system interrupt. A subroutine is executed if the specified key was pressed.

key_num

The following values can be used for *key_num*:

Key	Value
F1 to F10	1 to 10
Cursor up	11
Cursor left	12
Cursor right	13
Cursor down	14

line_num

Specifies the line number of the subroutine that will be executed when the specified key is pressed.

KEY (*key_num*) ON

Enables checking during the interrupt.

KEY (*key_num*) OFF

Ends interrupt checking.

KEY (*key_num*) STOP

Suppresses interrupt checking until the next KEY (*key_num*) ON.

Note: After an interrupt for a specified key is executed, the keyboard buffer is empty. Thus, further reading with INKEY$ is not possible. When KEY () STOP is used, the subroutine is not executed if the condition is true. Instead, a flag is set for the next KEY () ON statement to indicate that condition is true. When KEY () ON is subsequently encountered, the subroutine is then executed. KEY () STOP is then reset to prevent an infinite loop. RETURN at the end of the routine re-enables key interrupt checking.

If ON ERROR GOTO is active, a branch to the error-handling routine suspends key interrupt checking. RESUME re-enables key interrupt checking. To suppress the re-enabling of key interrupt checking, issue a KEY () OFF command in the appropriate routine.

ON PLAY   interrupt programming (S)

ON PLAY (*num_notes*) GOSUB *line_num* PLAY
ON | OFF | STOP

Checks the number of notes when the PLAY buffer is checked. If the number of notes is less than or equal to *num_notes*, the appropriate subroutine is executed. This can be used to reinitialize PLAY to continually play music in the background.

num_notes
> The number of notes remaining in the buffer, still to be executed by the subroutine.

line_num
> The starting line number of the subroutine.

PLAY ON Enables interrupt checking.

PLAY OFF
> Disables interrupt checking.

PLAY STOP
> Stops interrupt checking until the next PLAY ON command.

When PLAY STOP is used, the subroutine is not executed. Instead, a flag is set for the next PLAY ON statement to indicate the condition is true. When PLAY ON is subsequently encountered, the subroutines are then executed.

PLAY STOP is then reset to prevent an infinite loop. RETURN at the end of the routine re-enables play interrupt handling.

If ON ERROR GOTO is active, a branch to the error-handling routine suspends play interrupt checking. RESUME re-enables play interrupt checking. To suppress the re-enabling of play interrupt checking, issue a PLAY OFF function in the appropriate routine.

ON TIMER   interrupt programming (S)

ON TIMER (*seconds*) GOSUB *line_num* TIMER
ON|OFF|STOP

The timer is read during the system interrupt and a subroutine is executed, depending on the result and the time specified.

seconds
> The interval at which the subroutine at *line_num* is to be executed. Values can range from 1 to 86400.

line_num
> The line number at which the subroutine to be executed is located.

TIMER ON
> Enables timer checking during the system interrupt.

TIMER OFF
> Ends the timer checking.

TIMER STOP
> Suspends checking until the next TIMER ON.

When STOP is used, the subroutine is not executed if the condition is true. Instead a flag is set for the next ON option to indicate that the condition is true. When TIMER ON is subsequently encountered, the subroutine is then executed. TIMER STOP is then reset to prevent an infinite loop. RETURN at the end of the routine re-enables the timer interrupt checking.

If ON ERROR GOTO is active, a branch to the error-handling routine suspends timer interrupt checking. RESUME re-enables timer interrupt checking. To suppress the re-enabling of the timer interrupt after RETURN or RESUME, a TIMER OFF statement is specified in the appropriate routine.

ON X GOTO/GOSUB   conditional jump (S)

ON *index* GOTO *list_of_line_numbers*
(or) ON *index* GOSUB *list_of_line_numbers*

Jumps conditionally to subprograms or subroutines by way of *index*.

index   A numerical variable, function, or calculation whose result
             is of type integer.

list_of_line_numbers
             A list of line numbers (separated by commas) to which
             execution will branch by means of the index.

If X=0, or X is greater than the number of line numbers specified, the
program continues at the line following the ON X GOTO/GOSUB line.
The line numbers do not have to be in ascending order. A line can
appear in the list more than once.

OPEN   open a file (S)

OPEN *filespec* FOR *mode* AS # *file_number*
[LEN= *record_length*]

Opens a file for read/write access, or for using a function.

filespec
             A file specification corresponding to MS-DOS conventions.
             filespec can specify a drive, path and an extension.
             filespec must be entered between quotation marks ("").

             If the drive is omitted, the current drive is the default. If the
             path is omitted, the current directory is the default. An
             extension is optional.

mode   Specifies the operation for the file that is being opened.

             INPUT   The file is opened so that data can be read from
                      it. The file pointer is placed at the start of the
                      file.

233

OUTPUT   The file is opened so that data can be written to it. The file pointer is placed at the start of the file. If an existing file is opened, any data present is overwritten. If the file does not exist, a file is created.

APPEND   The file is opened in the OUTPUT mode, but the file pointer is placed at the end of the file so that it can be extended. If the file does not exist, a file is created.

file_number

A reference number that is subsequently used for file access as long as the file is opened.

LEN= *record_length*

If LEN is specified instead of a mode, the file is opened as a random-access file. *record_length* sets the length of the record in bytes. The *record_length* ranges from 1 to 32767 bytes. LEN is not separated from the other parameters by a comma.

OPEN   open a file (S)

OPEN "mode", # *file_number*,
filespec[, *record_length*]

This is the second variant of the OPEN command. Supported to maintain compatibility with previous versions of GW-BASIC.

file_number,

A reference number that is subsequently used for file access for as long as the file is opened.

filespec

A file specification corresponding to MS-DOS conventions. *filespec* can specify a drive, path and an extension. *filespec* must be entered between quotation marks ("").

If the drive is omitted, the current drive is the default. If the path is omitted, the current directory is the default. An extension is optional.

mode   Specifies the operation for the file that is being opened:

I   The file is opened so that data can be read from it. The file pointer is placed at the start of the file.

O   The file is opened so that data can be written to it. The file pointer is placed at the start of the file. If an existing file is opened, any data present is overwritten. If the file does not exist, a file is created.

A   The file is opened in the OUTPUT mode, but the file pointer is placed at the end of the file so that it can be extended. If the file does not exist, a file is created.

R   The file is opened for random-access.

record_length
Record length must be specified for mode R. LEN=... is omitted from this variant. The record length is separated from the other parameters with a comma. *record_length* can range from 1 to 32767.

OPEN COM   open communication channel (S)

```
OPEN "COM channel:[baud_rate] [,parity]
[,word_width] [,stop_bits] [,RS] [,CS[time]]
[,DS[time]] [,CD[time]] [,BIN] [,ASC] [,LF]" [FOR
mode] AS #[file_num] [,LEN=length]
```

Opens and initializes the serial interface for communications.

channel Specifies the interface number. Normally there is only one serial interface present, so you would use 1.

baud_rate
Sets the number of bits per second for data transfer. This value must match the baud rate of the device through which you are trying to communicate. If this specification is omitted, *baud_rate* defaults to 300. Possible values are: 75, 110, 150, 300, 600, 1200, 1800, 2400, 4800, 9600.

parity Sets parity for data transfer. This value must match the setting on the peripheral device. The default is N (no parity). The following abbreviations can be used:

N	no parity
E	even parity
U	odd parity
S	space
M	mark

word_width

Sets the number of bits per character. The default is 7 bits. Possible values are 5, 6, 7, and 8 bits per character.

stop_bits

Sets the number of stop bits sent after each character. This value must match the setting of the peripheral device in question. Unless otherwise specified, 2 stop bits are sent if the baud rate is less than or equal to 110. For all other baud rates, one stop bit is sent. Another possible value is 1.5.

RS   Suppresses the RTS (Request To Send) signal during transmission.

CS*time*   Waits for the CTS (Clear To Send) signal from the peripheral device. *time* sets the maximum waiting time in seconds. After this length of time a Device timeout is signaled.

DS*time*   Waits for the DSR (Data Set Ready) signal from the peripheral device. *time* sets the maximum wait time in milliseconds. After this length of time, a Device timeout is signaled.

CD*time*   Waits for the CD (Carrier Detect) signal from the peripheral device. *time* sets the maximum wait time in milliseconds. After this length of time, a Device timeout is signaled.

BIN   Specifies that data received is to be treated as binary data. All characters are processed unchanged. CR or LF is not interpreted as the end of a line. The EOF character (&H1A) is ignored.

ASC   Handles received data as ASCII data. The tab character (CHR$(9)) is converted to spaces (CHR$(32)). CR or LF is read as an end of line. The transfer ends when EOF (&H1A) is received.

LF   Specifies that an LF (&H0A, 10 decimal) is to be sent after every CR (&H0D, 13 decimal). This option is mainly for output to a printer that does not automatically perform a linefeed after a carriage return.

mode   Sets the transfer mode:

> INPUT = receive
> OUTPUT = send

If you do not specify FOR mode, the transfer takes place in random mode, meaning that simultaneous input and output are possible.

file_num
            Specifies the file number for input/output. Possible values range from 1 to 15.

length   Specifies the record length for data transfer. The default values are 256 bytes for INPUT and 128 bytes for OUTPUT. If you called GW-BASIC with the [/C] parameter, the record length cannot be longer than the values specified therein.

The baud_rate, parity, word_width and stop_bits parameters must be specified in the order that they are shown above. All other parameters and options can be in any order. Using BIN and LF together is meaningless, because CR and LF are ignored when BIN is active. The transfer is concluded with a CLOSE #filenum.

OPTION BASE   initialize arrays (S)

OPTION BASE 0 | 1

Sets the lower limit of all array indexes to start at 0 or 1.

0   All arrays in the program have starting indexes of 0.

1   All arrays in the program have starting indexes of 1.

OR   combine comparisons (O)

IF *condition_1* OR *condition_2* THEN *statement*

Combines multiple comparisons. The statement is executed if either *condition_1* or *condition_2* is true.

condition_1, condition_2
> Comparisons using the relational operators =, <>, <=, =>, <, or >.

OUT   write data to a port (S)

OUT *port,value*

Writes a value to a data or control port.

port   The port to which the data is written. Possible values are 0 to 65535.

value   Each port can accept a single byte of data, so values from 0 to 255 are allowed.

Consult other sources regarding I/O ports before you experiment with OUT. **Improper values can cause a system crash.**

PAINT   fill shapes with color (S)

PAINT[STEP] (*X,Y*) [,*mode*] [,*border_color*]

Fills an enclosed area with a given color and/or pattern.

(*X, Y*)   (*X,Y*) without STEP specifies the absolute coordinates of the point. STEP (*X, Y*) specifies the position relative to the last position addressed on the screen. *Y* can range from 0 to 199. *X* can range from 0 to 319 or 0 to 639, depending on the resolution.

mode   Specifies whether the area is filled with a color or a pattern. If COLOR has a value from 0 to 3, then it specifies the color to be used. Otherwise you can specify an 8 x 64-bit mask as the pattern (64 bytes). This pattern is then drawn in the default color set by COLOR. The pattern is specified with CHR$.

border_color

Specifies the border color surrounding the region to be filled. This border color is set by border with a value ranging from 0 to 3.

Note: If even a single point in the area is not set, the color or pattern will "leak" through this hole and fill other regions.

PEEK   read memory location (F)

X = PEEK(*offset*)

Returns the 8-bit value of the specified memory address in the current segment.

offset   The address within the segment (0 to 65535).

PLAY   program tone sequences (S)

PLAY *string*

Outputs the set of tones defined in a string.

string   Can contain the following specifications for defining the tones to be created:

MF (modeforeground)

Generates tones in the foreground. A new PLAY statement cannot be executed until the current one is completed.

MB (modebackground)

Generates tones in the background. The program continues to execute. A maximum of 32 characters for generating tones can be passed.

MN (modenormal)

> Generates tones of normal length (7/8 of the length specified by L).

ML (modelegato)

> Generates *legato* (smooth) tones, as specified in the string by L.

MS (modestaccato)

> Generates *staccato* (short) tones, 3/4 of the length specified with L.

Ox (octave)

> Specifies the desired octave with x. The value for x can range from 0 to 6.

>

> Raises the tone by one octave, up to a maximum of 6.

<

> Lowers the by one octave, down to a minimum of 0.

A to G[-][+|#]

> A musical note from A to G. The number sign or plus sign raises the note one half-tone (sharp), while the minus sign lowers the note one half-tone (flat).

Nnote_number

> Sounds one of the 84 possible notes within the seven available octaves. Values can range from 0 to 84. 0 produces a rest.

Pnote_length

> Produces a rest. The length of the rest corresponds to the note_length, that can be a value from 1 to 64. note_length=4 yields a quarter-note rest.

Lnote_length

> Sets the duration of the subsequent notes. note_length can be specified in the range 1 to 64. If L with a parameter follows a note, L applies to this note only.

T tempo

> Sets the tempo for the tone generation—the number of quarter notes per minute. *Tempo* can range in value from 32 to 255.

.   The period causes the tone generation to run one and a half times longer (3/2) than the values set by L and T. Multiple periods increase the value correspondingly.

X*string_var*;

Executes *string_var*. This corresponds roughly to a "musical subroutine." Remember to include the semicolon after the variable.

Variables can also be used for numerical parameters. These can be indicated in the string as follows:

"T=Tempo;"

Note that (in contrast to X *string_variable*) an equal sign (=) must be used.

PMAP   convert coordinates (F)

X=PMAP(*coordinate*),*mode*

Converts the coordinates changed with WINDOW.

coordinate

Specifies an X or Y coordinate converted according to *mode*.

mode=0   Specified X coordinate set with WINDOW and converted to an absolute coordinate.

mode=1   Specified Y coordinate set with WINDOW and converted to an absolute coordinate.

mode=2   An absolute X coordinate, converted to the coordinate axes set with WINDOW.

mode=3   An absolute Y coordinate, converted to the coordinate axes set with WINDOW.

POINT   determine graphic point color (F)

n= POINT (X, Y)

Returns the point color at the given coordinates.

(X,Y)   Specifies the coordinates of the point being tested. The result
          is between 0 and 3 and indicates the color number of the
          point based on the current palette.

n   Can be 0, 1, 2 or 3:

0   Returns the physical X coordinate
1   Returns the physical Y coordinate
2   Returns world X coordinate
3   Returns world Y coordinate

POKE   write a value to a memory location (S)

POKE *offset, value*

Writes a value into a memory location in the current segment.

offset The address of the memory location within the segment.
          Values can range from 0 to 65535.

value   The value to be written to the location. Values can range
          from 0 to 255.

POS (0)   determine cursor position (F)

X=POS (0)

Determines the current column position of the cursor.

PRESET   clear graphic point (S)

PRESET[STEP] (*X*, *Y*) [, *drawing_color*]

Clears a point on the graphic screen at the specified coordinates.

(*X*, *Y*) and STEP

> With STEP, (*X*, *Y*) specify the position relative to the last position addressed on the screen. For PRESET without STEP, (*X*, *Y*) are absolute coordinates.
>
> Y can range from 0 to 199. X can range from 0 to 319 or 0 to 639 depending on the resolution.

drawing_color

> Specifies the point color. If *drawing_color* is omitted, the point is set in the current background color, clearing it. Values can range from 0 to 3.

PRINT   output to the screen (S)

PRINT [TAB(*column*)] [SPC(*number*)] [*expression*...] [;] [,]

Displays data of any type on the screen.

column   Moves the cursor to a tab column on the screen in the current output line. *column* can have a value from 1 to 80, or from 1 to 40, depending on WIDTH.

number   Prints the specified number of spaces in the current output line.

expression

> Specifies the data to be printed. *expression* can be constants, variables, and numerical or string expressions. The data can be of any type, and types can be mixed. They are separated by one of the following separators:
>
> ;   Begins printing the next value at the next screen column while suppressing the carriage return. This

allows multiple expressions to be printed on the same line.

,   Begins printing the next value at the next tab stop (every 8 columns).

If the expression does not fit on the current line, the output is automatically continued on the following line. When printing numeric values, the first position represents the sign of the number. For positive values a space is printed. For negative values a minus sign (-) is printed.

The keyboard can also open files for screen output:

```
OPEN"CONS:" FOR OUTPUT AS #1
PRINT#1,PRINTER OUTPUT$
```

PRINT#, PRINT# USING and WRITE# are also output statements. After output, the file must be closed with the CLOSE statement.

PRINT USING   formatted output (S)

PRINT USING *mask; expression*

Displays formatted data on the screen.

mask   A string constant or variable that set the formatting characteristics for *expression*:

Masks for Numerical Data

"#####"

This mask formats integers. Each # stands for a digit in the number to be printed. If a sign is required, you should add another #. Real numbers are rounded off before they are printed.

"#####.##"

This mask formats decimal numbers. The # characters before and after the decimal point determine the number of places to be printed before and after the decimal point. If you don't provide enough # characters after the decimal, the value is rounded to the number of places specified.

`"+#####.##"` [or] `"#####.##+"`
> A plus sign (+) at the start or end of the mask displays the sign of the number before or after the value.

`"#####.##-"`
> A minus sign at the end of the mask displays a negative sign at the end of the value. Positive values are printed without a plus sign. The minus sign can appear only at the end of the mask.

`"#####.##^^^^"`
> Displays a value in exponential notation (scientific notation). The ^^^^ characters stand for E or D, the sign (+/-) and two digits that represent the powers of ten.

`"**#####.##"`
> If two asterisks are placed at the beginning of the mask, the spaces that are normally printed in the mask if the value is smaller than the width of the mask are replaced by asterisks.

`"$$#####.##"`
> The dollar sign ($) at the start of the mask causes a dollar sign to be placed before every value. It is not possible to use this with the scientific notation ^^^^. When used in combination with the asterisk mask as in the previous example, only one dollar sign is specified (**$#####.##).

`"#######,.##"`
> A comma in the mask prints the digits of the value in groups of three, separated by commas (e.g., 1,254,267.80). Use this format with numbers that have four or more digits.

Masks for Strings and Characters

`"\        \"`
> This mask specifies the number of characters to be printed. The backslash (\) characters stand for one character each. The spaces between the \ characters represent additional characters. For example, if you put five spaces between the \ characters, a total of 7 characters are printed.

`"&"`   The ampersand prints the string as unformatted.

`"!"`   The exclamation point prints only the first letter of a string.

"_" [underline]

> If PRINT USING finds the underline character in the mask, the characters that follow it are printed without further formatting. This allows you to include characters that normally are not allowed in the mask.

"#####.## *text*"

> Text within the mask is printed at the relative position in the mask.

The semicolon is used as a separator between the mask and the expression.

expression

> This is the data to be printed. *expression* can be constants, variables, results of calculations, or results of functions. The data can be of the same or different types, but they must be able to be formatted by the mask.

If the specified value is larger than the mask can format, PRINT USING indicates this by placing a percent sign (%) preceding the output. This can destroy any subsequent formatting. If the maximum number of printable places cannot be exactly determined in advance, a larger mask should be selected, or you should include a test for value size in your program.

PRINT#   write data in a file (S)

PRINT# *file_number, expression, ...* [; | ,]

Writes data to a file.

file_number

> The reference number used in the OPEN command for this file.

expression

> Data to be written to the file. Can be constants, variables, or the result of functions or calculations. Multiple expressions can be specified if they are separated by commas. The expressions can be of different types.

; | ,   After writing an expression to the file, PRINT# outputs CR/LF (&H0D/&H0A) as a separator. This sequence can be suppressed by placing a semicolon (;) after *expression*. The data is stored with separators, but cannot be read with INPUT#.

,   A tab is written to the file. Eight spaces are sent to the file before the next expression is written.

The file number must match a file number previously used in an OPEN command. If expressions of different types are written, they must be assigned to variables of the proper types with INPUT# when reading the file.

PRINT# USING   write formatted data (S)

PRINT# *file_number* USING "mask"; *expression*

Formats data output to a file.

file_number
> The reference number used when the file was opened.

"mask"   Specifies the formatting characteristics for *expression*. See PRINT USING in the **Output-Screen** section for complete descriptions of "mask".

expression
> The data to be written. These can be constants, variables, results of calculations or functions. The data can be of any type, but the "mask" must be of a design suitable for handling the specific types.

PSET   set graphic point (S)

PSET [STEP] (*X, Y*) [,*drawing_color*]

Sets a point on the graphic screen at the specified coordinates.

STEP   When used with STEP, (*X, Y*) specify the position relative to the last position addressed on the screen.

(X, Y)   Using PSET without STEP, *(X, Y)* are the absolute coordinates. Y can range from 0 to 199. X can range from 0 to 319 or 0 to 639, depending on the resolution selected.

drawing_color
        Specifies the point color. Values can range from 0 to 3.

PUT   display stored graphic

PUT *(X, Y)*, *array* [, *mode*]

Displays a graphic stored in an array with GET.

(X, Y)   Specifies the upper left point of the graphic in X and Y coordinates. Y can range from 0 to 199. X can range from 0 to 319 or 0 to 619, depending on the resolution.

array   The array that contains the graphic to be output.

mode   Specifies how the stored graphic is to be output:

        PSET   The graphic output is exactly as it was read.

        PRESET   The graphic is inverted, meaning that a point stored as set is displayed as cleared and a point stored as cleared is set on the screen.

        XOR   The graphic is XORed point by point with the area where it is output.

        AND   The graphic is ANDed point by point with the area where it is output.

        OR   The graphic is ORed point by point with the area where it is output.

PUT#   send data from the COM buffer (S)

PUT# *file_num, num_chars*

Writes a specified number of characters from the buffer to the serial interface.

The parameters correspond to those of the GET commands. Again, *num_chars* cannot be larger than the record length specified in OPEN COM.

The data is written into the buffer with the commands PRINT#, WRITE#, and PRINT# USING.

PUT#   write data in a random-access file (S)

PUT# *file_number* [, *rec_num*]

Writes a disk file record from the buffer defined by FIELD.

file_number
> The reference number used when the file was opened.

rec_num
> The record number to be written. If omitted, PUT# writes the record at which the file pointer is currently set. *rec_num* can be a value ranging from 1 to 16,777,215.

PUT# writes as many characters from the buffer as specified by the record length in the OPEN command.

If an incorrect record number is specified, the error message Illegal function call is returned. If the sum of the field lengths in the FIELD command are less than the record length, the data following the buffer in memory is written to the file.

RANDOMIZE   generate random seed (S)
RND   generate random number (F)

```
RANDOMIZE [number]
RND [number]
```

Sets the numerical basis for random numbers and generates a random number.

number   Specifies the limit of the random number to be generated. If RND is used without a parameter, GW-BASIC uses the same sequence for generating random numbers. *number* can be a value between -32768 and +32767.

If you call RANDOMIZE without *number*, you are asked to enter a number for the random number seed:

RANDOM NUMBER SEED (−32768 TO 32767) ?

The starting value and sequence are determined by your input.

READ..DATA   internal data tables (S)

```
READ variable [,variable...]
DATA text | value
```

Defines and reads fixed data values within a program.

variable

Specifies a variable of any type. The data must correspond to the data type of *variable*. Several variables can follow one READ statement.

text | value

Specifies the data assigned to the variables. The data that include commas must correspond to the data types of the variables. Individual data is separated by commas. Strings can be enclosed in quotation marks (""). Numerical values are separated by commas only. Data types can be mixed within a DATA line.

REM   insert comment (S)

REM *text*|' *text*

Inserts text into a program containing a comment.

text   Any string of characters. BASIC ignores all of the text
           following REM until the next program line.

REM allows you to place comments that describe the purpose of
different parts of a program.

RENUM   renumber lines (C)

RENUM [*new_starting_line*|.][,*from_line*|.]
[,*increment*]

Renumbers the lines of the current program.

new_starting_line
           Specifies the new starting line number of the range.

from_line
           Specifies the line number at which renumbering will start. If
           omitted, BASIC will start renumbering at the first line of
           the program.

increment
           Specifies the interval between successive line numbers. The
           default value is 10.

.   The period can be used in place of the current line.

RENUM replaces the line numbers of the current program. The first
program line to be replaced is *from_line*. It is replaced by
new_starting_line. The second line number is replaced by
new_starting_line + *increment* etc.

RENUM also renumbers the branch destinations of ON ERROR GOTO,
GOTO, GOSUB, etc., but not conditional execution with IF...THEN
involving the system variable ERL. ERL stores the number of the line

that the last error occurred. The following line is not changed by RENUM:

```
20 IF 1230=ERL THEN Statement
```

The following test is handled correctly by RENUM:

```
20 IF ERL=1230 THEN Statement
```

RESTORE   set DATA pointer (S)

RESTORE *line_number*

Set the DATA pointer for READing a specified line of data.

line_number
> Specifies the line number that contains the first DATA item to be read. If no line number is specified, the pointer is set to the first DATA line in the program.

RESUME   continue program after error (S)

RESUME [*line_num*|NEXT|0]

Continues program execution after handling an error using an ON ERROR GOTO statment.

line_num
> Specifies the line number at which the program execution is to continue.

NEXT
> If you specify NEXT, the program continues at the statement immediately following the statement that caused the error.

0
> The statement that caused the error is executed again. This is the same as specifying RESUME without parameters.

RIGHT$ dissect strings (F)

X$ = RIGHT$ (*string, num_chars*)

Returns the rightmost *num_chars* of a string.

string Specifies the string to be dissected. Array elements can be specified.

num_chars

        The number of characters, starting at the rightmost end of the string, that are to be returned.

RUN execute current program (C)

RUN [*starting_line*| .]

Executes the current program.

starting_line

        Specifies the line number at which execution begins. If omitted, the first line of the program is assumed.

.   The current line number can be abbreviated to a period.

RUN initializes all numeric variables to zero, string variables to a null string and array variables to undefined. RUN then executes the program in memory at *starting_line*. If *starting_line* is not specified, execution begins at the first program line.

RUN load and execute a program (C)

RUN *filespec*[,R]

Loads and executes a program from disk.

filespec

        Specifies the name of the BASIC program to be loaded from disk. *filespec* can specify a drive, path, and extension. *filespec* must be entered between quotation marks ("").

If the drive is omitted, the current drive is the default. If the path is omitted, the current directory is the default. If the extension is omitted, a .BAS extension is assumed.

,R   Indicates that any open files are to remain open. If omitted, any open files are closed before RUN executes the program.

RUN initializes all numeric variables to zero, string variables to a null string and array variables to undefined. RUN then loads the program into memory and executes the program.

SAVE   save a program (C)

SAVE *filespec* [,A|,P]

Writes the current program in memory to disk.

filespec
            Specifies the name of the BASIC program being saved. *filespec* can specify a drive, a path, and an extension. *filespec* must be entered between quotation marks ("").

            If the drive is omitted, the current drive is the default. If the path is omitted, the current directory is the default. If the extension is omitted, an extension of .BAS is assumed.

A   Saves the current program to disk in ASCII format. If omitted, the program is written in compressed format.

P   Saves the current program to disk in protected format. After a program is saved in protected format, it cannot be listed or edited.

SAVE writes a copy of the current program in memory to a disk file named *filespec*. If *filespec* already exists, it is overwritten.

SCREEN   select screen page (S)

SCREEN [*mode*] [,*color*] [,*output_page*]
[,*display_page*]

Set the text mode and text color, select the output and display pages.

mode   Sets the operating mode of the screen:

0	Text mode	80x25 or 40x25
1	Graphics mode	320x200 pixels
2	Graphics mode	640x200 pixels
x	Graphics mode	640x400 pixels
	↑(Version 2 only)	↑(mono cards only)

color   For 1, the color set with COLOR remains the same. For 0, the text color is set to the value 7 (light grey) and the background to 0 (black).

output_page
          Specifies the page to which the text will be output. An 80x25 screen has four pages (0 to 3) available, and a 40x25 screen has eight pages.

display_page
          Specifies which page will be displayed. An 80x25 screen has four pages (0 to 3) available, and a 40x25 screen has eight pages.

Your choice of display and output pages depends on whether your graphics card supports this mode. As a general rule, color graphics cards do support it. Refer to your hardware documentation to see if your monochrome graphics card supports this mode.

SCREEN   determine character and attribute (F)

X=SCREEN(*line,column*[,0|1])

Returns the ASCII code or attribute of a character displayed on the screen.

line, column
          The coordinates of the character on the screen. Depending on the WIDTH, the column can have a value between 1 and 80, or 1 and 40.

0|1   If you specify 0 here, SCREEN will return the ASCII code of the character in question. For 1, the display attribute of the character is returned.

SCREEN   select graphic mode (F)

SCREEN[*mode*] [,*color*] [,*output_page*]
[,*display_page*]

Switches to the graphic mode and sets the resolution.

mode   Sets the graphics mode:

0	text mode
1	medium-resolution graphic mode
2	high-resolution graphic mode
100	special mode for other cards

color   If *color* = 1 when SCREEN is called, the current color is
retained. If *color* = 0, the default colors (black background
and white foreground color) are set for the given mode.

output_page,*display_page*
There is only one page in the graphics mode, so the
parameters here are ignored.

SHELL   execute other MS-DOS programs (C)

SHELL *filespec*

Calls a .COM, .EXE, or .BAT program from GW-BASIC.

filespec
Specifies the program to be executed. The specification must
be enclosed in quotation marks and is the same as it is
entered at the MS-DOS command level. It is possible to use
a string variable, but no string operations are allowed
following SHELL.

COMMAND.COM must be on the disk in the current drive because MS-
DOS requires this for all SHELL actions. If not, GW-BASIC returns
the message File not found and continues with the program. On
the other hand, GW-BASIC does not display an error message if it
cannot find the program to be executed. After executing the SHELL
command, GW-BASIC continues the program at the command
following the SHELL command. You can also call COMMAND.COM

through SHELL and work on the MS-DOS command level. After EXIT you are returned to GW-BASIC. If *filespec* is omitted, COMMAND.COM is automatically loaded.

SOUND   output variable tone (S)

SOUND *frequency, duration*

Outputs a tone of variable frequency and duration.

frequency
> The pitch of the tone to be created. The value for *frequency* can range from 37 to 32767.

duration
> Length of the resulting tone measured in clock ticks (18.2 per second). Possible values range from 0 to 65535.

SPACE$ return spaces (F)

X$ = SPACE$ (*number*)

Returns a string consisting of a specified number of spaces.

number   Specifies the number of spaces to be returned.

STOP   stop running program (S)

STOP

Halts the execution of the program.

The following message is displayed on the screen:

Break in *line_number*

Line_number is the program line containing the STOP command. Program execution can be continued using the CONT command.

STR$ number→string (F)

STR$ (*expression*)

Converts a numerical value to a string.

expression
> Can be a constant, the result of a calculation, a numerical variable, or the result of a numerical function.

STRING$ fill string with characters (F)

X$ = STRING$ (*number, char*)

Returns a string consisting of a specified number of a single repeated character.

number Specifies the number of characters to be repeated.

char   The character to be repeated. *char* can be a constant, variable, or the result of a string function.

SWAP   exchange variable contents (S)

SWAP *variable_1, variable_2*

Exchanges the contents of two variables of the same data type.

variable_1, variable_2
> Both variables must be of the same type. Array elements can be exchanged.

SYSTEM   exits GW-BASIC (C)

SYSTEM

Exits the BASIC interpreter and returns to the MS-DOS command level. The contents of the current program in memory are <u>not</u> automatically SAVEd.

TIME$
system time (F,S)

X$ = TIME$ or TIME$ = X$

Returns or sets the MS-DOS system time.

TIME$ has the following format:

> 10 TIME$ = "hrs:min:sec"
> (or)
> 10 TIME$ = "hrs:min:sec:hsec"

TIMER
access system clock (F)

X = TIMER

This function returns the time elapsed since 0:00 hours (midnight) in the format *seconds:hundredths*.

Some versions return the elapsed time since the PC was turned on, independent of the set time.

TRON | TROFF
activate/deactivate trace (C)

TRON | TROFF

Turns the trace facility on or off. If the trace facility is active (TRON), BASIC displays the number of the program line as it is executed. This allows you to trace the program execution.

TROFF deactivates the trace facility.

VAL

string→number (F)

`VAL(string_expression)`

Converts a string with numerical contents to a numerical value.

`string_expression`
> Can be a string constant, variable, or the result of a string operation.

The contents of the string are representable as a numerical value. If VAL finds a character within the string that cannot be represented as a value, the conversion is terminated without an error message, and the numbers converted up to that point are returned.

VARPTR

access to variable memory (F)

`X=VARPTR(variable)` or `X=VARPTR(# file_num)`

Determines the offset of a variable in the data segment (DS).

`variable`
> Any variable types supported by GW-BASIC can be used here, including arrays. The variable must be assigned a value before this function is called.

`file_num`
> The second variant of the VARPTR function returns the address of the first byte of the FCB (File Control Block) for sequential files. For random-access files it returns the address of the first byte of the FIELD buffer. file_num corresponds to the file number used when the file was opened.

The DEF SEG command has no effect on this function.

Note: Variable addresses are changed by garbage collection. The result of the function cannot be used throughout the entire program—the address should be recalculated every time it is needed.

VARPTR$ access to variable storage (F)

X$=VARPTR$(*variable*)

Determines the variable type and offset address of a variable in the data segment (DS). The first byte of the string returned contains information about the type of variable:

> CHR$(2) = integer
>
> CHR$(3) = string
>
> CHR$(4) = single-precision
>
> CHR$(8) = double-precision

The second and third bytes contain the address of the first byte of the variable, in the format low byte/high byte:

> address = low_byte + 256*high_byte

variable
> Any of the variable types supported by GW-BASIC can be used here, including arrays. The variable must be assigned a value before this function is called.

The VARPTR$ function cannot be used on FCBs or random-access buffers! The DEF SEG command has no effect on VARPTR$.

Note: Garbage collection changes the addresses of variables.

VIEW   define window for graphics (S)

VIEW [SCREEN] (*X1,Y1*)-(*X2,Y2*)[,*bkgd_color*]
[,*border_color*]

Specifies dimensions and color of a window used to display graphics.

(*X1,Y1*)-(*X2,Y2*)
> Specifies the lower left and upper right coordinates of the screen, and defines the window size.

bkgd_color
>The background color of the window. Values can range from 0 to 3.

border_color
>Specifies the border color outlining the window. This outline is drawn only if space is available. If the window is placed at any corner, only the lines visible within the screen are drawn.

After VIEW, all the coordinates used in graphic commands are applied relative to the WINDOW border. For example, coordinates of 10,10 are read as 10 pixels down and to the right of the border drawn by the window. If absolute coordinates are desired, use VIEW with the SCREEN option. This gives the upper right corner of the window the coordinates 0,0.

VIEW PRINT   set text window (S)

VIEW PRINT [*from_line*] [TO] [*to_line*]

Defines a text window.

from_line, to_line
>Only ranges composed of complete lines can be defined as text windows. Enter the first line of the range as *from_line*, and the last line of the range as *to_line*.

WAIT   wait for port to change (S)

WAIT *port, mask_1, mask_2*

Halt program execution until a given bit pattern is read from a port. The value read from the port is combined with the masks in the following manner:

>*value_read* XOR *mask_1* AND *mask_2*

If the result is zero, the port is read until the result is not equal to zero. The bit pattern calculated is then available for processing, and execution of the program will continue.

port   A value between 0 and 65535.

mask_1,mask_2
           The values for use in the formula.

Note: WAIT can create an infinite loop that cannot be broken with
            Ctrl+C or Ctrl+Break.

WHILE..WEND   program loop (S)

WHILE *condition statement*
WEND

Execute statements as long as a condition is true.

condition
           A logical expression (data comparison, etc.) supported by
           GW-BASIC.

statement
           All of the commands and functions supported by GW-
           BASIC can be used here. *statement* can extend over
           multiple program lines.

Note that the loop is executed as long as the condition is true. An
infinite loop results if the condition is never true due to an error or
incorrect data.

Multiple conditions joined with AND or OR can be specified, one of
which can provide a "forced end" to the loop. The loop can be exited at
any time with GOTO. However, this can result in the error message
Out of memory.

WIDTH   set line length for COM (S)

WIDTH "COM *channel*:",*num_chars*

Sets the number of characters sent before a CR (&H0D) is sent.

channels
           Specifies the serial interface being addressed. Normally only

one interface is installed, so this value defaults to 1. Values can range from 1 to 4.

num_chars

> The number of characters to be sent before a CR (&H0D) is sent.

WIDTH   set number of screen characters/line (S)

WIDTH *num_chars*

Specifies the number of characters per line for screen output.

num_chars

> Specifies either 40 or 80 characters per line. Enter either 40 or 80.

WIDTH automatically clears the entire screen before setting the width. Only one mode is possible at a time.

WIDTH   set characters per printer line (S)

WIDTH LPRINT *num_chars* WIDTH "LPT
printer_num; ", *num_chars*

Sets the number of characters per line to be printed.

num_chars

> Specifies the number of characters sent to the printer before a CR/LF sequence is sent. The number of characters can range from 0 to 255.

printer_num

> The number of the interface connected to the printer. Can be 1, 2, or 3.

The default value for printer output is 80 characters per line in some versions of GW-BASIC.

WINDOW   change coordinates (S)

`WINDOW[ [SCREEN] (X1,Y1)-(X2,Y2)`

Defines the coordinate system for the current window. This is normally in world coordinates. World coordinates have 0,0 as the center of the screen. The *X* values above the center are positive and below the center are negative: The *Y* values to the right of the center are positive, and to the left of the center are negative.

`(X1,Y1)-(X2,Y2)`

These parameters apply to the lower left and upper right corner of the window and specify the new border values. The assignment can be changed with the `SCREEN` option. `(X1,Y1)` then refer to the upper left corner and `(X2,Y2)` refer to the lower right corner of the window.

WRITE   output to the screen (S)

`WRITE [SPC(number)] [expression...] [,]`

Output data to the screen.

`SPC(number)`

Prints the number of spaces specified by `number` in the current output line.

`expression`

The data to be printed. `expression` can be constants, variables, results of calculations, or results of functions. The data can be of mixed types. One of the following separators is used to separate the data.

`,`

A comma moves GW-BASIC to the next tab (every 8 characters) before printing the next data item.

The `WRITE` command is similar to the `PRINT` command, with the following differences:

• All expressions must be enclosed in quotation marks and separated by commas.

- Formatting with USING is not possible.

- The TAB function cannot be used with WRITE.

- The semicolon (;) cannot be used to suppress the linefeed.

WRITE#   write data to a file (S)

```
WRITE#file_number[SPC(number)]
[expression...] [,]
```

Outputs data to a file.

file_number
> The reference number used in the OPEN command.

SPC(*number*)
> Writes the specified number of spaces to the file.

expression
> The data to be written. These can be constants, variables, results of calculations or functions. The data can be of any type. If more than one type is specified, the following separator is used:

,   Outputs a tab, writing eight blank spaces to the file before the next data item is written.

The WRITE# statement corresponds to the PRINT# command, with the following exceptions:

- All expressions are enclosed in quotation marks and separated by commas.

- Formatting with USING is not possible.

- WRITE# cannot be used with TAB.

- The semicolon (;) cannot be used to suppress a linefeed.

Math Functions

Addition

Addition is indicated with the plus sign (+):

> RESULT = *expression_1* + *expression_2*

Subtraction

Subtraction is indicated with the minus sign (−):

> RESULT = *expression_1* − *expression_2*

Multiplication

Multiplication is indicated with the asterisk (*):

> RESULT = *expression_1* * *expression_2*

Division

Division is indicated with the slash (/):

> RESULT = *expression_1* / *expression_2*

A backslash (\) is used for integer division:

> RESULT = *expression_1* \ *expression_2*

Exponentiation

Exponentiation is indicated with the caret (^):

> RESULT = *expression_1* ^ *expression_2*

Extended math functions

X = ABS (*expression*)

Returns the absolute value of *expression*. The degree of precision corresponds to the type declaration for the variables used in the expression.

X = Y AND Z

When two values are combined with AND, the bits are evaluated so that the resulting bit is reset if the corresponding bit in either Y or Z is reset, or if a bit is set if the corresponding bits in <u>both</u> Y and Z are set. AND can be used to clear specific bits.

X = ATN(*expression*)

The angle of the arctangent is calculated and returned (in radians) in single-precision. If GW-BASIC was called with the [/D] parameter, the calculation is performed in double-precision.

X = COS(*expression*)

The cosine of *expression* is calculated and returned in radians in single-precision. If GW-BASIC was called with the [/D] parameter, the calculation is performed in double-precision.

X = Y EQV Z

When two values are combined with EQV, the bits are evaluated so that the resulting bit is set if the corresponding bits in Y and Z are the same. Otherwise the resulting bit is reset.

X = EXP(*expression*)

The constant e is raised to the power of *expression* and the value returned in single-precision. If GW-BASIC was called with the [/D] parameter, the calculation is performed in double-precision.

X = FIX(*expression*)

Returns the integer portion of *expression*. Any fraction following the decimal point is truncated. The result has the same precision as the variables in *expression*. Both positive and negative values are allowed.

X = Y IMP Z

When combining two values with IMP, the bits are evaluated so that if the corresponding bits in Y and Z are the same, the resulting bit is set. If a bit is set in Y and reset in Z, the resulting bit is reset. If a bit is reset in Y and set in Z, the resulting bit is set.

X = INT (*expression*)

Returns the greatest-integer function value for *expression*. The result corresponds to the variables in the expression. Both positive and negative variables are allowed.

X = LOG (*expression*)

Returns the natural logarithm of the expression in single-precision. If GW-BASIC was called with the [/D] parameter, the calculation is performed in double-precision. *Expression* must be greater than zero.

X = *expression_1* MOD *expression_2*

Returns the remainder of an integer division (modulo).

X = NOT Y

NOT manipulates the bits so each bit set in Y is reset, and each bit reset in Y is set (inverted).

X = Y OR Z

When two values are combined with OR, the bits are evaluated so that the resulting bit is set if the corresponding bits in either Y or Z are set. OR can be used to set specific bits.

X = SGN (*expression*)

Returns the sign of *expression*. SGN returns +1 if the sign is positive, -1 if it is negative, and 0 if the expression is equal to zero.

X = SIN (*expression*)

The sine of *expression* in radians is calculated and returned (in radians) in single-precision. If GW-BASIC was called with the [/D] parameter, the calculation is performed in double-precision.

X = SQR (*expression*)

Returns the square root of *expression* in single-precision. If GW-BASIC was called with the [/D] parameter, the calculation is performed in double-precision. The expression must be greater than or equal to zero.

X = TAN (*expression*)

The tangent of *expression* in radians is calculated and returned in single-precision. If GW-BASIC was called with the [/D] parameter, the calculation is performed in double-precision.

X = Y XOR Z

When two values are combined with XOR, the bits are evaluated so that the resulting bit is reset if the corresponding bits in <u>both</u> Y and Z are equal. Otherwise the resulting bit is set.

Appendix B – GW BASIC Keywords

ABS	ENVIRON$	LOC
AND	EOF	LOCATE
ASC	EQV	LOF
ATN	ERASE	LOG
AUTO	ERDEV	LPOS
BEEP	ERDEV$	LPRINT
BLOAD	ERL	LSET
BSAVE	ERR	MERGE
CALL	ERROR	MID$
CALLS	EXP	MKDIR
CDBL	FIELD	MKD$
CHAIN	FILES	MKI$
CHDIR	FIX	MKS$
CHR$	FN	MOD
CINT	FOR	NAME
CIRCLE	FRE	NEW
CLEAR	GET	NEXT
CLOSE	GOSUB	NOT
CLS	GOTO	OCT$
COLOR	HEX$	OFF
COMMON	IF	ON
CONT	IMP	OPEN
COS	INKEY$	OPTION
CSNG	INP	OR
CSRLIN	INPUT	OUT
CVD	INPUT#	PAINT
CVI	INPUT$	PEEK
CVS	INSTR	PLAY
DATA	INT	PMAP
DATE$	IOCTL	POINT
DEF	IOCTL$	POKE
DEFDBL	KEY	POS
DEFINT	KILL	PRESET
DEF'SNG	LCOPY	PRINT
DEFSTR	LEFT$	PRINT#
DELETE	LEN	PSET
DIM	LET	PUT
DRAW	LINE	PUT#
EDIT	LIST	RANDOMIZE
ELSE	LLIST	READ
ENVIRON	LOAD	REM

RENUM	SPC	TRON
RESTORE	SQR	USING
RESUME	STEP	USR
RETURN	STICK	VAL
RIGHT$	STOP	VARPTR
RMDIR	STR$	VARPTR$
RND	STRING$	VIEW
RSET	SWAP	VIEW
RUN	SYSTEM	WAIT
SAVE	TAB	WEND
SCREEN	TAN	WHILE
SGN	THEN	WIDTH
SHELL	TIME$	WINDOW
SIN	TIMER	WRITE
SOUND	TO	WRITE#
SPACE$	TROFF	XOR

Appendix C – Exercise Solutions

Solutions to Exercises in Section 2.2.1

1.   a) legal
   b) legal
   c) AUTO is illegal (GW-BASIC keyword)
   d) legal
   e) IF is illegal; see c)
   f) DATE$ is illegal (system variable)
   g) 4NAME% is illegal (starts with a digit)
   h) 255 is illegal; see g)
   i) legal

2.
```
10 INPUT A,B,C,D
20 PRINT A;B
30 PRINT C;D
40 END
```

3.
```
10 REM ENTER HEIGHT H AND
20 REM AND BASE B IN INCHES
30 INPUT "ENTER H,B";H,B
40 A=B/2*H
50 PRINT "THE AREA IS";A;"SQUARE INCHES"
60 END
```

4.
```
10 INPUT "ENTER HEIGHT IN CM";CM
20 REM CALCULATE IDEAL WEIGHT
30 IW=CM-100
40 REM CALCULATE 10 PERCENT
50 PR=IW/100*10
60 IW=IW-PR
70 PRINT "YOUR IDEAL WEIGHT IS";IW;"KG"
80 END
```

This problem could also be solved with a shorter program. Lines 30, 50, and 60 could be gathered into one line, as the following example shows:

```
30 IW=(CM-100)-(CM-100)/100*10
```

This line is harder to read since you can't tell right away what calculation is being performed. Some readers will no doubt point out that this style of programming helps to save memory space. That's right, of course—but as a programmer, you must make some compromise between readability and length of the program. If you don't have to worry about memory space, you should write your program so that it can be understood easily. This will also help you understand your own programs later if you have to make changes.

5.
```
10 INPUT "HEIGHT, LENGTH, DEPTH IN CM";H,L,D
20 REM CALCULATE VOLUME
30 V=H*L*D
40 REM CALCULATE LITERS
50 V=V/1000
60 PRINT "AQUARIUM CONTAINS";V;"LITERS"
70 END
```

In this program the variables for the height, length, and depth (H, L, and D) are first assigned values in cm. Then in line 30 the volume is calculated in cubic cemtimeters. In line 50 the calculated volume is divided by 1000 and we have the volume of our aquarium in liters.

6.
```
10 INPUT A,B,C,D
20 PRINT"A";A
30 PRINT"B";B
40 PRINT"C";C
50 PRINT"D";D
60 END
```

If these problems gave you any trouble, read through the appropriate sections again. Then you should be able to understand and solve them.

Solutions to Exercises in Section 2.3.4

1.
```
10 REM CLEAR THE SCREEN
20 CLS
30 REM CREATE RANDOM NUMBERS
40 R1=INT(6*RND(1))+1
50 R2=INT(6*RND(1))+1
60 REM OUTPUT RESULT
70 PRINT "ROLL 1:";R1,"ROLL 2:";R2
80 END
```

Your program should look something like this. Obviously, the solutions we present here are only *suggested* solutions. There are many

ways of solving any problem. If you repeat the program with RUN
<RETURN> you will see there is no difference in the numbers printed.
As we mentioned before, RANDOM only produces random numbers
when a random source is used as a seed value. In line 20 the screen is
cleared with the command CLS.

Lines 40 and 50 assign newly-created random numbers to the variables
R1 and R2. If you had problems with the upper and lower bounds, read
the section on random numbers again. Adding the following lines will
make the program much more random:

```
32 PRINT "PRESS A KEY"
34 COUNT=COUNT+1
36 K$=INKEY$:IF K$="" THEN 34
38 RANDOMIZE(COUNT)
```

Line 36 contains some statements which may not be familiar to you.
These will be covered in detail in later sections.

2.
```
10   REM ENTER VALUES OF TRIANGLE SIDES
20   INPUT "ENTER A,B,C IN INCHES";A,B,C
30   REM CALCULATION OF S
40   S=.5*(A+B+C)
50   REM CALCULATE SURFACE AREA
60   F=SQR(S*(S-A)*(S-B)*(S-C))
70   REM OUTPUT AREA
80   PRINT"THE AREA OF THIS TRIANGLE ";
90   PRINT"IS";F;"SQUARE INCHES"
100  END
```

With this program you must note that S must be calculated first
because it is used in the calculation of the area. The conversion of the
formula into BASIC should not have presented any difficulties.
Nevertheless, be sure that you don't use standard mathematical notation
when writing programs. When in doubt, use plenty of parenthesis to
make your formulas clearer.

3.
```
10 INPUT "TYPE A KEY FOLLOWED BY RETURN";A$
20 A=ASC(A$)
30 PRINT"THE ASCII VALUE OF ";A$;" =";A
40 END
```

If you have already tried this program out, you may have tried to enter a
comma or just a <RETURN> to find out the ASCII value of one of
these "characters". But the computer printed an error message. This is

one of the disadvantages of the INPUT command, since it uses the comma to separate variables, for instance. If you press just <RETURN>, *nothing* is assigned to the string variable—that is, this variable is empty. Since the computer naturally cannot determine the ASCII value of nothing, an error message is printed.

4.
```
10 G=9.81
20 INPUT "HOW MANY SECONDS";T
30 S=.5*G*T^2
40 PRINT"THE OBJECT FELL FROM ";
50 PRINT"A DISTANCE OF";S;"METERS"
60 END
```

Line 10 is interesting here. The variable G is assigned the value 9.81 at the start of the program. This procedure is called variable initialization. This means that you assigned certain values to various variables at the start of the program. Its advantage is that only the variable has to be called up in the program and not the entire number, which can be quite long under certain circumstances. This can, in turn, save memory space in large programs with more variables.

5.
```
10 INPUT "HOW MANY GALLONS USED";G
20 INPUT "HOW MANY MILES TRAVELLED";MI
30 V=G/MI*100
40 PRINT"CONSUMPTION PER 100 MI IS";V;"GALLONS"
50 END
```

This program is self-explanatory. If you solved all of these problems to your own satisfaction, you can now go on to the next section. If you are uncertain about anything, go through the appropriate passages again.

Solutions to Exercises in Section 2.5.9

1. a) is correct

2. You get the expression B$ = "DRIPS"

3. You get the expression ROTOR back again.

4. B$=MID$(A$,4,1)+MID$(A$,8,1)+MID$(A$,6,1)+
    MID$(A$,10,1)¶

This is one possible solution.

Solutions to Exercises in section 3.2.1

1.
```
10   REM ENTER ANNUAL INCOME
20   INPUT "ANNUAL INCOME IN $";IC
30   IF IC > 50000 THEN 70
40   REM CALCULATE 33 PERCENT
50   TX=IC*33/100
60   GOTO 90
70   REM CALCULATE 51 PERCENT
80   TX=IC*51/100
90   PRINT"TAX TO BE PAID:";
100  PRINT" $";TX
110  END
```

In line 20 the annual income is read. The value entered is assigned to the variable IC. In line 30 the income is checked to see if it is over $50,000. If this is not the case, 33 percent of the income is calculated and printed. If the income is greater than $50,000, 51 percent is calculated in line 80 and displayed.

2.   This problem could be solved in at least two ways. First the solution which uses the IF...THEN structure:

```
10 REM SUM 1 TO 100
20 A=A+1
30 S=S+A
40 IF A < 100 THEN 20
50 PRINT"SUM OF 1 TO 100 =";S
60 END
```

In line 20 we have our counter for the individual summands from 1 to 100. Line 30 calculates the sum of the values of A so far, 1+2+3+4 and so on. Line 40 performs the comparison to see if all values have been summed. The final summation of the numbers from 1 to 100 is finally printed in line 50.

The second solution results from the fact that we are dealing with an *arithmetic* series here—that is, the difference between successive terms is a constant. The sum can be calculated from the formula,

Sn=n/2 (A1+An)

n is the number of terms in the series, A1 the first term, and An is the last term. According to this, the second solution offers a solution in general. The program could look something like this:

```
10 INPUT "NUMBER OF TERMS";N
20 INPUT "FIRST TERM";A1
30 INPUT "LAST TERM";AN
40 REM CALCULATION
50 SN=N/2*(A1+AN)
60 REM OUTPUT
70 PRINT"THE SUM IS";SN
80 END
```

3.
```
10 REM 6 OUT OF 49
20 Z=Z+1
30 L=INT(49*RND(1))+1
40 IF Z > 6 THEN END
50 PRINT L;
60 GOTO 20
```

In this program the END command is not placed at the end of the program. There is no need to place the END command in the last line of the program. The program should otherwise be easily understood.

4. For this problem you must note that only the last values of A and Z are printed. The PRINT command stands outside the actual loop. Your solution therefore must be:

52   9

If you got an 8 as the second value, remember that the program jumps to line 20 as long as Z is less than 9. Not until Z equals 9 is the condition no longer fulfilled and the output in line 40 is performed.

5.
```
10 REM ENTER STRING AND SUBSTRING
20 INPUT"ENTER STRING";A$
30 INPUT"ENTER SUBSTRING";B$
40 I=I+1
50 C$=MID$(A$,I,LEN(B$))
60 IF C$=B$ THEN PRINT"FOUND":END
70 IF I > LEN(A$) THEN PRINT"NOT FOUND":END
80 GOTO 40
```

This problem was rather difficult. Your program need not match the one above to the last detail. But it should contain something similar to the formation of the comparison string in line 50, since this is the real problem. The statement of the problem makes reference to an arbitrary string—that is, independent of which and how many characters are searched for. The MID$ function must be informed as to the length of the string to be found via the LEN function. The counter in line 40 takes care of always moving the position of C$ one place to the right in A$. The comparison to see if the string to be found (B$) matches the current string in C$ takes place in line 60. Line 70 asks if the entire length of A$ has already been searched and B$ was not found. The following example will help clarify the function of the program:

String A$ = "INFORMATION", this is to be searched for the string B$ = "FORMAT".

Number of characters in B$=6, so the following substrings are generated:

1. INFORM

2. NFORMA

3. FORMAT

String 3 is the string we are looking for.

That was a tough nut to crack. Make sure that you have understood all the details of this program. If you are still unsure, work through the program step-by-step once.

Solutions to Exercises in Section 3.3.2

1.
```
10 REM HARMONIC SERIES
20 CLS
30 PRINT"ADD UP TO WHAT SUM?"
40 PRINT
50 PRINT
60 INPUT S
70 Z=1
80 SH=SH+1/Z
90 Z=Z+1
100 IF Z = 50*INT(Z/50) THEN PRINT Z;"ADDITIONS"
110 IF SH < S THEN 80
120 PRINT"AFTER";Z;"TERMS, THE SUM IS";SH
```

In lines 20 to 60 the screen is cleared and then the user is requested to enter the sum to be generated. Line 70 sets the counter to 1 and in line 80 the sum is formed from the individual terms. After this the counter is incremented by one in line 90. Line 100 checks to see if the counter has reached 50 or a multiple of 50. An appropriate output is to be made after every 50 terms. Other multiples can also be tested with this technique. The value 50 need only be replaced by the number to be tested for. If the counter is a multiple of 50, the command after the THEN is executed. Line 110 checks if the entered sum has already been reached. Line 120 outputs the passes required after the sum is reached, as well as the sum itself.

2.
```
10   REM QUADRATIC EQUATION
20   CLS
30   PRINT"ENTER THE COEFFICIENTS A,B,C"
40   PRINT
50   INPUT A,B,C
60   IF A=0 THEN 20 : REM A MUST BE <> 0
70   D=B*B+4*A*C
80   IF D < 0 THEN 140
90   X1=(-B+SQR(D))/(2*A)
100  X2=(-B-SQR(D))/(2*A)
110  PRINT"SOLUTION FOR X1 =";X1
120  PRINT"SOLUTION FOR X2 =";X2
130  GOTO 150
140  PRINT"NO REAL SOLUTIONS!"
150  END
```

The conversion of the problem into a program should not have presented any difficulties. Note the case in which A is zero. According to the formula, a division must be made by 2*A. Since division by zero is not allowed, we must exclude this case from the beginning.

3.   First the screen is cleared and then comes the output ILLEGAL VALUE. The important thing here is that you must recognize that the command directly following the GOTO command was executed.

Solutions to Exercises in Section 4.1.2

```
1.   10  REM READ NAMES
     20  DIM Y$(6)
     30  FOR I=1 TO 6
     40  INPUT "NAME";Y$(I)
     50  NEXT I
     60  REM 1ST ALPHABETICAL NAME
     70  Y$(0)=Y$(1)
     80  FOR I=2 TO 6
     90  IF Y$(0) <= Y$(I) THEN 110
     100 Y$(0) = Y$(I)
     110 NEXT I
     120 PRINT"1ST NAME ";Y$(0)
     130 END
```

The first part of the program should be pretty straightforward, since it was presented previously in some examples. Since you know that a total of 6 names are to be read, a FOR...NEXT loop can be used.

The second part of the program was, admittedly, somewhat trickier. If you solved this problem yourself, you may now pat yourself on the back. We talked about the temporary storage of values in an earlier section. It is precisely this technique which you must use again here. Which string variable you used for this is actually not so important. The array element Y$(0) is ideal for this purpose since it has no other use in the program. So in line 70 the contents of element Y$(1) are stored in Y$(0). In line 80 the FOR...NEXT loop begins with the start value 2. We can skip the value 1 since we don't need to compare the first element with itself. In line 90 the individual names are compared with each other in order. If the name in Y$(0) is "less than" the one currently in Y$(1), a branch is made to line 110 and the loop variable is incremented by 1. If the string in Y$(0) is "greater than" that in Y$(I), then Y$(0) is assigned the name in Y$(I). Once the loop variable has reached the value 6, the desired name is in Y$(0). It is then printed in line 120.

A word about comparing strings: If two strings are compared for greater or less than, each letter of the two strings are compared with each other. The deciding factor is the ASCII values of the individual characters. The string WIND is less than the string WINS because the ASCII value of D=68, and S=83.

2.
```
10 REM READ NUMBERS
20 DIM X(6)
30 FOR I=1 TO 6
40 X(I)=INT(100*RND(1))+50
50 NEXT I
60 REM FIND LARGEST NUMBER
70 X(0)=X(1)
80 FOR I=2 TO 6
90 IF X(0) >= X(I) THEN 110
100 X(0)=X(I)
110 NEXT I
120 PRINT"LARGEST NUMBER ";X(0)
130 END
```

This program has the same structure as the program from problem 1. If you got the solution to problem 1, you then have the solution to problem 2. The difference is only in the type of array (numerical) and the random number generation in line 40. The comparisons for finding the largest number are based on the same principle as in problem 1. In line 90 we test only for greater than/equal to, since we want to find the largest number.

3.
```
10 REM ASSIGNMENT RULE FOR SEQUENCE
20 DIM X(6)
30 FOR I=1 TO 6
40 X(I)=I*I-I
50 NEXT I
60 REM OUTPUT ARRAY
70 FOR I=1 TO 6
80 PRINT X(I)
90 NEXT I
100 END
```

The values in this problem are created by the multiplying the loop variable I with itself and then subtracting I from that total. This solution is intended only to be a suggestion. If you got the same results in a different manner, naturally your solution is right as well.

Appendix D – ASCII Character Set

Dec.	Hex.	Character	Dec.	Hex.	Character	Dec.	Hex.	Character	Dec.	Hex.	Character
0	00		32	20		64	40	@	96	60	`
1	01	☺	33	21	!	65	41	A	97	61	a
2	02	●	34	22	"	66	42	B	98	62	b
3	03	♥	35	23	#	67	43	C	99	63	c
4	04	♦	36	24	$	68	44	D	100	64	d
5	05	♣	37	25	%	69	45	E	101	65	e
6	06	♠	38	26	&	70	46	F	102	66	f
7	07	•	39	27	'	71	47	G	103	67	g
8	08	◙	40	28	(	72	48	H	104	68	h
9	09	○	41	29	)	73	49	I	105	69	i
10	0A	◙	42	2A	*	74	4A	J	106	6A	j
11	0B	♂	43	2B	+	75	4B	K	107	6B	k
12	0C	♀	44	2C	,	76	4C	L	108	6C	l
13	0D	♪	45	2D	–	77	4D	M	109	6D	m
14	0E	♫	46	2E	.	78	4E	N	110	6E	n
15	0F	☼	47	2F	/	79	4F	O	111	6F	o
16	10	►	48	30	0	80	50	P	112	70	p
17	11	◄	49	31	1	81	51	Q	113	71	q
18	12	↕	50	32	2	82	52	R	114	72	r
19	13	‼	51	33	3	83	53	S	115	73	s
20	14	¶	52	34	4	84	54	T	116	74	t
21	15	§	53	35	5	85	55	U	117	75	u
22	16	▬	54	36	6	86	56	V	118	76	v
23	17	↨	55	37	7	87	57	W	119	77	w
24	18	↑	56	38	8	88	58	X	120	78	x
25	19	↓	57	39	9	89	59	Y	121	79	y
26	1A	→	58	3A	:	90	5A	Z	122	7A	z
27	1B	←	59	3B	;	91	5B	[	123	7B	{
28	1C	∟	60	3C	<	92	5C	\	124	7C		
29	1D	↔	61	3D	=	93	5D	]	125	7D	}
30	1E	▲	62	3E	>	94	5E	^	126	7E	~
31	1F	▼	63	3F	?	95	5F	_	127	7F	▨

Dec.	Hex.	Character	Dec.	Hex.	Character	Dec.	Hex.	Character	Dec.	Hex.	Character
128	80	Ç	160	A0	á	192	C0	└	224	E0	α
129	81	ü	161	A1	í	193	C1	┴	225	E1	ß
130	82	é	162	A2	ó	194	C2	┬	226	E2	Γ
131	83	â	163	A3	ú	195	C3	├	227	E3	π
132	84	ä	164	A4	ñ	196	C4	─	228	E4	Σ
133	85	à	165	A5	Ñ	197	C5	┼	229	E5	σ
134	86	å	166	A6	ª	198	C6	╞	230	E6	µ
135	87	ç	167	A7	º	199	C7	╟	231	E7	τ
136	88	ê	168	A8	¿	200	C8	╚	232	E8	Φ
137	89	ë	169	A9	⌐	201	C9	╔	233	E9	Θ
138	8A	è	170	AA	¬	202	CA	╩	234	EA	Ω
139	8B	ï	171	AB	½	203	CB	╦	235	EB	δ
140	8C	î	172	AC	¼	204	CC	╠	236	EC	∞
141	8D	ì	173	AD	¡	205	CD	=	237	ED	φ
142	8E	Ä	174	AE	«	206	CE	╬	238	EE	ε
143	8F	Å	175	AF	»	207	CF	╧	239	EF	∩
144	90	É	176	B0	░	208	D0	╨	240	F0	≡
145	91	æ	177	B1	▒	209	D1	╤	241	F1	±
146	92	Æ	178	B2	▓	210	D2	╥	242	F2	≥
147	93	ô	179	B3	│	211	D3	╙	243	F3	≤
148	94	ö	180	B4	┤	212	D4	╘	244	F4	⌠
149	95	ò	181	B5	╡	213	D5	╒	245	F5	⌡
150	96	û	182	B6	╢	214	D6	╓	246	F6	÷
151	97	ù	183	B7	╖	215	D7	╫	247	F7	≈
152	98	ÿ	184	B8	╕	216	D8	╪	248	F8	°
153	99	Ö	185	B9	╣	217	D9	┘	249	F9	•
154	9A	Ü	186	BA	║	218	DA	┌	250	FA	·
155	9B	¢	187	BB	╗	219	DB	█	251	FB	√
156	9C	£	188	BC	╝	220	DC	▄	252	FC	η
157	9D	¥	189	BD	╜	221	DD	▌	253	FD	²
158	9E	₧	190	BE	╛	222	DE	▐	254	FE	•
159	9F	ƒ	191	BF	┐	223	DF	▀	255	FF	

Appendix E – Error Messages

GW-BASIC's error numbers and messages are divided into the following groups:

Error 01 to error 30   Program and syntax errors

Error 50 to error 76   File management and peripherals

The following error numbers generate `Unprintable error` messages: 21, 28, 56, 59, 60, 65, and 78 to 255.

The following error numbers are not used and display varying messages, depending on the version of GW-BASIC:

Error 73   usually Advanced Feature

Error 77   usually Deadlock

The following two error messages do not have error numbers:

Can't continue after SHELL
This message is sent to the program or data area if GW-BASIC is destroyed after a SHELL program is executed. The PC will respond with the MS-DOS prompt.

Can't run BASIC as a child from BASIC
This message is produced by some versions if you try to call the interpreter again with SHELL.

01 NEXT without FOR
During program execution a NEXT is discovered that was not preceded by a FOR. This error usually occurs in nested FOR...NEXT loops from which FOR was deleted.

02 Syntax error
The interpreter cannot identify the instruction that it is supposed to execute. You either entered the keyword incorrectly, entered an illegal parameter, forgot special characters like parentheses, commas, or semicolons, or entered too many characters in a program line.

03 RETURN without GOSUB
The interpreter encountered a RETURN without first having executed a GOSUB. This error usually occurs in nested GOSUB/RETURN sequences.

04 Out of data

READ attempted to read more data than was available in DATA statements. Check the DATA lines. Also, RESTORE could have been specified with an incorrect line.

05 Illegal function call

This error has a wide variety of causes:

- The record number for GET#/PUT# for a random access file is 0 or negative.
- USR command without previous DEF USR.
- The value of a mathematical operation was illegal.
- An illegal parameter was passed to a function.
- You tried to index an array with a negative number.

06 Overflow

The result of a calculation is too large. Check the arguments.

07 Out of memory

The program is too large, so there is not enough memory for the variables and stack. Or the instructions could be nested too deeply and/or are too complex, meaning that you have too many FOR/NEXTs, WHILE/WENDs, and/or GOSUB/RETURNs open at one time. Make sure that subroutines are not exited using GOTO, that FOR...NEXT and WHILE...WEND loops are terminated, and the calculations and expressions are as simple as possible. Perform garbage collection regularly with FRE("") when you use several string operations at one time.

08 Undefined line number

You are trying to reference a nonexistent line number in a statement such as GOTO or GOSUB. Check the line number that is being called.

09 Subscript out of range

You attempted to address an array element that is either beyond the dimension set with DIM, or less than the lower index boundary set by OPTION BASE. Check the indices.

10 Duplicate definition

An array was redefined with DIM, or an array being used with default dimensioning was redimensioned with DIM. It is also possible that OPTION BASE was used after arrays were referenced. To redimension an array, it must first be deleted with ERASE. OPTION BASE must be used at the beginning of the program before all DIMs.

11 Division by zero
You attempted to divide a value by 0. Check the value before the division to see if it is zero.

12 Illegal direct
You tried to execute a command in direct mode that can only be allowed in program mode. Use the command within a program only.

13 Type mismatch
The variable types used in a string or mathematical operation do not match. Check the variable types.

14 Out of string space
String memory will overflow if too many string operations and not enough garbage collections are used. Keep string operations to a minimum, and execute garbage collections often with FRE("").

15 String too long
A string longer than 255 characters was created. Check the operation and the contents of the variables used.

16 String formula too complex
The string operation you tried to perform is too complex for the interpreter. Divide the operation into several smaller operations.

17 Can't continue
You either used a CONT without a previous STOP, or you changed the program or variable contents after a STOP.

18 Undefined user function
A function was called in the program with FN or USR that has not been defined with DEF FN or DEF USR.

19 No RESUME
After an ON ERROR GOTO, the interpreter discovered your error-handling routine did not contain a RESUME.

20 RESUME without ERROR
A RESUME was encountered in the program but an error did not occur. Check the routine.

22 Missing operand
An operand within an operation is missing.

23 Line buffer overflow
You entered a line in direct mode that was longer than 255 characters. Shorten the line or write a program to execute the line.

24 Device timeout
The expected answer was not received from a peripheral device within the specified time. See that the device is present and turned on. For COM operations you can specify longer delay times for CS *time*, DS *time* and CD *time*. You can also trap the error with ON ERROR GOTO and IF ERR=24 THEN RESUME. This generates an infinite loop at worst.

25 Device fault
The addressed device does not exist. Check the call.

26 FOR without NEXT
There is no NEXT for the FOR to be executed, or loops are not nested correctly.

27 Out of paper
The printer sent an "out of paper" error code.

29 WHILE without WEND
A WHILE occurred in the program without a corresponding WEND.

30 WEND without WHILE
A WEND was encountered without a WHILE having been executed.

50 FIELD overflow
You tried to make the field larger than the record length specified in OPEN. Check the specified variable lengths or the LEN=*rec_len* parameter.

51 Internal error
An error occurred within the interpreter that was the interpreter's fault.

52 Bad file number
You tried to access a file that was not opened with OPEN, or the file number lies outside the range 1 to 15, or the maximum number of files is already open. Check your input or the /F parameter when calling GW-BASIC or the entry in CONFIG.SYS.

53 File not found
The file addressed cannot be found. Check the drive, path, filename, and extension.

54 Bad file mode
You tried to use a file in a way that does not correspond with its mode. In other words, you tried to use PUT# or GET# on a sequential file or to read something from the printer.

55 File already open
You tried to use a file number that is currently in use in another OPEN command. Choose a different file number or close the other file. The same error is printed if you try to KILL an open file or change its name with NAME. In these cases the file must first be closed.

57 Device I/O error
An error occurred during output to the diskette or printer. It is possible that the floppy diskette is not formatted, is write-protected, or cannot be written to for some other reason. If this error occurs with a hard disk, there can be a problem with the disk itself. For a printer, either the printer device is not turned on is not online, or sent an error code that cannot be interpreted. Check the printer device.

58 File already exists
When you change the name of a file with NAME, you gave the specification of an existing file as *new_filespec*. Choose a different name.

61 Disk full
Your disk is full. Insert a new disk or clean up disk space.

62 Input past end
You tried to read past the end of a sequential file. Use EOF to check for the end of the file.

63 Bad record number
The specified record number is either 0, negative, or larger than the maximum record number (16,777,215).

64 Bad file name
The filename used has illegal characters or has too many characters. See the MS-DOS manual for valid characters, or shorten the name.

66   Direct statement in file

A statement without a line number was discovered while loading a file. The loading process is terminated. Check the program and insert line numbers as needed.

67   Too many files

There is not enough room in the directory on the disk to store the entry for the file. Use a different diskette or subdirectory.

68   Device unavailable

An attempt was made to access a nonexistent device with OPEN.

69   Communication buffer overflow

The receive buffer for the COM interface has exceeded it capacity. Either set a larger buffer with /C: *buffer* when calling GW-BASIC, select a lower baud rate if the data cannot be processed fast enough, or use ON ERROR GOTO.

70   Disk write protected

It was found during file output that the diskette is write-protected. Remove the write-protect tab, or use another diskette.

72   Disk media error

The disk controller has discovered irregularities during data transfer. There can be several reasons for this:

- There is something physically wrong with the diskette.
- The read/write head cannot be positioned correctly.
- The diskette contains defective sectors.
- The read/write head is dirty.

Check the disk with CHKDSK.COM, and copy the files to another disk. If you can't find the reason for the problem, see your dealer to have the drive(s) checked.

74   Rename across disks

You specified different drives in the file specifications for renaming.

75   Path/file access error

The given path/file specification contains an error.

76   Path not found

The path specified for a file access is not correct.

Appendix F – Number Systems & Logical Operators

The computer can distinguish only two conditions in its electronic circuits, namely ON and OFF. These two conditions must be transformed into a number system. The binary system is used for this. In the binary system, numbers are represented using only the digits 0 and 1. The 1 stands for the condition ON and the 0 for the condition OFF. To explain the binary system we will first start with the decimal system.

A decimal number can be converted into a number in any arbitrary number system. We can also write the decimal number 5678 like this:

$$5678 = 5*1000 + 6*100 + 7*10 + 8*1$$

(or)

$$5678 = 5*10^3 + 6*10^2 + 7*10^1 + 8*10^0$$

In mathematics, a number raised to the power of zero is always 1. In the decimal system the numbers can be represented as a sum of individual products of base 10. Each digit is assigned a specific power of ten.

power—>	10^3	10^2	10^1	10^0
	5	6	7	8

This number is often represented with the subscript 10 to distinguish it from the other number systems in this section.

(5678_{10})

The binary system

The binary system is based on the same principle of individual powers but with the difference that the base is 2. The result is that only the digits 0 and 1 are used. To convert the binary number 1011_2 into a decimal number, we proceed as follows:

The places of the individual digits, as in the decimal system, correspond to individual powers, in this case the powers of two. If we now want to convert the binary number, we write each digit under its corresponding power of 2. The whole thing is then simply added together and we have our decimal number.

$$2^3 \quad 2^2 \quad 2^1 \quad 2^0$$

$$1 \quad\quad 0 \quad\quad 1 \quad\quad 1$$

The result is the following sum of products:

$$1*2^3 + 0*2^2 + 1*2^1 + 1*2^0 = 11$$

(or)

$$1*8 + 0*4 + 1*2 + 1*1 = 11$$

The result is the decimal number 11. To convert a decimal number into a binary number, we proceed as follows:

Say we want to convert the decimal number 167 into a binary number. First determine the highest power of 2 in this number. In our case it's:

$$2^7 = 128$$

This value is subtracted from the number to be converted. The same thing is done for the remainder of 39. The highest power of 2 here is:

$$2^5 = 32$$

The highest power of 2 is then:

$$2^2 = 4 \text{ rem } 3 \text{ etc.}$$

Once we have found all of the powers of 2 in the number, write a 1 under the powers of 2 which are in the number. A zero is written under all other powers of 2. This then looks like this:

2^7	2^6	2^5	2^4	2^3	2^2	2^1	2^0
1	0	1	0	0	1	1	1

If we then form the sum of the products of the powers of 2 under which a 1 stands, we get our decimal number back, namely 167.

Bit and byte

Above we used a decimal number less than 256. It required 8 digits in the binary system, or 8 powers of base 2. The smallest unit of information which a computer processes is called a *bit* (*bi*nary dig*it*). A bit can have two conditions or values:

A set bit has a value of 1. A cleared bit has a value of 0.

All eight bits together make up one byte.

A large number composed of only zeros and ones is difficult for us to read. For this reason, a number system that is easier for us to read is usually used when working with computers.

The hexadecimal system

In the hexadecimal system the base is the number 16. For this you have 16 (including zero) different "digits." In order to be able to distinguish the digits which are to represent values greater than 9, the letters A-F are used. The following sequence of decimal numbers:

0 1 2 3 4 5 6 7 8 9 10 11 12 13 14 15 16 17 18 etc.

becomes the following in hexadecimal notation:

0 1 2 3 4 5 6 7 8 9 A   B   C   D   E   F   10 11 12 etc.

We will practice working with this number system using examples. We will first convert hexadecimal numbers into decimal numbers. The index 16 is used to designate the hexadecimal numbers.

$$2 E 0 C_{16}$$

$$= 2*16^3 + 14*16^2 + 0*16^1 + 12*16^0$$

$$= 2*4096 + 14*256 + 0*16 + 12*1 = 11788_{10}$$

You can see that here the digits 2E0C are assigned specific powers of 16. Here is another example:

293

$$0 \ A \ B \ C_{16}$$

$$= 0*16^3 + 10*16^2 + 11*16^1 + 12*16^0$$

$$= 0*4096 + 10*256 + 11*16 + 12*1 = 2748_{10}$$

It is no problem to convert from binary numbers if we make a detour via the hexadecimal numbers. The following examples clarify this.

Examples:

$$0101 \ 1011_2 = 5B_{16} = 5*16^1 + 11*16^0 = 91_{10}$$

$$1100 \ 0011_2 = C3_{16} = 12*16^1 + 3*16^0 = 195_{10}$$

$$1010 \ 1010_2 = AA_{16} = 10*16^1 + 10*16^0 = 170_{10}$$

Notice that a string of eight binary digits (bits) is divided into two halves. Each half is converted into one hexadecimal digit. In the first case the first and third bits were set in the left half. This yields:

$$5_{16}$$

In the right half the first, second, and fourth bits were set, which yields:

$$B_{16}$$

So we get the hexadecimal value of 5B. The two-place hexadecimal number can be easily converted to a decimal number.

These halves of four bits each are also called nybbles or nibbles (both spellings are currently in use).

In conclusion, we'll show you how to convert decimal numbers into hexadecimal numbers. The method uses the same principle as that for converting decimal numbers to binary numbers. Say you want to convert the number 49153 into its hexadecimal equivalent. First find out the largest power of 16 contained in the number. In this case it is:

$$16^3 \ \text{or} \ 4096$$

The number 49153 is then divided by 16^3. This results in:

12 with a remainder of 1

Now we have almost reached our goal. The values of 16^2 and 16^1 are not contained in the number. The only thing left is 16^0 which is present once. Here is the notation in the number representation:

$$49153 = 12*16^3 + 0*16^2 + 0*16^1 + 1*16^0$$

12_{10} corresponds to hexadecimal C

0_{10} corresponds to hexadecimal 0

0_{10} corresponds to hexadecimal 0

1_{10} corresponds to hexadecimal 1

Now we have our hexadecimal number:

$$C001_{16} = 49153$$

Here's a partial listing of a conversion table to help you see the relationship between the different number systems:

Decimal	Hexadecimal	Binary
0	00	0000 0000
1	01	0000 0001
2	02	0000 0010
3	03	0000 0011
4	04	0000 0100
5	05	0000 0101
6	06	0000 0110
7	07	0000 0111
8	08	0000 1000
9	09	0000 1000
10	0A	0000 1010
11	0B	0000 1011
12	0C	0000 1100
13	0D	0000 1101
14	0E	0000 1110
15	0F	0000 1111
16	10	0001 0000
17	11	0001 0001

The logical operators

The logical operators (some of which are also called boolean operators after English mathematician George Boole) are encountered in almost every program. Comparisons and bit manipulations are made possible by these operators. GW-BASIC offers you six logical operations:

```
NOT, AND, OR, XOR, EQV, IMP
```

These three operators are sufficient to attain the most complicated logical combinations.

In digital electronics some of these operators are found in various combinations in integrated circuits (such as AND, NAND, OR, NOR, and XOR gates).

As we already know, the computer can distinguish between just two states: ON and OFF. Because of this, the computer has only a two-value predicate logic. It can determine only if a statement is true or false. A statement is something like:

$$2 < 3 \text{ (two is less than three)}$$

This statement is a true statement. The computer does not tell us this decision by outputting "true" or "false," but through a corresponding number. If the statement is true, as in the previous example, the computer outputs a value other than zero.

Enter the following sequence of commands into the computer:

```
PRINT 2<3   (<RETURN>)
```

Output: −1

The value is other than zero, the computer views the statement as true. In most cases, a true statement results in a value of -1. Let's create a false statement:

```
PRINT 3<2
```

Output: 0

The value is equal to zero. The computer indicates that the statement is false. A false statement has the value zero and only the value zero as the result.

The two logical operators combine two values with each other, in which they are compared bit by bit (remember the binary number?). Now we'll discuss the operators individually.

NOT

The operator NOT has the result that a true statement returns a false result and a false statement returns true. The following overview should clarify this.

Operator	Value	Result
NOT	-1	0
	0	-1

Examples:

```
PRINT NOT 0
```

Output: -1

```
PRINT NOT -1
```

Output: 0

AND

The operator AND returns a true result only if both conditions are true.

Operator	Value 1	Value 2	Result
AND	0	0	0
	0	-1	0
	-1	0	0
	-1	-1	-1

Example:

```
PRINT 0 AND 0, 0 AND 1, 1 AND 0, 1 AND 1
```

Output: 0 0 0 1

Another example will clarify the function of AND:

PRINT 23 AND 12

Output: 4

In order to understand this result, we take a look at the bit patterns of the values 12 and 23.

The bit pattern of 23 is:

    00010111

The bit pattern of 12 is:

    00001010

These two bit patterns are then combined with AND:

    00010111

AND 00001010

    00000010   = 4

Notice that only when both bits are true (1) is the result true (1).

OR

The operator OR yields a true result if one or both of the two statements is true.

Operator	Value 1	Value 2	Result
OR	0	0	0
	0	-1	-1
	-1	0	-1
	-1	-1	-1

Example:

PRINT 0 OR 0, 0 OR 1, 1 OR 0, 1 OR 1

Output: 0   1   1   1

Another example should clarify the function of OR.

Example:

PRINT 23 or 12

Output: 31

In order to understand this result, we will take another look at the bit patterns of the values 12 and 23. The bit pattern of 23 is:

00010111

The bit pattern of 12 is:

00001010

These two bit patterns are then combined with OR:

```
    00010111
OR  00001010
    00011111    = 31
```

Just like the mathematical operators, the logical operators also have a priority. NOT has the highest priority, AND the second highest, followed by OR, XOR, EQV, and IMP, in that order. This means that a negation is preformed first, before AND or OR. Naturally, the order can be changed by parenthesizing the logical expressions.

XOR

Exclusive OR is something we generally mean when we use "or" in every-day language. For example, when one friend says to another: "I'll ride by bike or I'll take my car," these two options are exclusive because he can't both ride his bicycle and drive his car. Either he drives the car, in which case he doesn't ride his bike, or he rides his bike and he doesn't drive his car. The result of a XOR function is true if only *one* of the two statements is true, if the two statements have different truth values.

You can check that the XOR does indeed operate in this manner by entering the following line into your computer:

```
PRINT 0 XOR 0, 0 XOR 1, 1 XOR 0, 1 XOR 1

Output:     0      1      1      0
```

The table for the XOR function looks like this:

Operator	Value 1	Value 2	Result
XOR	0	0	0
	0	-1	-1
	-1	0	-1
	-1	-1	0

The XOR function can be created using NOT, AND, and OR:

$$Q = (X \text{ AND NOT } Y) \text{ OR } (\text{NOT } X \text{ AND } Y)$$

Q is the result of the operation and X and Y are the two operators. This is the equivalent of the statement Q = X **XOR** Y.

EQV

The logical operator EQV is the negation of the operator XOR. The table for EQV looks like this:

Operator	Value 1	Value 2	Result
EQV	0	0	-1
	0	-1	0
	-1	0	0
	-1	-1	-1

The function EQV returns a true value if the two statements have the same truth value.

IMP

The logical operator results in a true value in three cases and false in only one, so that the table for this operator looks like this:

Operator	Value 1	Value 2	Result
IMP	0	0	-1
	0	-1	-1
	-1	0	0
	-1	-1	-1

On the following page we've placed all of these logical operators in a table, in their order of precedence.

Index

<stdin	3	CGA (Color Graphics adapter)	174, 191
>stdout	3	CHAIN	187
		channel	235
ABS, or absolute function	40	char	258
Addition	267	CHDIR 1	88, 290
address	3	CHR$	43, 188, 239
AL	198	CINT (Convert to INTeger)	39, 188
Algorithms	7	CIRCLE	178, 189
ALL	187	CLEAR	57, 189
Alt key	59	CLOSE	190, 237, 244
AND	184, 248, 263, 268	CLS	60, 190
APPEND	234	COLOR	190, 192, 255
arc_end	189	Color monitor	191
arc_start	189	Color table	191
array	105, 207	column	243
ASC(X$)	43, 184	COM	229
ASCII codes	18, 149, 283	COMMAND.COM	256
ASCII file	225	COMMON	187, 193
ATN	3	Composite monitor	191
ATN	3, 268	computations.	144
AUTO	54, 184	COMSPEC.	201, 202
		condition	228
background color	191, 192	Conditional program jumps	64
BAS	221	CONFIG.SYS	288
BASIC	8, 251	connector	62
baud_rate	235	CONT	156, 93, 257, 287
BEEP	185	control_string	213
BIN	236, 237	COS	3, 36, 268
BLOAD	196	CPU	198
border color	239	CR	236
branch	81	CR/LF	212, 264
branches	61, 81	CSNG	39, 194
BSAVE	185, 196	CSRLIN	194
bubble sort	153, 154	CTS	236
BX	198	cursor keys	5
		CVD	194
calculated jump commands	81	CVI	194
CALL	101, 186	CVS	194
carriage return	25		
CD	236		
CDBL	39, 186		

DATA	97, 114, 119, 187, 250, 286
Data flowcharts	11
data_space	190
DATE$	195
DEF FN	40, 195, 196, 287
DEF SEG	185, 196
DEF USR	197, 286, 287
DEFDBL	197
DEFINT	197
DEFSNG	197
DEFSTR	197, 199
delay loop	71
DELETE	56, 187, 198
dest_string	226
dev	220
DIM	106, 117, 193, 199, 286
dir	200
direct mode	24
display_page	255, 256
Division	267
Documentation	15
Double-precision real	33
DRAW	199, 175, 200
drawing_color	248
DSR	236
duration	257
DX	198
EDIT	57, 201
editing	54, 57
EGA	174, 191
ELSE	64, 210
END	26, 61, 97, 193
end_value	205
ENVIRON	201
ENVIRON$	202
EOF	185, 202, 227, 236, 289
EQV	268
ERASE	57, 203, 286
ERDEV	203
ERDEV$	203
ERL	91, 203, 251
ERR	91

ERR	91, 204
ERROR	204
error-handling routine	91
EXIT	257
EXP	3, 37, 268
Exponentiation	267
Extended math functions	267
extended character set	172
extension	157
FAC	198
FCB	260, 261
FIELD	225, 260
filenum	237
FILES	205
filespec	157, 187, 205, 220
first_char	225
FIX	39, 268
flags	154
FN	195, 196, 287
FN F(X)	40
FOR	69, 100, 119, 205, 237
foreground	192
FRE	95, 206
frequency	257
GET	150, 207, 208, 248, 249
GOSUB	209, 251
GOTO	61, 81, 206, 209, 233, 251, 263
graphics	171
GRAPHICS.COM	58, 216
HEADER	147
HEX$	42, 209
IF	64, 82, 182, 210, 251
IMP	268
increment	184, 251
index	105
indexed variable	105
individual computation operations	34
INKEY$	94, 145, 210, 230
INP	210

INPUT	21, 118, 145, 211, 212, 218, 233, 237,	MID$	48, 225, 226
		MKD$	226
input routines	148	MKDIR	188
INPUT$	94, 208, 212	MKI$	226
INSTR	212, 213	MKS$	226
INT	38, 269	ML(modelegato)	240
Integer	33	MN(modenormal)	240
IOCTL	213	MOD	269
IOCTL$	213	mode	233
		Monochrome monitor	191
KEY	214, 230	MS(modestaccato)	240
KEY	ON 214	Multi-dimensional arrays	117
KILL	159, 215	Multiplication	267
LCOPY	216	NAME	159, 227, 289
LEFT$	47, 151, 216	NEW	34, 56, 97, 228
LEN	49, 151, 210, 217, 234	NEXT	69, 72, 100, 119, 205, 237, 252
LET	23, 217	Nnote_number	240
LF	236	NOT	228, 269
LINE	217, 218	Numerical functions	36
LINE INPUT	22, 218	numerical output	27
line number	4		
line numbering	54	OCT$(X)	42, 228
linear flowchart	19	OFF	214
linefeed	25	ON	81, 214, 233
LIST	5, 56, 99, 214, 219	ON COM	228
LIST command	5	ON ERROR GOTO	92, 229, 232, 251
LLIST	220	ON KEY	214, 229
LOAD	84, 158, 221	ON PLAY	231
LOC	221, 222	ON TIMER	232
LOCATE	148, 222	ON...GOTO command	82
LOF	221, 223	One-dimensional arrays	103
LOG	37, 269	OPEN	233, 234, 246
logical operators	34	OPEN COM	208, 235
LPOS	223	OPEN command	161
LPRINT	223	OPTION BASE 108, 187, 207, 237, 286
LPRINT USING	224	OR	238, 248, 263, 269
LSET	224	OUT	238
		OUTPUT	234, 237
MB(modebackground)	239	Output volume	14
menu	144	Ox(octave)	240
MERGE	163, 187, 225		
MF(modeforeground)	239		

PAINT	238
palette	178, 192
parity	235
PATH	157, 201, 202
PC BASIC	1
PEEK	196, 239
PLAY	167, 231, 239
PMAP	241
Pnote_length	240
POINT	242
POKE	101, 196, 242
port	238
POSition	96, 242
PRESET	243, 248
PRINT	24, 82, 96, 100
PRINT USING	27, 244
Program flowcharts	13
program mode	24
programs	7
PROMPT	202
PSET	199, 247, 248
PUT	248
Radian measurement	36
radians	36
Random numbers	41
RANDOMIZE	250
raster	218
READ	97, 114, 119, 250
rec_num	249
record counter.	160
record_length	234
REM	32, 88, 251
RENUM	54, 251
RESTORE	98, 187, 252, 286
RESUME	91, 252
RETURN	209
RIGHT$	48, 253
RMDIR	188
RND	41, 250
RSET	224
RTS	236
RUN	4, 56, 253

SAVE	157, 187, 225, 254
scan_code	215
SCREEN	218, 254, 255, 256
Screen control	60
screen color	177
seconds	232
segment_addr	196
sequential files	160
SET	201
SGN	38, 269
SHELL	256
shift	215
SIN	3, 36, 269
Single-precision real	33
Sorting procedures	153
SOUND	165, 257
SPACE$	52, 257
SPC	45, 265, 266
SQR	37, 269
STEP	206, 247
STOP	193, 257
STR$	51, 258
string	33, 46, 199, 213, 214, 253
STRING$	52, 258
subscripts	199
Subtraction	267
SWAP	258
SYSTEM	258
Tempo	241
TAB	45, 266
TAN	3, 36, 270
text	250
text output	27
text_color	190, 193
THEN	64, 82, 182, 210, 251
three-dimensional array	122
TIME$	259
TIMER 2	32, 259
toggle	215
TROFF	56, 259
TRON	56, 259

unconditional program branch   61
user-friendly   144
USING   224, 247, 266
USR   197, 287

VAL   50, 260
value   217, 238
variable   33, 203
VARPTR   196, 260
VARPTR$ 196, 261
VIEW 194,   261, 262

WAIT   262
WEND   74, 263
WHILE   74, 263
WIDTH   60, 222, 263, 264
wildcard characters   158
WINDOW   262
WRITE   31, 265, 266,

XOR 2   48, 270

Optional Diskette

For your convenience, the program listings contained in this book are available on an IBM 3 1/2" or 5 1/4" formatted floppy disk. You should order the diskette if you want to use the programs, but don't want to type them in from the listings in the book.

All programs on the diskette have been fully tested. You can change the programs for your particular needs. The diskette is available for $14.95 plus $2.00 ($5.00 foreign) for postage and handling.

When ordering, please give your name and shipping address. Enclose a check, money order or credit card information. Mail your order to:

Abacus Software
5370 52nd Street SE
Grand Rapids, MI 49512
Phone (616) 698-0330
FAX (616) 698-0325

Or for fast service,
Call Toll Free **1-800-451-4319**

To order, fill out this form and send to Abacus along with proper payment, or call **Toll Free 1-800-451-4319.**

Qty.	Title	Price

Name:_____

Address:_____

City:_____ State:____ Zip:_____

Country:_____ Phone:____/_____

MI residents add 4% sales tax	
Add $4 S/H (U.S. and Canada) or Foreign orders add $12 per item	
Check/ Money Order **TOTAL**	

Charge order to my: ☐ VISA ☐ MC. ☐ Am.Ex.

Card #: ☐☐☐☐☐☐☐☐☐☐☐☐☐☐☐☐ Exp. Date: ___/___/___

SEE LIST OF AVAILABLE TITLES ON REVERSE SIDE

PLEASE HELP US

So that we better understand who you are and what types of books interest you, please answer the following questions and return this prepaid card to us. THANK YOU

Computer:
☐ IBM/ PC or compatible   ☐ Atari ST   ☐ Macintosh
☐ Commodore 64   ☐ Commodore 128   ☐ Apple II/ GS
☐ Amiga   ☐ Other: _____

I purchase most computer books from:
☐ Retail book store   ☐ Discount book store   ☐ Mail order
☐ Retail computer store   ☐ Discount computer store   ☐ Publisher direct

I learned of this book from:
☐ Magazine ad   ☐ Book review   ☐ Recommendation
☐ Store display rack   ☐ Catalog/ Brochure   ☐ Library

Suggestions for new books:_____

This book's title:_____

Your name:_____

Address:_____

City:_____ State:_____ Zip:_____

Purchased from (Store name):_____

City:_____ State:_____ Zip:_____

☑ Available book titles for IBM/ PC and compatibles

PC BEGINNERS SERIES

☑ PC for Beginners	$18.95
☑ MS-DOS for Beginners	18.95
☑ GW-BASIC Prog'ing for beginners	18.95
☑ Microsoft Works for beginners	18.95
☑ Ventura Publisher for beginners	18.95
☑ Lotus 1•2•3 for beginners	18.95
☑ Excel for beginners	18.95
☑ Microsoft Word for beginners	18.95
☑ dBASE IV for beginners	18.95
☑ UNIX/ XENIX for beginners	

PROGRAM REFERENCE GUIDES

☑ dBASE III Plus	$9.95
☑ GW-BASIC	9.95
☑ Lotus 1•2•3	9.95
☑ Microsoft Word	9.95
☑ MS-DOS	9.95
☑ Multiplan	9.95
☑ Turbo C	9.95
☑ Turbo Pascal	9.95
☑ WordPerfect	9.95
☑ Wordstar	9.95

To order call **Toll Free 1-800-451-4319.**

NO POSTAGE
NECESSARY
IF MAILED
IN THE
UNITED STATES

 **Abacus**

5370 52nd Street S.E.
Grand Rapids, MI 49502-8107